D1457330

The Measure of Paris

STEPHEN SCOBIE

The University of Alberta Press

Published by
The University of Alberta Press
Ring House 2
Edmonton, Alberta, Canada T6G 2E1

LIBRARY AND ARCHIVES CANADA CATALOGUING IN PUBLICATION

Scobie, Stephen, 1943-
      The measure of Paris / Stephen Scobie.

(Wayfarer series)
Includes index.
ISBN 978-0-88864-533-3

      1. Paris (France)—In literature. 2. Paris (France)—History—20th century. 3. Paris (France)—
Civilization—20th century. 4. Paris (France)—Biography. 5. Canadian literature—20th century—
History and criticism. I. Title. II. Series: Wayfarer series (Edmonton, Alta.)

PS8101.P38S36 2010   C810.9'3244361   C2009-906594-0

All rights reserved.
First edition, first printing, 2010.
Printed and bound in Canada by Friesens, Altona, Manitoba.
Copyediting by Meaghan Craven.
Proofreading by Kirsten Craven.
Indexing by Judy Dunlop.

The University of Alberta Press is committed to protecting our natural environment. As part of our
efforts, this book is printed on Enviro Paper: it contains 100% post-consumer recycled fibres and is
acid- and chlorine-free.

The University of Alberta Press gratefully acknowledges the support received for its publishing
program from The Canada Council for the Arts. The University of Alberta Press also gratefully
acknowledges the financial support of the Government of Canada through the Book Publishing
Industry Development Program (BPIDP) and from the Alberta Foundation for the Arts for its
publishing activities.

CONTENTS

ACKNOWLEDGEMENTS

THIS BOOK IS IN LOVING MEMORY of my late wife, Maureen
Scobie (1940–2001). She had lived in Paris before me; she introduced
me to the city, and to her love for its history. We lived there together
for two extended periods, in 1975–76 and in 1985, both times at 19, rue
Rousselet. She was the first to show me the stained glass glories of
Ste.-Chapelle, the Impressionist paintings in Jeu du Paume, and many
other secrets of the city. The photo of her sitting at the tip of Île de la
Cité, taken in 1972, has been the talisman I have carried with me ever
since her death.

This book is also for my dear friend and companion, Eunice Scarfe.
Eunice has also shared Paris with me: on one occasion, her driving
skills guided our rented car backwards out of the narrow alley of
rue Rousselet. And I remember her smiling in the winter sun of the
Luxembourg Gardens. Her critical acumen and inquiring mind have
been immensely instructive for this book. But her greatest gift to *The
Measure of Paris* is the title, which was her inspiration.

I remember with pleasure many friends who have accompanied
me through the streets of Paris: Doug, Sharon, Terry, Madelyn, Katie,

Don. But most of all, Lola Lemire Tostevin and Gerry Shikatani, not only for their Parisian companionship, but also for the generosity with which they permitted me to discuss their works in such detail— such permission given, I should add, without even asking to see in advance what I had written about them.

Thanks for gracious hospitality go to a series of Parisian land-ladies: Mesdames Warnier, Vincens, Ventura, et Muret. And, for many years, to the Hôtel Michelet-Odéon and the Hôtel St.-Pierre. Special thanks also to Adrienne Clarkson, John Ralston Saul, and Michael Ignatieff.

Among the many scholars who invited and welcomed me to academic conferences on Canadian studies, my thanks to the late Michel Baridon, Marta Dvorak, Jean-Michel Lacroix, Jacques Rancourt, and Héliane Ventura.

My thanks to the Universities of Alberta and Victoria for support over many years, not least for the study leaves which enabled me to live for extended periods in Paris. And to all the students who have endured my obsession, *merci*. At the University of Alberta Press, my very grateful thanks to Peter Midgley and all his associates— including the anonymous readers of this manuscript, who provided invaluable help with details of French translation and punctuation.

Two sections of this book have appeared in earlier versions. Part Two was included in *American Modernism Across the Arts*, ed. Jay Bochner and Justin D. Edwards (New York: Peter Lang, 1999). Chapter 8 was included in *Literary Environments: Canada and the Old World*, ed. Britta Olinder (London: Peter Lang, 2006).

Every reasonable effort has been made to obtain permission to reprint two poems by Jacques Réda ("Rue Rousselet" and "L'Automne Rue Rousselet"). These poems appeared in *Amen, Récitatif, La tourne*, published in 1999 by Éditions Gallimard (Poésie).

←-- INTRODUCTION -->

The Measure of Paris

PARIS IS AN INFINITE CITY: beyond all description, beyond all measure. So it may seem that the title of this book, *The Measure of Paris*, is inherently paradoxical. Yet "measure" is also an integral part of the Parisian ethos; intensely civilized and acculturated, the city invites the gestures of measurement which it can never satisfy.

One possible measure of Paris may be found on the rue de Vaugirard,[1] carved in marble and set in a wall under some arcades, just across the street from the French Senate in the Palais du Luxembourg. It is a *mètre étalon*, a standard measure of exactly one metre, against which all other metres may be judged. It was set in this wall in 1796, at the time that the post-Revolutionary government was instituting the metric system. Sixteen such metres were installed in public places throughout Paris, to be seen and to be measured, to be used by citizens as the new standard; today, only two survive, and the only one that is still in its original mural location is the one on rue de Vaugirard.

From this measure, a two-minute walk will take you to the Café de la Mairie du VIème Arrondissement, habituated by Djuna Barnes; or

to 27 rue de Fleurus, home of Gertrude Stein and Alice B. Toklas. A couple of minutes more will bring you to St.-Germain-des-Prés, and to my personal measure of Paris: the Café Bonaparte, rue Guillaume Apollinaire.

The "measure of Paris" is a phrase that may be read two ways. On the one hand, it sets Paris up as the definitive standard (étalon) by which many things (cities, cultures, histories, literatures) may be measured: the judgement of Paris passed upon the world.[2] On the other hand, Paris is itself to be measured. It is perhaps the most discussed city in the world: it has been painted, filmed, written about interminably, talked about in a million civilized conversations in cafés and salons. People never tire of attempting to "measure" Paris, or of offering their own personal accounting of its history, its allure, the endless fascination of its sheer existence.

Paris is the measure by which the modern Western world determined itself. "The capital of the nineteenth century," Walter Benjamin called it; the phrase is echoed by David Harvey in his 2003 book *Paris, Capital of Modernity*. Modern politics was born in the frenzy and idealism of the Jacobin clubs in the Quartier de l'Odéon;[3] modern literature began with the "Paris Spleen" poems of Charles Baudelaire; modern art began with the Salon des Refusés in 1863 and settled solidly in Paris for the next sixty years. Benjamin traces the whole sociology of the modern city to the Parisian arcades,[4] and to the *flâneurs* who wandered through them. Paris reigned supreme in the timeless arts of fashion and cuisine, and laid claim to the quintessential twentieth-century art of cinema.

The capital of the nineteenth century persisted as such well into the twentieth. In the years from 1907 till 1914, the cultural history of the age was written, on an almost daily basis, in the canvases painted by Georges Braque and Pablo Picasso; and then rewritten, one word at a time, in the pages of Guillaume Apollinaire and Gertrude Stein. By the 1920s, Paris had become a self-created and self-perpetuating myth, the city of expatriates, where Sylvia Beach toiled and sacrificed to produce the first edition of James Joyce's *Ulysses*: February 2, 1922, Shakespeare and Company, 12 rue de l'Odéon.

By the later twentieth century, assertions of Paris as the measure of the world were becoming more sporadic, and perhaps more desperate. Certainly there was a continuing display in philosophy, from Existentialism through to Deconstruction; and there was the glorious outburst of the Nouvelle Vague in 1960s cinema: Godard, Resnais, Truffaut, Rohmer, Chabrol. But by the end of the twentieth century, one would be tempted to say that Parisian ascendancy had passed, that Paris was no longer the measure. (Not that it had been replaced by any single centre—not even New York—rather, it had been submerged in the unmeasured mediocrity of globalization.) "One would be tempted"—except that the temptation itself is an all too easy rhetorical trope, which I discuss in Part One of this book, "Paris Perdu"—to give in to the nostalgic tendency to see the glory, and the measure, of Paris as being always in the past. I'd like to resist it, even here.

But people are always taking the measure of Paris. Books multiply; my shelves groan under their weight.[5] Paris is a city in which text—

the written and the spoken word—is so important that it demands more words in return. What Jacques Derrida (that great Algerian Parisian) called the supplement of writing is in force here too. The impulse to write about Paris is irresistible: Paris is written as poetry, as history, as politics, as sociology, as memoir, as urban geography, as autobiography. In the 1920s (or rather, in the 1920s as seen in retrospect), a highly particular subgenre developed: the "Paris in the 20s memoir," in which it seemed that every expatriate who had ever set foot in Montparnasse felt compelled to tell his (or sometimes her) story.

A "measure" is also a unit of poetry, or of dance ("'Now tread we a measure!' said young Lochinvar"—Sir Walter Scott). To measure Paris may be to look at it objectively, to take its historical or political measure; but it is also to appreciate, and partake of, its poetry. That marble line, so rigidly fixed on the wall of the rue de Vaugirard, also dances.

Or at least walks. Because walking—the activity of strolling around the streets of the city—has become one of the most crucial measures of Paris. The one who walks—in the French phrase, which has more or less been taken over into English, the flâneur—is a key image of Parisian discourse from nineteenth-century writers like Balzac and Baudelaire to twentieth-century theorists like Benjamin or Michel de Certeau. Certeau speaks of *"la geste cheminatoire."* **"La geste"**—which Collins/Robert defines as "a collection of epic poems centred around the same hero"—is only subtly different from **"le geste"**—gesture. Both meanings are appropriate. The flâneur's gesture could be translated as "the long poem of walking" (with Walter Benjamin, perhaps, as its epic hero).

This book, then, is an attempt to survey some of these measures of Paris, and to take part in its long poem of walking. The book began as an account of a very particular measure of Paris—the city as it appeared in the writing of certain Canadian writers who had lived there[6]—but it quickly exceeded that measure. While Canadian writers—John Glassco, Sheila Watson, Mavis Gallant, Gail Scott, Gerry Shikatani, Lola Lemire Tostevin—remain central to my account, I could not entirely exclude the American expatriate writers, especially Djuna Barnes and Gertrude Stein. They are a vital and unique measure of Paris. Nor could I exclude (even though it is sampled very selectively) the vast body of cultural history (such as *The Arcades Project*), which seeks to provide another measure of Paris. Nor, finally, could I exclude my own experience of the city, the many times in which I, too, have taken a small and personal measure.

Thus, the stance and tone of this book shift from chapter to chapter—sometimes as literary criticism, sometimes as cultural history, sometimes as personal memoir. What holds the book together is Paris itself: Paris as the measure of all that I attempt to say about it.

Part One, "Paris Perdu," provides a parameter for the whole. It is a cautionary prelude, guarding against a common trope in Parisian writing: the tendency to see Paris always in a nostalgic glow, or to idealize the city in an image of its past glory, a glory that is assumed to have faded. This trope recurs in every age of Parisian writing: the city always is not what it used to be. I am sure that I am guilty of such nostalgia myself (my ideal Paris dates from the mid-1970s); all I can do is be aware of it and draw attention to it. The key instance here is attitudes towards the Baron Haussmann and his reconstruction of the city in the 1860s; but I also look at some more recent writing by Mavis Gallant. In this manner, "Paris Perdu" sets a caveat around everything that follows.

Part Two, "I is an other," then turns to the most characteristic form of Parisian measure, autobiography. As I have suggested, the "Paris in the 20s" memoir is crucial to the measure of Paris as cultural mythology. But autobiography is not a simple or transparent stance for a writer; it involves quite complex narrative presuppositions. This section attempts to explore the theoretical status of autobiography, with detailed examples coming from the Parisian memoirs of Gertrude Stein, Robert McAlmon, Kay Boyle, John Glassco, and Gail Scott. Like Part One, this section functions both as a study in its own right and as a cautionary prelude to all later references to these writers' autobiographical accounts.

Part Three, "What Pleasure in a Name," is perhaps the core of the book. It began as a simple note on the prevalence of specific street names in Parisian writing. These writers never simply say "I went from A to B"; they will say "I left A and took rue B to avenue C, passed through place D to boulevard E, avoided impasse F, then took rue G until I arrived at H"—all the street names lovingly recorded. My "simple note" on this stylistic quirk expanded under my hands into a major study; it opened up a whole ethos of Parisian topography. Street names are, in the most basic sense, the measure of Paris. They are the indices by which you place yourself, or determine your direction. My study of street names took me to the heart of Benjamin's image of the flâneur; of Sheila Watson's "devious routes"; of Mavis Gallant's stance during the contested days of May 1968; of Gail Scott's ambivalent position in contemporary Paris; and of John Glassco's ethics of pleasure. What had seemed a simple indulgence in exact naming proved to be a measure of my experience of the city.

Part Four, then, "Parisian Sites," turns to a deeper exploration of specific locations in Paris. It looks at particular sites associated with the wanderings of Gertrude Stein and Djuna Barnes; and it dwells upon a specific address—19 rue Rousselet—whose associations range from a German poet to a Québécois painter, from my own personal history to that of a Governor General of Canada.

The Canadian association is then intensified in Part Five, "Canadian Visions." This section is perhaps the closest to the original intent of the book, a study of the image of Paris as it appears in Canadian writing. This section analyzes the importance of Paris in the work of two Canadian writers: the novelist Lola Lemire Tostevin (*Frog Moon*) and the poet Gerry Shikatani (*Aqueduct*). "Canadian Visions" is written from the stance of the literary critic—but the next, and final, section, "Personal Postscripts," is written as autobiography, memoir, poetry, diary. All the theoretical caveats registered in Part Two should be applied here. I look back to my own measure of the city, as I first saw it in 1970, as well as in a particularly memorable visit in 2002.

And though my book ends here, the city does not. There is no last word. A final paradox: the "measure" of Paris is finite, the rue de Vaugirard's "étalon" is just so long, and no longer. But the city itself is infinite. Paris never ends.

PART ONE --> *Paris Perdu*

...(la forme d'une ville

Change plus vite, hélas! que le coeur d'un mortel)

...(the form of a city

changes, alas, faster than the human heart)

> —CHARLES BAUDELAIRE, *Le Cygne, À Victor Hugo* (*The Swan, To Victor Hugo*)

From 1900 to 1930, Paris did change a lot. They always told me that America changed but it really did not change as much as Paris did in those years that is the Paris that one can see, but then there is no remembering what it looked like before and even no remembering what it looks like now.

> —GERTRUDE STEIN, *Paris France*

← 1 CONSPIRACY THEORIES →

"Ineluctible intolerable oblivion"

PARIS IS LOST TO US. The whole city has gone to hell. The Paris we once knew and loved has disappeared under a ruinous assault: demolition of glorious old buildings, construction of hideous new ones, the wanton destruction of whole neighbourhoods and their traditional way of life, all replaced by ugly and soulless highways, shopping centres, libraries, HLMs, etc.[1] It's as if the city planners of Paris were deliberately trying to destroy everything unique, distinctive, or beautiful about it. What was once the most lovely city in the world is now absolutely, irretrievably lost. Paris perdu—this is the end.

Does the above paragraph sound familiar? It should. In one form or another, this rhetoric—the whole discursive trope that I would here like to sum up as "Paris perdu" (Paris lost)—has been prevalent in writing about the city for hundreds of years. I just now invented the particular wording of the above paragraph, but its sentiments have been expressed, repeatedly, at least since the early nineteenth century, and in fact far earlier. The details may change—from Haussmann's boulevards to Mitterrand's *grands projets*—but the form of the trope remains the same. Paris perdu: which I am tempted to translate into English, via one verbal expansion and one intertextual leap, as "Parisdise Lost."[2]

If the first paragraph above was invented, this next one, in all its glorious paranoia, in its feeling of being on the edge of parody, is, I am delighted to say, not parodic at all, but for real:

> In one of the basements of City Hall is the headquarters of a society, secret but powerful, composed of architects and officials. Its aim is to make the capital ugly. It is called the Society of the Enemies of Paris. For several years it has redoubled its activity and has had countless victories; it exhorts shopkeepers to cover the most noble facades with signs;[3] it uses timid architects to elaborate bizarre plans and extravagant elevations; it discovers and designates the places where insane constructions will be best placed to outrage an admirable monument or ruin a beautiful perspective....

This paragraph might have been written yesterday; it might have been written in the 1850s, as Baron Haussmann commenced his reconstruction of Paris; it certainly might (without any hint of parody at all) have formed part of Louis Chevalier's hysterical rant, *The Assassination of Paris* (published in France in 1977 and in America in 1994). In fact, it was written by an architectural critic called André Hallays, and it was published in 1909 (cited in Evenson, 159). The date, in the end, scarcely matters. The trope persists, irrespective of time. Indeed, my main subject here is the very persistence of the trope; only in a secondary sense am I interested in its individual manifestations with regard to specific architectural projects.

And partly, I admit, I am writing out of a very self-conscious impulse to resist the same kind of nostalgic idealism in myself. It's not that I totally disbelieve what the "Paris perdu" critics say, far less that I approve of every modern building that has gone up in Paris. Certain experiences of the city are indeed lost, even for me, in my late-coming lifetime. But I am suspicious of the way that the "Paris perdu" rhetoric surrounds what has been lost with a romantic haze: loses it a second time, so to speak, in idealized nostalgia. Once you notice this trope *as trope*, it becomes much more difficult (fortunately) to take it seriously.

Witness, for example, the supremely paranoid Louis Chevalier, as he declaims, in *The Assassination of Paris*:

> Vanishing, this is the theme of my book, the certainty that in a few years, easy enough to calculate, no one will have any idea of what Paris was. In barely fifteen years it will be gone except when we conjure up its image—always inadequate—from books. There will no longer be the faintest imprint of a footstep, as it was possible to find in an earlier time, no longer the smallest stone where one sat daydreaming or grafting the city's past onto one's own. Ineluctible intolerable oblivion. (11)

These lines were published in 1977. By the time they appeared in English translation, seventeen years later, Chevalier's "barely fifteen years" had come and gone, and his point had (surely) been proved wrong. Paris had certainly changed (drastically, and not always for the better), but to say that there is no longer "any idea of what Paris was" is simply ridiculous. All that remains of Chevalier's argument is the force of the rhetorical trope, the nostalgic longing for an idealized past, the refusal to accept the pragmatic adjustments of the literal present.

Or here is English historian Richard Cobb, writing in 1980:

> The old Halles is a sad desert; the Marais has become a museum....
> The quartier Saint-Merri has been frozen into a network of voies
> piétonnes, one of the surest ways of congealing a once-living quarter
> into the slow death of fashion, tourism, sex-shops, antique-shops and
> expensive boutiques....The VIe has been lost beyond hope....the VIIe
> is similarly infected, the quartier Saint-Séverin is totally ruined.
> (117–18)

And he concludes "There will be no more novelists of the VIe, for there is no life there any more to write about" (180), an opinion that must come as something of a surprise to the past twenty-five years of French novelists.

Even Cobb's sympathetic editor, David Gilmour, feels compelled to comment in his introduction that

Like many nostalgic people, he [Cobb] believed that places first seen in his youth were in their prime at that moment, and that all subsequent changes have been bad. This gives his writing an elegiac quality, the historian and the poet combining to record and commemorate a disappearing world. (x)

Much as I love Richard Cobb's writings about Paris, his editor's comment seems to me a generous estimation. Certainly it points to the personal nature, or at least the personal *timing* of all such statements. The love for any particular manifestation of Paris *"depends on where your memories begin"* (my italics)—as Adrian Rifkin says, in a passage considerably more sensible and balanced than anything in Chevalier or Cobb:

...where were the good old days? When did Belleville really start to be rebuilt? The simple answer is—as soon as it was built, or as soon as a writer's identity detaches itself from childhood. Both of these. There has not been a moment from 1859 until today when demolition and construction have not gone on, from the hovel to charity or municipal housing, and now luxury flats; when industries have not evolved and faded, from the shoe trade to the Chinese restaurant; when the population has not shifted and moved on....

So in the end, a lot depends on where your memories begin. The points at which the past becomes felt as loss, in emotion or topography, can be the focus for quite contradictory perceptions of the city. (204)

In his wide-ranging history, *Paris: Biography of a City*, Colin Jones traces the phenomenon even farther back, over many centuries:

The history of Parisian nostalgia is as long as the history of Paris itself. Present in the writing of the Emperor Julian, it is also evident in one of the earliest detailed descriptions of the city we have from the

Middle Ages—Guillebert de Metz's "Description of the City of Paris,"
dating from the early fifteenth century. Paris "had been in its flower"
in his youth it seems (ah! when else?). On such nostalgic longings for
le vieux Paris a whole literary tourist industry would be built in the
twentieth century. (xxi)

Thus, any perception of Paris has a personal dimension, which
depends on an interaction between the history of the city and *your*
history of the city. "A lot depends on where your memories begin":
indeed. The Canadian painter Joseph Plaskett, in his charming auto-
biography, *A Speaking Likeness*, recalls the adjustments that had to be
made by a bright young man arriving in Paris not in 1920 but in 1950:

Violet le Duc and Baron Haussmann ruined medieval Paris, replacing
it with an image more glamorous to the popular mind—"the city
of light." By 1950 the Paris of artistic legend, the Montmartre of
Toulouse-Lautrec and the Montparnasse of Modigliani, was begin-
ning to resemble a vacated stage set....But isn't that the point—the
idea of the movable feast? Paris was losing some of its pre-eminence
to New York, but the art activity was neither static nor stagnant.
New generations of artists find new places to congregate. When I
arrived, Saint-Germain-des-Prés had supplanted Montparnasse as a
Mecca point and that was exactly where I had chosen to live. I was in
the centre for twelve years. (57-59)

Plaskett here is much more sensible than Cobb. He recognizes
that the city changes, and that there is nothing to be gained by
lamenting some outdated image of "the city of light," Montmartre or
Montparnasse, far less "medieval Paris." Instead, he looks at the city
as it is, and moves straight to the centre.

But if the intensity, and sometimes the extravagance, of "Paris
perdu" lamentations are rooted in personal emotions, memories of
childhood, individual configurations of nostalgia and desire, they are
also, in Paris, public and political. The transformation of the cityscape
has been determined, to a much greater extent in Paris than in most
other Western capitals, by the political heads of state. From Napoleon

III to Pompidou and Mitterrand, French emperors and presidents have seen the architecture of Paris as their visible legacy. Thus, any aesthetic reaction to the startling design of the modern art museum at Beaubourg cannot avoid the fact that its official name is the "Centre Pompidou," any more than one's distaste for the dehumanizing vistas and caged trees of the new Bibliothèque Nationale can be detached from the fact that Mitterrand personally chose and approved the plans. In Paris, architecture is politics.[4]

Or, as Lebbeus Woods puts it, "Architecture is war. War is architecture" (310).[5] "Building is by its very nature an aggressive, even warlike act," Woods writes. "For one thing, buildings are objects that disrupt existing landscapes. Older buildings, perhaps much-loved, must be torn down. Fields and farms are taken over" (311). Furthermore, such aggression always carries social and political implications. "The wrecking machines that leveled houses and urban blocks were no less destructive to culture than if they had been the tanks and artillery of an attacking army....Nor can it be denied that the fabric destroyed is always that of an "inferior" class of culture (whether it be agrarian or simply old and in the way of progress)..." (311–12).

The specific reference Woods has in mind for these comments is the blasting of highways through New York under Robert Moses in the 1930s, but the comments would apply equally as well to the central test case of all "Paris perdu" arguments: the career and accomplishments/demolishments of the Baron Haussmann.

←-- 2 THE BARON OF ALPHAVILLE[1] -->

GEORGES-EUGÈNE HAUSSMANN (1809–1891) was the appointed
Prefect for the Seine region, including Paris, from 1853 until 1870. As
such, he was responsible for all public works in the city, exercising an
obsessive control over everything from the large-scale construction
of new streets and boulevards to the minutest details of the design of
drinking fountains (not to mention the sewers). Working in the name
of the Emperor Napoleon III, Haussmann was more than a meticulous
administrator with a fanatical eye for detail; he was a visionary who
reshaped the entire city to the form of his own imagination.

While Haussmann may be the single most influential figure in the
history of the transformation of Paris, he by no means stands alone.
Many of his plans were worked out in close collaboration with the
Emperor, and certainly with his support. Many of the projects for the
redesigning of Paris both precede Haussmann—such as the reforms
carried out by his predecessor, Claude-Philibert Barthelot, Comte de
Rambuteau—and succeed him—such as the completion of the boule-
vard named after him, as well as the boulevard Raspail. Or take this
statement:

*We need...open public markets, water fountains which work, regu-
larly laid-out crossroads, new theatres. We must widen the narrow
and unhealthy streets, and openly reveal hidden monuments and
make them visible.*

These words may sound like a Haussmann manifesto; but in fact they
were written by Voltaire, in 1749 (quoted in Jones, 208).

Until recently, no one much liked Haussmann. No matter that he
created, almost single-handedly, the "look" of Paris—tree-lined boule-
vards, star-shaped intersections, uniform five-storey buildings with
mansard attics—that most twentieth-century visitors have identified
as the essence of the city: Haussmann was cast, always, as the major
villain of "Paris perdu" scenarios.

Walter Benjamin called him "the artist of demolition" (Buck-Morss,
89). Richard Cobb described him as "The Alsatian Attila" (165), hinting
none too subtly that no real *Frenchman* could have so assaulted Paris.
(While Haussmann's family did come from the debatable border
territory of Alsace, he himself was born in Paris.) "In examining
Haussmann's career," writes the admirably balanced and fair-minded
John Russell, "we must never forget that he was one of the most
obnoxious of recorded beings....Even such friends as he had were
forced to admit that Haussmann was a brute—heavy of eye and tread,
stiff, coarse, demanding, humorless, and vain" (212). David A. Bell
uses a striking if obvious comparison when he writes that "the great
boulevards sliced through old neighbourhoods like a guillotine blade
through flesh" (19). Walter Benjamin delights in repeating the infa-
mous remark attributed to a supposedly naive Madame Haussmann:
"It is curious that every time we buy a house, a boulevard passes
through it" (132).[2]

Recently, however, there has been somewhat of a revisionist
tendency, and a more positive view of Haussmann may be emerging.
See, for example, two books, both of which appeared in 2000: Georges
Valance's *Haussmann le Grand*, and Michel Carmona's *Haussmann*.[3]
The implications of Valance's title are made more explicit in the 2002
English translation of Carmona, whose one-word original title is
expanded to *Haussmann: His Life and Times, and the Making of Modern*

Paris. There is also a curious 2001 novel by Paul LaFarge, *Haussmann, or the Distinction*, which, though qualified by many layers of contrivance and irony, is not ultimately unsympathetic to the Baron.

Such revisionist writers perceive a genuine vision in Haussmann's reconstructions. Richard D.E. Burton comments that "Haussmannization was less an experiment in city planning than an epistemological revolution translated into buildings and streets. It supplanted one conceptual model, the organic, the prerational, the feudal, with another, the organized, the rational, the modern" (269). In his novel, LaFarge enters imaginatively into the mindset of his protagonist:

> *The old skeptic[4] would have had convulsions of spite if he could have seen what a fuss his still-unenlightened countrymen made over the demolition of a church or two—didn't they see that the path of reason is straight, leads straight from one great mind to another; it cuts a gleaming roadway through time....The Baron sometimes believed, looking at the map of his works, that the civic order he created—the improved circulation of carriages, the sewers and the clean drinking water—was a benefit attendant on a greater, spiritual transformation....He would save the city not from congestion but from unreason, the gathering dark of a thousand years of thoughtless acts; he would sacrifice its stone confusion, to the last house, in order to save the few gestures of any true clarity (the Champs-Elysées, the Louvre, the Madeleine) which had been written as if by accident in the tangled and mediocre pages of the city's history. (119)*

The main charge against Haussmann (apart from financial corruption and abuse of power) is that, in driving through his rationalized plan of grand boulevards flanked by buildings of uniform height, he destroyed the historic city: not only the architecture of narrow, twisting streets and dark, dilapidated buildings, but also the social fabric of neighbourhoods, especially working-class neighbourhoods, with the rich texture of communal life that supported them.

The crudest form of the accusation is that the broad boulevards were designed to facilitate military action—cavalry charges and even artillery—against revolutionary insurgents, and to render impossible the effectiveness that street barricades had enjoyed in, for example, 1830. (An effective barricade needs a narrow street.) Walter Benjamin, for instance, asserts that "The true goal of Haussmann's projects was to secure the city against civil war. He wanted to make the erection of barricades in the streets of Paris impossible for all time" (23). This story has been repeated so often that it has taken on something of the character of an urban myth,[5] but historians like David H. Pinkney have tended to downplay it: "the enforcement of public security was only one of [Haussmann and] Napoleon's purposes and probably not the most important" (36). Patrice Higonnet dismisses it outright: "by 1860 the military uselessness of barricades was well known.... Benjamin might have noticed this as well, had he not been so influenced by the disdain for Haussmann's Paris that was so common in the 1930s, especially among the Surrealists" (171). Colin Jones, however, takes it more seriously:

> Boulevards certainly made the deployment of barricades, the stock-in-trade of traditional Parisian radicalism, rather obsolete (they were already more of symbolic than military value, according to Friedrich Engels)....The width of the boulevards allowed detachments of cavalry to be used effectively...[and] permitted the rapid deployment of police. (318–19)

Haussmann himself was ambiguous on this point. Carmona, the most pro-Haussmann of the recent biographers, quotes him as writing that "when I combined [two boulevards] in this way I never gave the slightest thought to their greater or lesser strategic importance" (231). Yet Carmona also writes: "although he denied that this [military advantage] was his sole concern he had no wish to disclaim it—on the contrary" (143).

But while the accusation of military advantage may remain problematic, there is no doubt that Haussmannization reinforced the ruling ideology in many much more subtle ways.[6] For one thing, there was a massive shift of population (mainly working class) out of the historic centre of the city. Pinkney reports that "Between 1861 and

1872 the ten central arrondissements lost 33,000 inhabitants while
the ten eccentric arrondissements added more than 200,000" (165).
This shift has continued ever since, and may still be seen today, in
the politicization of the *banlieues* as sites of resistance (such as was
the case during the 2005 riots) to the ruling authority of the French
state, from Chirac to Sarkozy. More and more, the centre of the city
is occupied by those in control of business, law, and administration
(or is devoted to tourists). The workers of Paris, or all social elements
capable of resistance, are relegated to the suburbs. "Where then have
the Parisians gone?" asks Richard Cobb, writing in 1985. "The older,
the more recalcitrant, the most intractable have *died*. The rest have
gone, reluctantly, to Alphaville" (182).[7] Thus, the social vitality (and
revolutionary potential) of the historic centre is dispersed to discon-
nected outlying areas, while the centre becomes a site for government
and museums, for the invisible workings of power, cloaked in a
cityscape of controlled and distanced spectacle.

Haussmann's tranformations may thus be seen not so much in
terms of the military as in terms of the visual. Again, Haussmann
is not the originator: rather, he is the one who brings to realization
earlier and traditional ideas of the visualization of power. Two centu-
ries earlier, notes Colin Jones,

> What distinguished the programme of Louis XIV and Colbert was
> an emphasis on monumentality. Particular emphasis was placed on
> public buildings, which would overpower the viewer with an impres-
> sion of strength and force, and care was taken to implant them in the
> city in such a way that they transformed the surrounding cityscape.
> (160)

Haussmann continued and institutionalized the primacy of the
visual sense and the perception of urban perspectives:

> The force of the Haussmannian boulevard lay far more in its political
> legibility — as proof of the creative power of the bourgeoisie — than
> in its resistance to barricades....The new boulevard...allowed the
> visual as well as the military penetration of the city....Visibility is the

key: *Haussmann's long perspectives made it possible to take in an entire avenue at a glance, to decipher and organize the city's space.* (Higonnet, 171–72)

The effect was most dramatic on the Île de la Cité, where Haussmann was restrained barely short of his "ambition of demolishing every private building on the island and making it the exclusive preserve of law, religion, and medicine" (Pinkney, 87). Only the lovely place Dauphine remains—described by John Russell as "that pink-and-gray triangle of which the last valiant fragment would have been destroyed by Haussmann, had he remained in office a year or two longer" (75), and more bizarrely by André Breton as the vagina of Paris.[8]

One of the earliest commentators on this transformation of the city's centre, although unknown at the time, was Jules Verne, in a science fiction novel called *Paris in the Twentieth Century* (an early precursor of Godard's *Alphaville*). Though not published until 1994 (English translation 1996), it was written in 1863, at the height of Haussmann's activities. Verne's futuristic vision is a fascinating mixture of hits and misses: he succeeds in imagining a fax machine, but, since he did not succeed in imagining the typewriter, the messages transmitted by fax are all handwritten. Verne's comments on Hausmannization, however, are so acute that they may well have been one of the reasons why the novel was not published in 1863. In the "future" Paris of the twentieth century, Verne writes,

lodgings were hard to find in a capital too small for its five million inhabitants; enlarging public squares, opening avenues, and multiplying boulevards threatened to leave little room for private dwellings. Which justified this bromide of the period: in Paris there are no longer houses, only streets!

Some neighbourhoods offered no lodging whatever to inhabitants of the capital, specifically the Île de la Cité, where there was room only for the Bureau of Commerce, the Palace of Justice, the Prefecture of Police, the cathedral, the morgue—in other words, the means of

being declared bankrupt, guilty, jailed, buried, and even rescued.
Public buildings had driven out houses. (72)

Haussmann's "civic cleansing" of the Île de la Cité also notably involved the demolition of the houses that crowded in front of the Cathedral of Notre-Dame, thus opening up the space, the *parvis*, which now enables us to stand far enough back from the front of the church to gain a clear and unobstructed view of the whole façade— again, the supremacy of the visual. In a provocative commentary on this effect, Ken-Ichi Sasaki, quoting the French architectural critic J. Hillairet, notes that the parvis is now six times larger than it was in the Middle Ages, and four times bigger than it was before Haussmann. While modern viewers may feel that they are now seeing the authentic mediaeval view, Sasaki argues that

> *the townscape, with its peculiar aesthetic requirements of* vision *[emphasis added], is an invention of modern times....[It] is our eye, our visual interest, that is modern. People before the mid-eighteenth century did not recognize the beauty of the façade of the Notre-Dame.... The original manner of appreciating this architecture [according to Hillairet] consisted in standing not in front of the façade but beneath the towers, physically receiving the effect of the stone mass and feeling as though the towers reached as high as the sky. (38)*

In other words, Sasaki argues, the original human sense perception for which Notre-Dame was designed was not sight but touch: not the separate stance of things seen from a distance in proper perspective, but close-up tactility, immersion in a space from which one is not distinct.[9] Here we begin to see the deeper ideological import of Haussmann's interventions: not just a simple question of cannon-fire down boulevards, but a redefinition of what it means to be an individual—in all the modernist, bourgeois, liberal definitions of that term—which also involves (an argument far too large for me to get into here) the supremacy of sight (perception at a distance) over the more immediate senses such as touch...

...and smell. In his fascinating essay "Utopia of an Odorless City" (1986), Ivan Illich traces the history of city-dwellers' tolerance for what we would now call bad smells: not only the open sewers that routinely ran down the middle of Parisian streets, but especially the smells of the dead, "the stench of shallow graves" (250). Illich writes:

> During the eighteenth century it became intolerable to let the dead contribute their aura to the city.[10] The dead were either excluded from the city or their bodies were encased in airtight monuments celebrating hygienic disposal, for which Père Lachaise became the symbol in Paris....This effort to deodorize utopian city space should be seen as one aspect of the architectural effort to "clear" city space for the construction of a modern capital. It can be interpreted as the repression of smelly persons who unite their separate auras to create a smelly crowd of commonfolk. Their "common" aura must be dissolved to make space for a new city through which clearly delineated individuals can circulate with unlimited freedom. (251)

The class implications here are clear. The "clearly delineated individuals" who can now "circulate with unlimited freedom," as flâneurs through urban space, are obviously not the same as the "smelly persons" who are now to be suppressed. The city that Haussmann creates is an ideological space, marked by visual distance (the sweeping perspectives of long avenues and boulevards, framed by buildings of uniform height, leading up to defining monuments such as the grandiose new Opéra or the venerable Notre-Dame) rather than by the messy proximities of touch and smell, neighbourhood and propinquity.

And yet, and yet. For all the theoretical acuteness of these critiques of Haussmann, I remain suspicious of the "Paris perdu" rhetoric that lurks behind them. It may be all very well to lament the disappearance of these hovels and slums clustered on the parvis of Notre-Dame, but would you really want to live in one? It may be all very well to argue for the communality of touch and smell, but do you really want open sewers running down the middle of your street? Would you really want to cancel out all the improvements Haussmann made to the Parisian sewer system? Would it really be preferable if Notre-Dame was still surrounded by stinking slums?

In other words, I am deeply suspicious of the nostalgia and romanticism implicit in many of the anti-Haussmann laments for the "authentic," "old" Paris lost, Paris perdu. Phrases like "authentic lived experience" set me on edge and get all my deconstructive suspicions going.[11] Paul LaFarge's novel contains a brilliant summary of these ambivalences. Just as he was able (in the passage cited earlier) to give expression to Haussmann's idealism without entirely endorsing it, so here he captures anti-Haussmann feeling both accurately and parodically, both giving it its due and acutely satirizing the fatuity of "Paris Perdu" rhetoric:

> [A]t midnight the guests drank a toast to that fabled place, Paris As It Was. This was a new city that came into being sometime around 1865. As the novelty of Haussmann's construction wore off, and people became accustomed to the conveniences it brought them, they began to take stock of what they'd lost. All of a sudden it seemed to them that a great many buildings had been torn down which ought to have been left standing, and that the streets which no longer existed had been the most picturesque, the richest in heritage, the quietest, and the least deserving of destruction. The boulevards are too wide; it was much better when they were alleyways! And the water does not taste as good as it once did....Give us back Paris As It Was! Because this city was perfectly irrecuperable they felt free to mourn it as much as they liked. (313–14)

Colin Jones reaches much the same conclusion:

> The more Paris was mythologized as the city of modernity...the more it nurtured a counter-myth of le Vieux Paris, an untidy but somehow authentic site, which had allegedly been much more to the human measure....This dystopian, disenchanted vision highlighted the extent to which the name of Haussmann and the cause of modernity were becoming scapegoats for the processes of intense social and cultural change. (340)[12]

The Prefect of Paris thus becomes the Baron of Alphaville: town planner becomes neighbourhood destroyer, visionary becomes vandal.

3 FROM THE TOUR EIFFEL TO
THE TOUR MONTPARNASSE -->

WHILE MUCH OF THE DEBATE over "Haussmannization" deals with questions of overall urban design (laying out of streets, boulevards affording heroic perspectives), the more pointed disputes attend to specific buildings. And here, one irony of the persistence of the "Paris perdu" trope is that some of Haussmann's most drastic interventions themselves became, in the course of time, precisely those venerable monuments that later generations of "Paris perdu" loyalists sought to protect. Even Benjamin, for example, acknowledges Haussmann's role in preserving and opening up the banks of the Seine. In "The Seine, the Oldest Paris," he quotes Fritz Stahl:

> The quays of Paris likewise owe their realization to Haussmann. It
> was only in his day that the walkways were constructed up above
> and the trees planted down below, along the banks; and these are
> what serve to articulate the form of that great thoroughfare, with its
> avenues and boulevards, that is the river. (798)

A hundred years later, these same quays would be under assault from Pompidou's determination to push through motorways for automobiles (an assault only partially resisted). Here, Haussmann's innovation becomes itself the ideal to be defended against a later vandal, Pompidou as a latter-day "Alsatian Attila."

Something surprisingly similar occurs in the case of Les Halles, where the old buildings (that is, nineteenth century) were demolished (mid 1960s) and moved to the outskirts. The vast food markets at the centre of Paris were for generations the heart and soul—or, more literally, the stomach, the guts, the intestines—of the city. "With Les Halles gone," writes Louis Chevalier, "Paris is gone" (246). But what precisely has *gone*? If it is simply the buildings, the glass and iron constructions put up by the architect Baltard, then these were, precisely, architectural innovations resisted in their own time and pushed through by, ahem, Haussmann (see Pinkney, 78). Another problem with the "Paris perdu" rhetoric is that one generation's architectural abominations become the next generation's prized monuments.

But of course the argument is that what was destroyed in the relocation of Les Halles from the centre to the periphery of the city was far more than the buildings themselves (whose Haussmannian origin was conveniently overlooked). Les Halles was not so much a place as a spirit: a centre of working-class population, a neighbourhood, a source of cultural vitality—and also, in the unabashed words of Richard Cobb, of "inexpensive prostitutes" (181).

Something of the attraction of the old Les Halles, and of the conscious or unconscious condescension implicit in attitudes towards it, can be seen in the account given by Robert McAlmon, in *Being Geniuses Together*, of a casual visit to "the markets" by a group of 1920s American expatriates, at the end of a long night's drinking. The tone is a typical McAlmon mixture of realism and cynicism, straight reportage and self-conscious irony.

It was a mistily glistening morning, the dazzle seeming to splinter before our befuddled eyes. We knew we were too late for the great show of meats, vegetables, and flowers, but as we walked we spoke

of the wholesale market's smell and beauty, and the soundness of the
market's working types. (59)

How much literary artifice is self-consciously displayed in the
repeated s/z sounds of that first sentence? How much irony, and/or
condescension, lurks behind that "soundness"? McAlmon's compan-
ions discourse learnedly on Renaissance Italian paintings and are "as
careless in expressing our disdains as we were in acclaiming our
enthusiasms, and at every bistro we stopped to have another cognac."
Again, does McAlmon's tone here dismiss or endorse the value of
aesthetic opinions elaborated under the influence of dawn cognacs in
Les Halles? They meet some old women, from whom they obtain some
flowers, later exchanged for vegetables; they meet some young
women ("street girls," still on the streets at dawn), who (cf. Cobb!)
"suggested that we go home with them, and mentioned prices, begin-
ning at thirty francs and coming down to five" (60). The Americans
decline, but donate the vegetables, in a conscious (unconscious?)
parody of the commercial dealings of the markets of Les Halles. The
passage (which McAlmon tosses off, with his usual insouciance, as a
mere anecdote) is full of ambivalent implications relating to the
implicit romantic idealization of the markets, in the rhetoric of
"Paris perdu."

The "old" (i.e., Baltard/Haussmann) buildings of Les Halles were
torn down ("architecture is aggression") in the 1970s. For a while there
was only a vast construction hole in the ground, literally dubbed *le
Trou*. The most witty use of this site was made by the Italian film
director Marco Ferreri, who filmed in it a parody Western, *Touche pas
la femme blanche*, in which the Halles/hole stood in for the Wild West
desert. This gesture was both parodic (an uncivilized wilderness in
the heart of Paris) and envious (if only we *could* genuinely recreate
the Wild West in the heart of Paris!). Most recent responses to the loss
of Les Halles, however, have concentrated not so much upon *le Trou* as
upon the banal shopping centre that has come to fill it.

The new Forum des Halles is not perhaps the most successful
modern building in Paris (to put it mildly),[1] but it continues a long
tradition of adventurous and controversial architecture. The central

example is of course the Eiffel Tower, widely scorned and savagely attacked when it was first built, and now the most enduring symbol of the city. The famous letter published in *Le Temps* in February 1887 by a committee of writers and artists may now stand as one of the canonical texts for the "Paris perdu" trope:

> We come, writers, painters, sculptors, architects, passionate lovers
> of the beauty, until now intact, of Paris, to protest with all our force,
> with all our indignation, in the name of unappreciated French taste,
> in the name of menaced French art and history, against the erection,
> in the very heart of our capital, of the useless and monstrous Eiffel
> Tower....
>
> It suffices to understand what we put forth, to imagine, for an
> instant, a ridiculously tall tower dominating Paris, like a gigantic
> black factory chimney, overpowering with its barbaric mass Notre
> Dame, Sainte Chapelle, the Tour Saint Jacques, the Louvre, the dome
> of the Invalides, the Arc de Triomphe, all our humiliated monuments,
> all our belittled architecture, which will be obliterated in this stupe-
> fying dream.
>
> And for twenty years we will see spreading out over the entire
> city, still vibrating with the genius of so many centuries, we will see,
> spreading like a blot of ink, the odious shadow of the odious column
> of tin.[2]

Vituperation of the Eiffel Tower was not *simply* an instance of "Paris perdu," though that was certainly part of it. Right from the start the Eiffel Tower was seen as a symbolic counterpart, in both religious and political terms, to its near-contemporary, the Basilica of the Sacré-Coeur at the height of Montmartre. Personally, I am by no means neutral on this topic. The Basilica of the Sacred Heart was erected after the 1870–71 Franco-Prussian War, by public subscription, in order to exculpate the sins of the Commune. Not, that is, the sins of the Parisian bourgeoisie who collaborated with the Prussians as they put down the Commune and decimated (literally) the working classes of Paris, lining them up by the hundreds against the walls of Père Lachaise and gunning them down—no, to exculpate the "sins" of those who had dared to proclaim socialism, the "sins" of feminists like Louise Michel, the "sins" of the slaughtered. Sacré-Coeur is (again, literally) a whited sepulchre; a monument to hypocrisy; a piece of fake Orientalism; an architectural travesty. I have never set foot inside it. I curse it every time I inadvertently catch a glimpse of it on the Paris skyline; I hate the fact that it is the first monument you see as you take the bus in to Paris from Charles de Gaulle airport; of all the buildings in the world, it is the one I would most like to demolish.[3]

The contrast between Sacré-Coeur and the Tour Eiffel was openly acknowledged at the time. Richard D.E. Burton records that the Tower's construction, "completed in 1889 to mark the centenary of the Declaration of the Rights of Man, would henceforth confront Sacré-Coeur...as an emblem in iron of modernity and rationality triumphing over obscurantism and guilt" (18). Iron was precisely the point (as Benjamin would later stress in *The Arcades Project*): for a Catholic reactionary like Huysmans, "iron was anti-art, anti-poetry, anti-God" (Burton, 195). By contrast, French writer Eugène-Melchior imagined the Tour Eiffel addressing its counterparts of Notre-Dame: "Old abandoned towers, you are no longer listened to. Do you not see that the world has changed its pole, and that it is spinning on my iron axis?... You were ignorance, I am Science" (quoted in Burton, 193).

The most notorious manifestation of anti-Eiffel Tower sentiment is the story of Guy de Maupassant dining there, on the grounds that it was the only place in Paris where he could look out a window and not see the Eiffel Tower. Roland Barthes made the definitive comment: "Like man himself, who is the only one not to know his own glance, the Tower is the only blind point of the total optical system of which it is the center and Paris the circumference" (*Eiffel Tower*, 4).

In a more literal, less metaphysical sense than Barthes', the Eiffel Tower is also a "blind point" in a good deal of the American and Canadian expatriate writing about Paris. It is very seldom even mentioned, and I cannot recall any novel or story with a key scene set there, or any poem that uses it as a central image. In John Glassco's *Memoirs of Montparnasse*, it appears only as a fatuous tourist expectation of Paris:

"Oh boy, I want to see the Latin Quarter and Montmartre and the Bastille and the Sacré Coeur and everything."

"You forgot the Eiffel Tower," I said.

"My God, yes." In the grey light of the rainy morning her expression suddenly grew rapt. "The Eiffel Tower!" (126)

In all of Mavis Gallant's short stories, I can recall only one passing reference to "a number of tourists [taking] pictures of the Eiffel Tower and the lighted water" ("A Report," *In Transit*, 210). Nevertheless, at least three of Gallant's books carry images of the Eiffel Tower on their covers[4]—so its semiotic force as *the* icon of Parisianness survives as a marketing tool, despite its textual absence.

The equivalent of the Eiffel Tower a hundred years later was the Centre Pompidou at Beaubourg, opened in 1976. As John Russell comments,

> *It was a building enormous in size, outrageous in color and design, and completely out of key with its surroundings. But it soon became clear that the Centre Pompidou was to the 1970s what the Eiffel Tower had been to the 1880s: an erection as indispensable as it was provocative. No sooner was it there than it was difficult to imagine Paris without it. (161)*

There were, of course, many people who were all too eager to imagine Paris without it, led of course by Louis Chevalier: "that frightful jumble of pipes and conduits and ducts that they have dubbed the gas works or the refinery" (260).

Yet Beaubourg has been a popular building ever since it was first opened—so popular that its carpeting had to be replaced years ahead of schedule. Some of this popularity is due to its amenities, especially an easily accessible public library, a rarity in Paris at that time. There is also its view, as John Russell (by far the most perceptive writer on Beaubourg) explains:

> *Those who detest Beaubourg—and there are still plenty of them around—like to say that people ride the exterior moving staircase*

to the top, take a quick look around, and go back down again. But
the truth is that these people see Paris from that moving staircase
as no one has ever seen it before. The Pompidou Centre is not a high
building. The visitor can "see more" from the Eiffel Tower, or from
the Sacré-Coeur. What he does not get from those higher points of
vantage is the feeling of participation, the instantaneity, the sense
of being way aloft and yet within hallooing distance of the ground,
that he gets at Beaubourg. Beaubourg gives him in no time at all the
texture of Paris, the inner life of Paris, the layered secrecies of Paris.
It shows him how Paris has changed, and it also shows him how it has
stayed the same. (161)

Russell is also illuminating in his commentary on the most scandalous
aspect of Beaubourg's design: the way that all its "pipes and conduits
and ducts" are exposed, all the normally concealed inner workings of
the building turned inside out and displayed on the exterior. Russell
realizes that something in this reversal was fundamentally offensive
to the conservative Parisian spirit:

What differentiates Beaubourg from every other building in Paris
is the total, the reckless, the unmitigated candor of its operation.
In many aspects of their lives, Parisians are a secretive, devious,
ungiving people. They mind their own business—so they would say—
and they expect other people to do the same. Buildings are there to
cover things up, not to leave them open to everyone who passes by
in the street. Not only does Beaubourg display its every last secret in
public, but it displays them in color. Nothing could be more abhor-
rent to the traditional Parisian. He would as soon show you his bank
balance as let you see his plumbing, his ventilation system, or the
material in his home computer. Beaubourg puts it all on view. (161)

Exactly what Russell is talking about can be seen in a comment by
Julien Green: "And what shall I say of the entrails that Beaubourg
exhibits with the idiotic satisfaction of a toddler baring its stomach?"
(119).

The whole point of Beaubourg (and of its comparison here to the Eiffel Tower) is its outrageousness, and the way that outrageousness is "completely out of key with its surroundings." One could also make an interesting contemporary comparison between Beaubourg and the Eiffel Tower, and the Tour Maine-Montparnasse (completed in 1973, three years before Beaubourg), erected on the site of the old Montparnasse railway station and situated so as to be visually framed by the length of the rue de Rennes looking south from Saint-Germain-des-Prés. Again we have a building out of key with its surroundings: a sleek, elegant, modernist highrise tower that would have fitted perfectly on 6th Avenue in New York. Its designers, Norma Evenson records, "consistently maintained that once completed it would become a source of pride and an attraction equal to the beloved Eiffel Tower" (194). This has not happened. It is hard to find anyone with a kind word to say about the Tour Montparnasse.[5] Like Beaubourg, it has a splendid view from the top, but the viewing platform has not become a major tourist attraction (despite, presumably, the Maupassant/Barthes advantage that it would be the one place in Paris where you would not have to see the Tour Montparnasse!). I think that the problem is that the design was not outrageous *enough*. By 1973, its modernist elegance was already somewhat passé. The very fact that it would have fitted so perfectly on 6th Avenue counted against it. (Beaubourg would *not* fit on 6th Avenue: its five-storey height does, curiously, echo its surroundings, but would be lost in New York.)

The most successful of President Mitterrand's *grands projets*—I.M. Pei's Pyramid at the Louvre—works because of the combination of outrageous incongruity (this glass and steel construction surrounded by classical stone and masonry) and curious appositeness (the reference to all the Egyptian antiquities in the Louvre, the echoes of pyramids in the crazier metaphysics of the Revolution—Pei's Pyramid is perhaps the only place in contemporary Paris where Robespierre would have felt at home[6]). It is precisely this combination that the Tour Montparnasse does not attain, thus rendering it a legitimate target of "Paris perdu" jeremiads.

If the covers of Mavis Gallant's books were to accurately reflect the architectural references of her stories, they would show, not the Tour

Eiffel, but the Tour Montparnasse. Probably because she lived in the neighbourhood, and had to see it every day, it is the most prominent architectural innovation in her fiction.

In a 1979 story, "Baum, Gabriel, 1935-( )," one of the characters says that "the Montparnasse railway station was to be torn down and a dark tower built in its place; no one believed him" (*Selected Stories*, 459). A few pages later, "the Montparnasse station had been torn down, and a dark ugly tower had been put in its place" (463). Two stories from 1993 make the same reference: "Across the Bridge" recalls "the old Montparnasse station, where the trains came in from the west of France. Hardly anyone remembers it now: a low gray building with a wooden floor" (136). And in "In Plain Sight,"

> From the window, if he leaned a bit to the right, he would see the shadow of the Montparnasse tower, and the office building that had replaced the old railway station with its sagging wooden floor. Only yesterday, he started to tell himself—but no. A generation of Parisians had never known anything else. (886)

These references in Gallant's fiction are reinforced in her essays. In "Paris: The Taste of a New Age," an essay written in 1981 and republished in the *Paris Notebooks*, Gallant makes explicit the meaning hinted at in those passing references in her stories. The Tour Montparnasse, she says,

> has been there forever....The old Montparnasse railway station, which the tower replaced, was there some fourteen years ago; there are people still living in the neighbourhood who went by it every day. Oddly enough, no one can quite say what it looked like. It was low, it was gray, and, yes, it was dirty and run-down. What else? The wooden floors sloped and creaked. There were always a few pimps hanging about, waiting to catch the Breton village girls as they stepped off the train. No one denies that the station was inefficient and had to be replaced. But a postcard view of it arouses no immediate recognition. It might as well have been torn down sixty years ago. What people do recall is that the streets around the station were not as shabby and anonymous as they seem now. There have

been few structural changes apart from the tower, which still makes the older buildings look dwarfed and absurd. The changes it has attracted (pizza parlours instead of family restaurants) seem to blind the mind's eye. The nature of a neighbourhood has been so funda- mentally altered by a single unnecessary structure that collective memory is wiped clean. (167–68)

In these passages, about the speed with which previous buildings on a site are forgotten, Gallant may simply be recording a common fact about urban memory and/or forgetfulness (many of us, seeing a new construction site, have difficulty remembering what was there before), or she may be deliberately recalling Gertrude Stein's comments in *Paris France* on the building of the boulevard Raspail: "there is no remembering what it looked like before and even no remembering what it looks like now" (15).

Based on her comments on the Tour Montparnasse, it would be easy enough to see Gallant simply as another "Paris perdu" moaner; but her discussion in this essay is in fact much more subtle and nuanced. A few pages later, she makes a very interesting, and apparently paradoxical, point:

Whatever is built in Paris is built in a void. There is no contemporary building to which a new structure can be likened. Critics reach back 400 years to make a point. The point is, inevitably, reactionary. (171)

Of course there are plenty of "contemporary buildings," so this "void" is paradoxical. But I take it that what Gallant means is that the new buildings do not form a tradition, and thus cannot provide a criterion, a measure. Each one of them—Beaubourg, the Pyramid, the Bastille Opera, the new Bibliothèque Nationale—is so utterly individual, even bizarre, that even at their best they cannot provide the kind of template that Haussmann laid down with the regularity of his boule- vards. Thus, Gallant concludes, critics have to "reach back 400 years" to find criteria for their judgements: and their judgements are thus "inevitably reactionary." That is, the persistence of the "Paris perdu" trope is both inevitable and enervating. If there is an architectural crisis in Paris, then "Paris perdu" is as much its cause as its effect.

Gallant's essay discusses Beaubourg at some length,[7] but I would prefer to concentrate on what she has to say about a much more modest construction in her own neighbourhood, not a *grand projet* at all, scarcely even a *petit projet*. In the early 1980s, Gallant lived just off the rue de Sèvres (just a couple of blocks away from my own haunts on the rue Rousselet). On the rue de Sèvres there is "a small, dim chapel of gentle ugliness," as Gallant describes it (161), owned by the Lazarist brothers and containing, as sacred relic, the body of Saint Vincent de Paul.[8]

> *In the 1970s, when the value of property in Paris began its heady ascent, the Lazarists sold nearly all that was left of their land.... The sale resulted in the construction of an undistinguished apartment block, a supermarket, and a shopping arcade. The arcade is in reality a bleak tunnel of storefronts linking Rue de Sèvres to Rue du Cherche-Midi. Above the Rue de Sèvres entrance is its name: "Passage Commercial." For once, a clear purpose has not been disguised by something like "Pompadour's Pathway." Some of the shops never found takers; their windows still carry glazier's chalk marks. Some opened and closed rapidly. There is always one with a "For Rent" sign in the window. Like so many of the arbitrary projects foisted on Paris, the arcade does not work because it was not needed. Urban change, now, has virtually nothing to do with urban requirements. A considerable amount of innovation seems to drain the street of its vitality rather than to infuse it with new energy. It is not blight that is settling in but a new sickness—new to Paris, at least: architectural anemia. (163)*

I have somewhat mixed reactions to this passage. I agree that this "Passage Commercial" is entirely undistinguished; I have walked through it many times, using it as a short-cut to the rue du Cherche-Midi, without ever being tempted to linger or actually shop in it; it certainly has none of the aura of Benjamin's arcades. But at the same time, it's still there. Twenty years after Gallant wrote her essay, it survives; its name has changed, from the functional "Passage Commercial" to "Galerie de Sèvrien," slightly more pretentious but still nowhere near as bad as Gallant's guess. The last time I walked through it, the shops seemed successful; there were no "glazier's chalk marks" on the windows; no "For Rent" signs. Indeed, as far as I could tell, it had expanded over the years. No one would pretend that this "Galerie" was one of the great shopping attractions of Paris; but neither is it a failure.

"Paris perdu" rhetoric always exaggerates: a neighbourhood is "ruined," a street is "lost forever," a city is "assassinated." "Ineluctible intolerable oblivion," moans Chevalier. In reality, a great city, especially Paris, is always more resilient. A city always changes and grows; it is a constant cycle of destruction and recreation. Not all the old buildings were masterpieces; not all the new ones are hideous (though some of them certainly are!). But nothing is, ultimately, *ruined*. The city is not lost. As Norma Evenson wittily puts it, "Contrary to rumor, Paris is alive and well and living in Paris" (xvii).

PART TWO

⟵-- "I IS AN OTHER" -->

Parisian Autobiography

WHEN PARIS IS REPRESENTED in art or in literature, the image is often as much mythological as it is real. Paris is a city that lends itself to romance and transgression, to nostalgia and desire. The effect is, of course, self-perpetuating: the accumulating image of Paris preconditions visitors to expect, to react to, and to add to that inherited image. Accounts of life in Paris, especially those written by foreigners, must always be read with a sceptical eye, alert as much to the mythology as to the reality.

While artists and writers have mythologized all periods of Parisian history, the decade of the 1920s is probably the most romanticized. "Paris in the 20s" has been remembered and/or mythologized, at least in American writing and popular culture, as a Golden Age. It was the era of the expatriates: when you could sit in cafés in Montparnasse and drink white wine with James Joyce, or challenge Ernest Hemingway to a round of boxing. If you were lucky, you could obtain (or fake) a Saturday evening invitation to 27 rue de Fleurus and sit at the feet of Gertrude Stein (no other position was permissable), admire the collection of Picasso and Cézanne on her walls, and wonder (discreetly) about the hovering presence of Alice B. Toklas. If you were ambitious yourself, in a literary way, you could submit your work to magazines like *This Quarter* or *Transatlantic Review*, or even entertain hopes of being published by a press like Contact Editions, run by the cynical and abrasive Robert McAlmon. Especially if you had just come from Prohibition-era America, the life of the Parisian cafés must have seemed like a decadent vision of paradise; and what's more, the exchange rate for the dollar was so favourable that even the most modest income enabled you to live like a lord. A Golden Age, indeed—and, like all mythological Golden Ages, it came equipped with its own ending, its fall from grace, its expulsion from paradise, in the shape of the Stock Market Crash of 1929, which sent so many of the expatriates (but not McAlmon or Stein) scurrying home. And once they got there, what was there left for them to do but write their autobiographies?

If Paris in the 20s was a myth, then it was a myth largely created by the expatriates themselves: and their primary vehicle for doing so was autobiography. The fashion was set by the immense success of Gertrude Stein's *The Autobiography of Alice B. Toklas*, published in 1933; and over the succeeding decades, practically everyone who had ever set foot in Montparnasse in the 1920s published a book about it. Autobiography became the method of memorializing, and mythologizing, a place and a time that receded, increasingly, into the image of the century's lost innocence—an innocence here paradoxically represented as a decadence. Lives and memoirs piled upon one another. Everyone from Ernest Hemingway to Jimmy the Barman committed themselves to paper. Morley Callaghan wrote a book about his notorious sparring-match with Hemingway, which takes several more hours to read than the fight itself lasted (and in 2003, it was made into an even more dull and interminable television film). From book to book, memories are revised, insults are exchanged, and old battles are re-fought. Gertrude Stein in 1933 contrived to be utterly nasty about Ernest Hemingway; Hemingway waited thirty years for his revenge, and then contrived to be perfectly foul about Gertrude (who was safely dead) and Alice B. Toklas (who wasn't). The Montparnasse memoirs are not always an edifying spectacle.

As they accumulate, these autobiographies take on the appearance of a multi-volumed novel, an overgrown version of Lawrence Durrell's *Alexandria Quartet*, in which the same characters and the same incidents appear and reappear from different perspectives, taking on the quality of myth. It is the mythological element that is explicitly responded to in fictional works like Alan Rudolph's film *The Moderns*, Howard Engel's detective fantasy *Murder in Montparnasse*, or Bill Richardson's graveyard pastiche *Waiting for Gertrude*. But the Montparnasse memoirs also provide a kind of test case for autobiography: they supply, indeed they flaunt, the possibility of external verification, a criterion of fact—or at least of consensus—against which any one account may be measured for its accuracy.

For autobiography has always been a deeply paradoxical genre.[1] On the one hand, autobiography makes its appeal to the special authority and authenticity of the participant: an eye-witness, and, even more, an I-witness. I know, the author tells you; I was there; I am in a unique position to tell you The Truth. But on the other hand, reading audiences always approach autobiography with a certain amount of scepticism; they know that autobiographers—especially politicians, though they are an extreme case—are likely to be engaged in self-justification. If old battles are being re-fought, guess who wins. That is, autobiography's basic premise of reliability—its promise of a uniquely privileged access to the subject's experience—is simultaneously the ground for its unreliability. As a genre, it hovers between its guarantee of authorial authenticity and its built-in inability to deliver on what it promises. It is the most trustworthy of genres and also the most untrustworthy.

In trying to cope with the paradoxical nature of the genre, recent criticism has been at pains to distinguish its various modes and narrative positions. Briefly, I would like to outline three distinct positions—which I will immediately proceed to modify.

THE AUTHOR. *By "the author," I mean the historically existing person who wrote the autobiography, about whom a certain number of facts may be ascertained from sources independent of the text of the autobiography itself.*

THE NARRATOR. By "the narrator," I mean the position taken by the author, the technical point of view from which she or he chooses to narrate the autobiography.

THE PROTAGONIST. By "the protagonist," I mean the character who appears as the principal agent in the narrated events, the person about whom the story is told.

The premise of autobiography is that all three of these narrative positions are occupied by the personal pronoun "I." Strictly speaking, this pronoun has three different referents—author, narrator, and protagonist—but in practice, there is always an undecidable slippage between the three. Autobiography in some ways *asserts* the identity of the three—it is this assertion that Philippe Lejeune calls "the autobiographical pact," the implicit promise of reliability made by authors to their readers—but at the same time, autobiography's fascination often resides in the *non*-identity of the three. In the classical autobiography, the protagonist is a young person who grows to become the author, who then creates the narrator as a means of showing the continuity between the protagonist and the author.[2] But in practice, this classical version is continually being disrupted by textual variations on the position of the "narrator." Nowhere is this disruption more evident than in the autobiographies of expatriate writers in the mythologized Paris of the 1920s.

Indeed, the various experiments with autobiographical structure contribute strongly to that mythology, by elevating the subjects of their books to the level of fiction, almost of myth. Both Gertrude Stein and Kay Boyle use their privileged position as narrator (or editor of the narrative) to cast their protagonists in glowing terms, as "geniuses." John Glassco uses his highly manipulated narrator to create an image of his protagonist as a beautiful, Adonis-like young man on the point of death—as, in fiction if not fact, a dying god. So the technical manipulations of the Paris autobiographies are not mere technical exercises: they are an essential part of the city's mythology.

⇢ THE MOST FAMOUS of these 1920s expatriate autobiographies is Gertrude Stein's *The Autobiography of Alice B. Toklas*, with its notorious narratological manoeuvre:

> *For some time now many people, and publishers, have been asking Gertrude Stein to write her autobiography and she had always replied, not possibly.*
>
> *She began to tease me and say that I should write my autobiography. Just think, she would say, what a lot of money you would make. She then began to invent titles for my autobiography. My Life With The Great, Wives of Geniuses I Have Sat With, My Twenty-five Years With Gertrude Stein.*
>
> *Then she began to get serious and say, but really seriously you ought to write your autobiography. Finally I promised that if during the summer I could find time I would write my autobiography.*
>
> *When Ford Madox Ford was editing the* Transatlantic Review *he once said to Gertrude Stein, I am a pretty good writer and a pretty good editor and a pretty good business man but I find it very difficult to be all three at once.*
>
> *I am a pretty good housekeeper and a pretty good gardener and a pretty good needlewoman and a pretty good secretary and a pretty good editor and a pretty good vet for dogs and I have to do them all at once and I found it difficult to add being a pretty good author.*
>
> *About six weeks ago Gertrude Stein said, it does not look to me as if you were ever going to write that autobiography. You know what I am going to do. I am going to write it for you. I am going to write it as simply as Defoe did the autobiography of Robinson Crusoe. And she has and this is it.* (309-10)

This apparently straightforward substitution of Stein for Toklas stems from many causes, and produces many complex and unpredictable effects. Biographically, it seems that the narratorial device was, in Karin Cope's words, an attempt "to patch up a huge battle between Stein and Toklas" (165); by adopting her lover's voice, by placing her at the centre of the narrative, Gertrude was reassuring and reasserting Alice's importance and centrality both to their personal life and to their public career. Equally, Cope sees both *The Autobiography of Alice B. Toklas* and its follow-up, *Everybody's Autobiography*, as "attempts to exit from passages in [Stein's] life when her narcissim—her sense of self—was particularly at risk. Both works arise from and address moments of deep crisis in her life, when she was not sure that her life as she knew it could go on" (164). Thus, the equivocal nature of the narrative "I" may also be seen to reflect real questions about Stein's sense of her own identity.

Whatever the biographical reasons, the effect is that the "I" (as is also the case with John Glassco) problematizes the whole stance of autobiography. Stein disrupts the solidarity of the autobiographical "I," conventionally allowed to slide silently back and forth between author, narrator, and protagonist. The authorial "I" is still Gertrude Stein—it is her name that will eventually appear on the title page,[3] in the position of the signature: *The Autobiography of Alice B. Toklas*, **by** Gertrude Stein—but the narratorial "I" is now the voice of Alice B. Toklas: mimed, fictionalized, yet also (by all accounts) rendered with marvellous accuracy. And while the protagonist is nominally Toklas, the principal agent of the narrative is Stein. Each voice echoes off the others, producing multiple levels of indeterminacy.

Take, for instance, one of the passages disparaging Ernest Hemingway:

> Later on when things were difficult between Gertrude Stein and Hemingway, she always remembered with gratitude that after all it was Hemingway who first caused to be printed a piece of *The Making of Americans*. She always says, yes sure I have a weakness for Hemingway. After all he was the first of the young men to knock at my door and he did make Ford print the first piece of *The Making of Americans*.
>
> I myself have not so much confidence that Hemingway did do this. I have never known what the story is but I have always been certain that there was some other story behind it all. That is the way I feel about it. (264–65)

Is this simply Stein having her cake and eating it too?—that is, insulting Hemingway, but evading responsibility for the insult, complacently admitting her own "weakness," while attributing the real malice to Toklas?[4] It is possible that this passage accurately depicts Toklas's feelings about Hemingway; but it is still Stein (the author) who chooses not only to include this passage in the Toklas narration but also to highlight it as one of the very few times in the book where Toklas disagrees with Stein, and one of the very few times in which the narrator expresses anything less than full confidence in the trustworthiness of her own narration. "I have never known what the story is," she admits, undermining her own status as narrator, but also allowing for the possibility that someone else *does* know. But who else could that person be but Gertrude Stein, the author who is here declining to share her secrets with her own narrator?

The narrator's self-deprecation fits also with the portrait of Toklas, as both narrator and protagonist, which the book is developing. As the suggested titles for her autobiography indicate, Toklas—or Stein-as-Toklas—portrayed herself always in a secondary role, as an attendant on greatness. The list of things that Toklas is "pretty good at" (housekeeper, gardener, needlewoman, secretary, editor, vet) defines her role in the household as that of an enabler: she creates the domestic space within which it is possible for Gertrude Stein to function as a genius—in Stein's own terms, as a writer and as a man. It is this domestic role of Toklas that is made literal in her position as the narrator of Stein's autobiography. Quite literally, she enables Stein to speak; her voice provides the site within which it is possible for Stein to convey her own vision of herself as if from a distance, as if from the place of *the other*.

Thus, Stein's use of Toklas as narrator dramatizes one of the continuing paradoxes of autobiography. The narrator must always be "the other," occupying that place of alterity from which the authorial "I" can look at the protagonist, and at herself, as if from a distance. Autobiography continually replays Rimbaud's aphorism, "Je est un autre"—"I is an other"—on which so many modernist schemes of identity are based. The narrator mediates between the past biographical "I" of the protagonist and the present biographical "I" of the author; but this mediation is possible only from a position that is always, to some degree, fictional. "I" is an other. By placing the narratorial "I" literally outside herself, in Toklas, Stein thematises that fictional distance; yet at the same time, since the "other" is, after all, her lover—and, furthermore, a lover of the same sex—Stein also cancels out that difference, and in paradoxical form reunites the various "I"s of "her" autobiography.

--> IN *MEMOIRS OF MONTPARNASSE*, John Glassco positions himself as an even more radically distanced "other," adopting the stance of a young man on the verge of death. When *Memoirs* was published in 1970, Glassco provided a "Prefatory Note," signed "J.G.," in which he explained that the first three chapters had been written "in Paris in 1928...soon after the events recorded"; whereas the rest of the book, the greatest part of it, "was written in the Royal Victoria Hospital in Montreal during three months of the winter of 1932-3, when I was awaiting a crucial operation." Having barely survived the operation, Glassco says, he set the manuscript aside, and "did not look at [it] again for thirty-five years" (xiii).

This account would appear to set up a straightforward division between the author (the John Glassco of 1970, who publishes the manuscript with minimal editing, and who signs the Prefatory Note); the narrator (the John Glassco of 1932, lying in his hospital bed in Montreal awaiting a potentially fatal operation); and the protagonist (the John Glassco of 1928, living a life of careless dissipation in Montparnasse). But immediately some slippages appear. For at least the first three chapters, the protagonist is also the narrator: and indeed, the protagonist makes quite a point of the fact that he is already, at a precociously young age, writing his autobiography. The 1932 narrator, despite his precarious position on the brink of death, quite conspicuously declines to distance himself from the protagonist, or to offer any moral condemnation of the excesses that have ruined his health and quite possibly lost him his life.[5] Even the author of the Prefatory Note does his best to deny the traditional identity of the three positions, insisting that "This young man is no longer myself... in my memory he is less like someone I have been than a character in a novel I have read" (xiii). (Note, however, that this fictionality exists "in my memory," not in my text: that is, it is the *protagonist*, not the *narrator*, whom Glassco here disclaims as fictional.)

Within the text of *Memoirs of Montparnasse*, there are many further hints that all is not as it seems. The narrator persistently describes the protagonist as a born liar, and the action is filled with references to fictional memoirs, forged memoirs, fake memoirs.[6] Despite these hints, many early readers of Glassco (including me) displayed a touching faith in the reliability of the Prefatory Note. Early responses to the book accepted the Note as an authentic account of the circumstances of composition. Many of Glassco's friends in the writers' circle of Foster, Québec, knew exactly what was going on, but kept admirably straight faces. It was not until after Glassco's death in 1981 that the full extent of his deception could be appreciated.[7]

The truth is: nothing in the *Memoirs* was in fact written in that hospital bed in Montreal in 1932; the bulk of the writing was done in 1964–65, with a fairly extensive revision in the late 1960s before its 1970 publication. In fact, Glassco may well have been prompted to write the first draft in response to the success of Morley Callaghan's *That Summer in Paris* (1963) and Ernest Hemingway's *A Moveable Feast* (1964), feeling—with a good deal of justification—that he could do a better job than either of them. And then, with the manuscript languishing, his revisiting of it in the late 60s may well have been prompted by his renewed correspondence with Kay Boyle, and by her 1968 republication of Robert McAlmon's *Being Geniuses Together*, with extensive editing and interpolated chapters by herself.[8]

Part of Glassco's pose, then, was to claim that these memoirs had in fact been the first in the field: written long before Hemingway or Callaghan, and at least contemporaneous with Stein. By creating the fictitious composition date of 1932, Glassco gleefully usurps the title of the earliest of the Paris-in-the-20s autobiographers. At the same time, the text ironically questions the authority of such a claim: Glassco at one point lays aside his manuscript because "I wondered if I was not too close to the events I was relating" (58). Yet it is precisely the prestige of being "close" that the faked date lays claim to.

The result is that Glassco's narrator—the dying young man in the Montreal hospital—is a figure as thoroughly fictional as Gertrude Stein's Alice B. Toklas. Like Toklas, the young man existed historically: what is fictional is not his illness or his location but his *writing*. Like Stein, then, Glassco fictionalizes the position of the narrator—but unlike Stein, and even more radically, Glassco also fictionalizes the position of *the author*. Conventionally, a Prefatory Note is one place where the author speaks in his own right, not as a narrator; but in Glassco, the Prefatory Note is the book's biggest fiction. Alternatively, one could say that the author of the Prefatory Note is turned into another narrator, while the position of author— the one position from which no lies should be tolerated—has been reserved for yet another figure: that is, for the John Glassco who left his manuscripts to Library and Archives Canada, and who thus assured—with, I believe, full intention and posthumous glee—that his deception would be uncovered.

Thus, the "J.G." who writes in the Prefatory Note that the young protagonist is "less like someone I have been than a character in a novel I have read" is himself, in effect, also a character in a novel he has read, or written. (In the surprisingly similar words with which Roland Barthes prefaced *his* autobiography, published five years after Glassco's, "Tout ceci doit être considéré comme dit par un personnage de roman.") Glassco's narrator becomes a fictional character, and his near-death experience is crucial to the ways in which this character is presented, and in which the image of his death becomes part of the mythology of 1920s Paris.

--> ROBERT MCALMON was the most notoriously unsuccessful of the American expatriates in Paris in the 1920s. He wrote hard, cynical, distinguished fiction, which went nowhere. He ran Contact Edtions, the most influential small press of the period. His autobiography, *Being Geniuses Together*, is in its first version the most conventional of the books I am looking at in this discussion, as it adheres to the classical form of minimizing or eliding any distinctions between author, narrator, and protagonist. It is in this book, more than anywhere else, that I hear what I take to be the authentic McAlmon voice—bitter, sarcastic, disillusioned, self-mocking, yet also acute, intelligent, and strikingly undeceived—the voice that I attempted to capture in my own portrait-poem *McAlmon's Chinese Opera* (1980). The original *Being Geniuses Together* was written in 1933-34, and published in London in 1938, where it suffered a not uncommon fate for McAlmon's books:

it was ignored. Within a year, the realities of the Europe of 1939 had eclipsed any nostalgia for the Paris of the 1920s. About McAlmon's book, Sanford J. Smoller records: "Reportedly, most of the unsold copies were destroyed during the Blitz by a bomb on the warehouse storing them" (xxxvi).

McAlmon returned to the period in 1945–47, when he wrote a novel called *The Nightinghouls of Paris*: a *roman à clef* with transparently thin disguises for all its characters. John Glassco and Graeme Taylor, here named Sudge Galbraith and Ross Campion, play a much more prominent role in the novel than they do in McAlmon's original memoir—and even there, their presence is mainly due to "creative editing" by Kay Boyle (see below). *Nightinghouls* was finally published, edited by Sanford J. Smoller, in 2007.

Being Geniuses Together itself disappeared until 1968, when it was reissued in a version assembled by Kay Boyle.[9] Boyle edited McAlmon's text quite extensively, cutting out some passages and adding others, including an account of Glassco and Taylor (Smoller, xxix). Neither in the 1968 edition nor in its 1984 reprint does she give any bibliographical indication of what changes she has made. It is a striking instance of editorial irresponsibility.

More drastically, Boyle adds to the text an autobiographical account of her own experiences in France in the 1920s, inserting her chapters in alternation with McAlmon's. But since the two narratives are not synchronized in time, the result is a discontinuous chronology. In practice, I suspect that most readers ignore the alternation, and read straight through the McAlmon chapters and straight through the Boyle chapters separately. But Boyle certainly intended the modernist collage effect of a disrupted time scheme.

What Boyle has done is to take McAlmon's title literally, and to attempt to produce a new, composite narrator, a role in which she and McAlmon can, at long last, be geniuses together. The narrator of the Boyle chapters portrays the Boyle protagonist as being obsessed with McAlmon; she presents, says Smoller, "a highly romanticized version of herself and her relationship with McAlmon....She is in love with him and is certain he feels the same about her" (xxvii). But the infatuation was not mutual. In *The Nightinghouls of Paris*, McAlmon is brutally dismissive: "A sense of failure and futility was embedded deeply in [Boyle's] soul, and she wrote, not well, but there was some authenticity in the black hysteria and incoherence of her writing" (37). In the McAlmon chapters of the joint *Being Geniuses Together*, Boyle is mentioned only briefly and indifferently. The editorial joining of the two is thus, to some extent, an exercise in emotional masochism, flaunting the fact that Boyle's devotion was not reciprocated. As the author/editor of the 1968 text, Boyle once again effaces herself in relation to McAlmon, burying her own life story inside his, accepting *his* title for *her* autobiography.

This subservient position accords also with the idealized portrait Boyle offers of herself as a young woman obsessed with the idea of service: "It was homage, service, to the spirit, perhaps, that I wanted to give....I wanted to find work in a bookshop (Sylvia Beach's), or with a publishing company (Robert McAlmon's), and give my daily allegiance to the words that others were able to put on paper" (113–14). In the Afterword added to the 1984 edition, Boyle continues this attempt to erase her own "I" from the "autobiography" she has created:

> *The pronoun "I" is an awkward one to deal with, and I do so with impatience; for I have come to believe that autobiography to fulfill a worthy purpose should be primarily a defense of those who have been unjustly dealt with in one's own time, and whose lives and work ask for vindication. (333)*

Thus, Boyle presents the "worthy purpose" of her own life and work as being the "vindication" of McAlmon's. The "awkward" pronoun "I" will be deferred from Boyle-as-editor to McAlmon-as-narrator.

Yet at the same time, it could be argued that Boyle's editing is an act of extraordinary arrogance and even aggression.[10] McAlmon died in 1956; he had no say in this presentation of his text. Boyle-as-editor claims for herself the position of being a "genius," "together" with McAlmon, posthumously creating a relationship that never existed in life. As McAlmon's title, *Being Geniuses Together* refers, ironically, to the whole large group of Paris expatriates; as Boyle's title, it refers, quite unironically, to only two people. She edits his text without full acknowledgement; she breaks up the chronology of his narrative with her own discontinuous chapters; on the front cover of the first edition (though not on the title page), her name appears before his. Her whole stance towards his text is one of appropriation.

I use this word, "appropriation," deliberately but obliquely, since it is a loaded term in contemporary cultural discourse. It now carries the connotation of an illegitimate or unauthorized exploitation of the life experience of another individual or group, or of the laying claim to a cultural authority to which the writer is not entitled. Appropriation thus expresses a deep-seated ambivalence. There is violence in it certainly: the experience of the other is devalorized, seen only as subservient to one's own. Yet at the same time the appropriating writer must, presumably, to some extent admire the experience being appropriated: admire it, envy it, desire it, perhaps even love it.

It is this kind of ambivalence that I sense, most strongly, in Boyle's treatment of McAlmon. Her editing of his text is appropriation in the most literal sense, of being unauthorized, since he was dead. It certainly expresses her love for him, and her desire to serve or vindicate him; yet the crude insertion of her own text into his, and the blatant appropriation of his title, may well be read as expressions of resentment for his neglect of her in the original text. Editing well is the best revenge.

The case is less clear in the instances of the other two books I have discussed so far, yet there, too, I believe that the author/narrator relationship could be seen as one of appropriation. We have no way of knowing whether, or in what fashion, Gertrude Stein may ever have asked Alice Toklas's permission to appropriate her voice; for what it's worth, my guess would be that the question never even occurred to Stein. Their whole relationship was based on the assumption that Gertrude's wishes, and Gertrude's genius, were paramount. Yet, as I suggested above, there is also the possibility that the *Autobiography* was written in Alice's voice as a way of appeasing her after a major quarrel. There is always a fine line between appropriation as an act of violence and appropriation as an act of desire, even love. In taking on her lover's voice, Stein may well have been usurping the place of the other; but the other was her love, a place which she already occupied, and which already, reciprocally, occupied her.

It may be more difficult to describe John Glassco as "appropriating" himself, since he certainly had, in some sense, the "permission" of the person being appropriated. Yet is there not also an element of resentment or aggression in Glassco's attitude toward his fictionalized 1932 narrator? The deathbed pose may on the one hand work to elicit the reader's sympathy for this young man in the Montreal hospital; but on the other, it deals out a terrible punishment to the carefree protagonist.

Glassco's narrator continually professes the ascendancy of pleasure over virtue, and of sensual dalliance over ascetic professionalism. I discuss this point in Chapter 10, where I note that Glassco in effect replays the classical Judgement of Paris, and comes down solidly on the same side as the Trojan prince. But, just as Paris was punished for his choice by the ruin of his city and his family, so Glassco-the-protagonist is punished, both by the onset of his illness, and by his 1960s author, who firmly returns him to the hospital deathbed—defining it, indeed, as the site of the narration.

Consider the very abrupt ending of the book, in which the protagonist's dalliance with Mrs. Quayle is cut off at precisely the moment of its supreme sensual fulfillment—"the land of sunshine and dancing. Spain" (200). Glassco explains that "My manuscript ended at this point. The operation was suddenly set forward a week, and there was no time to start on Chapter 27" (201). However, since we now know that these medical circumstances are entirely fictional, this explanation for cutting off the narrative at this point can no longer be sustained. The question remains: why in fact *does* the narrative end at this point, unmotivated by the circumstances of its actual composition? And the only answer can be that this ending ensures that the narrator remains in that Montreal hospital, unreleased by the text, confined to his bed of pain.

--> I HAVE ARGUED that the position of the narrator in autobiography is always, to some degree, fictional. Even if the fictionalization is not dramatized explicitly (as in Stein's adoption of Toklas's voice) or implicitly (as in Glassco's designed-to-be-discovered subterfuge about the hospital bed narrator), some degree of fictional distance is necessary to the creation of even the most conventionally conceived "autobiography." Indeed, a couple of recent Canadian writers who have dealt with their Parisian experience in ways which seem, at least superficially, to be fairly straightforwardly autobiographical have nevertheless both chosen to describe their books as novels. The subtitle "A Novel" appears on both Lola Lemire Tostevin's *Frog Moon* (1994) and Gail Scott's *My Paris* (1999). In Part Five, "Canadian Visions," I will discuss the degree to which Tostevin sets up an ironic distance between narrator and protagonist in the crucial Parisian chapter of that "novel." Here, I concentrate on Gail Scott.

Seventy years after the classic Paris-in-the-20s memoirs (but bearing them in mind as a model [especially Stein's]), Gail Scott revisits the paradoxical position of author/narrator in an "autobiography" that goes to remarkable stylistic lengths to insist upon its own status as "a novel." While the book may initially appear to be a straightforward account of Gail Scott's six-month stay in Paris (which actually happened, and may be independently documented), the figure of the protagonist that gradually emerges is treated with sufficient distance, irony, and even mockery that it may well be best to regard her as a fictional character.

In addition, Scott writes in an idiosyncratic and fractured prose style that in some ways poses the most drastic challenge in any of these Parisian memoirs to the centrality and authority of the autobiographical "I." Some readers (including many of my students) have found this style so disconcerting as to render the book almost unreadable; I, on the other hand, suspect that it is more radical in theory than in practice.

At first sight, *My Paris* may seem to present itself in a conventional memoir form, almost as a diary. Each numbered section seems to correspond to a single day in the protagonist's six-month stay in Paris. But if so, there would be some 180 numbered entries, as against the actual 120. And Scott's narrator at one point admits: "Also lying by writing day 40. Because sometimes no entries for ages. Or several in a sitting" (51). So the book's most ostentatious gesture towards factual

autobiography—the numbering of daily sections—is revealed as ficti-
tious. The "diary" format of *My Paris* cannot be relied on.

Further, the "novel" is full of snide comments at the protago-
nist's expense. The narration continually insists on the protagonist's
insecurities and failings: everything from her skin diseases to her
lack of a chic Parisian fashion sense, from her awkward accent to
the overstated paranoia about her lack of proper visa papers. This
ironic discrepancy is explicitly stated in several passages that pit
the "narrator" against the "author." I'm not at all sure that Gail Scott
is here using these terms in the same sense that I have outlined
earlier in this chapter. I sense that her "author" is at times closer to
my "protagonist"; and also, that her use of it invokes Barthesian or
Foucauldian notions of "the death of the author." Certainly, there are
several points in the novel where the traditional "authority" of the
author is directly challenged by the narrator.

The initial calling of attention to the discrepancy between author
and narrator occurs in the (unnumbered) prologue "Narrator on
author":

> *Narrator on author: she kept an old postcard of a white "Saltimbanque"*
> *stuck on the fridge....That time she thought she saw her Saltimbanque,*
> *in the Luxembourg. Dancing along a pathetic low railing, inches off*
> *the ground. Balancing as if on a highwire tightrope. Toeing tremu-*
> *lously to the left. To the right. Bowing to the audience. (No one was*
> *watching.) He seemed a white-painted clown. Possibly from "the*
> *south." Or else a scared nomad. With nowhere to go. (9)*

Here, Scott's use of the term "author" does seem to be close to what I
have designated the "protagonist": the main character in the action,
someone who rather self-consciously sticks an old postcard on the
fridge. Thus, the author/protagonist is portrayed as someone whose
own experience of Paris is pre-conditioned by artistic images,
such as this postcard portrait, of a painting by Watteau perhaps, or
Picasso. The postcard preconditions her to see "her Saltimbanque,
in the Luxembourg"—probably an actual person, dancing in the
Luxembourg Gardens, but also with the overtone of a Saltimbanque

painting, in the Luxembourg Museum. The Saltimbanque becomes
not only what she *expects* to see, but also (implicitly) an image for
herself—*her* Saltimbanque. Over the course of the novel, the protag-
onist will emerge as something of a clown, something of an acrobat.
Here she pre-emptively suggests both identifications. The book will
perform a whole series of balancing acts, "Toeing tremulously to the
left. To the right," as Scott balances between English and French,
Canada and Québec, Montreal and Paris, et cetera. The "scared
nomad. With nowhere to go" refers to her own position within the
book, but this position is in turn held in ironic contrast to the racial
and political victims for whom having nowhere to go is not at all
metaphorical or literary, but simply real.[11]

Section #39 is even more precise in its critique of the authorial
voice:

> *Me lying here thinking how to write. More progressive chronicle.*
> *Maybe author déjà vu by narrator. Instead of usual reverse.*
> *Permitting latter to float beyond limitations. Biases. Of former....*
> *It going to be one of those clear scintillating almost-autumn days.*
> *Can't wait to "live" it. (50)*

To start with, the possible pun on "lying" casts the whole section into
doubt. The equivocation is repeated at the beginning of the very next
section, #40: "Also lying by writing day 40" (51). The word "progres-
sive," applied to her own account, may invoke a whole register of
political judgements, of the kind that the protagonist rather vaguely
subscribes to, but it may also simply indicate the linear progression of
narration in a "chronicle" (a more neutral term than "autobiography,"
suggesting an uninflected chronology of events). The following lines
claim for the narrator's voice the wider view usually ascribed to the
authorial function, and it is here that the echoes of "author" as used
by Barthes and Foucault are clearest. The narration itself, a purely
linguistic position, is claiming the right to go "beyond [the] limita-
tions" of a predetermined authorial personality. Language exceeds the
author. No construct of authorial "personality" can reduce to an arti-
ficial coherence the multiple linguistic possibilities of the narrative

voice. Yet at the same time, the narrator acknowledges her intertextual dependence on previous images. She knows what "those clear scintillating almost-autumn days" are *supposed* to feel like and she "can't wait" to translate that theoretical knowledge into the reality of "lived" experience. However, the quotation marks around "live" indicate both its ambivalence (as something that may not truly be "lived"), and its citational quality, as something whose "lived" quality would necessarily be pre-inscribed.

This ambivalence is restated in the most spectacular instance of the narrator inserting the "author" into the textual play:

> *In bistro window—seeing statuesque woman. With silver pageboy.*
> *Once encountered. Stepping from row of lindens. On les Invalides.*
> *Waving gaily. Invitingly. I waving back. "Gail-y." Too. (119)*

This passage is full of ambivalent wordplay: the woman who is also a statue; the haircut that is also a sexually attractive young boy; the possible reference to Unter den Linden, notorious site of 1920s Berlin bisexuality; the bilingual pun on "invalid" (in both its English senses); even the doubled sense of bis-tro. All of these dualities culminate in the use of the author's proper name, Gail, in its improper sense, gaily. Gail-y: Gail (in French) here. "Gail-y too" is both doubled (two) and addressed in the familiar second person (tu). The author's signature is (in its only appearance in the whole novel) doubled, divided from itself. "Gail-y" signs the author's presence at the same moment as it distances that presence into a gesture (a reciprocal gesture) of sameness/difference, identity/desire—all the central themes of a lesbian, "gay" discourse.

This ambivalence about authorial and/or narrative identity is most pervasively realized in the novel by its consistent equivocation around the pronoun "I." Although the word is not entirely omitted from the book, it is frequently repressed in constructions using the participle rather than the predicate form of the verb (a trait that I will discuss shortly), or else by the substitution of the impersonal "one," always conspicuously qualified within quotation marks:

And "one" walking there near millennium. Mid countless objects
representing point of convergence. Between 19th and 20th. Feeling
certain of genius. It being task of museum to make "one" feel lucid.
Grizzled feats having been laid out for "one's" unique consumption....
"One" feeling certain marvellous to be had. (127–28)

In this passage, the first and fourth occurrences of "one" seem to
be simply disguised or deferred forms of "I," referring to personal
actions or feelings of the protagonist. The second and third occur-
rences are more generalized, suggesting that "one" is not just a single
individual but rather a representative member of a larger group (such
as museum-goers). This double sense problematizes the singularity
of the "one," and suggests that the suppressed "I" may not be entirely
distinct and individualized. Rather, the narrator's personal pronoun
will fluctuate between the individual and the general, and between
appearance and disappearance. The subject (as Scott has said) is lost
in the text of the city.

This loss is most apparent in the book's consistent replacement
of the active predicate verb by the present participle, which serves
not only to elide the privileged position of the active subject but also
to render all the actions of the novel as amorphously continuing
rather than decisively accomplished. These syntactic tactics are
fully conscious and theorized, as is shown by several of Gail Scott's
comments on her own work.

In an e-mail to me (August 2000), Scott wrote:

The narrator is mocking the author in the intro and then in one of the
entries [39], implying that the author gets overwhelmed by the figure
of the narrator created by the text. This is a post-modern relationship
I suppose inasmuch as the narrator (writing subject) of the text occu-
pies a place between subjective and objective which is neither author
nor character. Using present participles reduces the weight of the
subject of the "sentence" as well, i.e., the author, or her stand-in,
brings the subject closer to the verb. The subject is lost in the text of
the city, small and Chaplinesque, and is a very different kind of voice,
therefore, than the voice normally narrating travelogues, which

latter voice I think still unconsciously brims over with nostalgia for
the traveller of 19th and early 20th [century] imperialism.

And previously, in an essay entitled "The Porous Text," published in
Chain (University of Hawaii, 1998):

> *The great American writer Gertrude Stein also wrote in English in a*
> *French context. She understood that French is axed on the verb, and*
> *did wonderful things with this, letting the way the French language*
> *moves permeate her American English. My way of letting French into*
> *English displaces the energy from the verb to the present participle.*
> *Perhaps this is the difference between the energetic confidence of a*
> *citizen whose republic stands for organisation and movement, and*
> *the subject of an ex-dominion with a foreign queen on its currency.*
> *The present participle does not go straightforward. The movement is*
> *gestural, swings forward and back, extending the writing subject into*
> *its environment. And the reverse. Linking within to without. It*
> *reduces the sentence to the smallest possible thinking unit. It leaves*
> *spaces in between. Breathers. With the present participle the*
> *narrator cannot assume a well-constituted "I." Being of America, but*
> *not American; Canadian, but the word doesn't fit. Québécoise, but in*
> *the wrong language. Instead of an identity, the narrator constructs a*
> *porous text, trying to take into account the complete situation (all the*
> *languages) in which the act of writing takes place.*

There are, obviously, many points of interest in these statements,
not the least of which is Scott's reflection on what it means to be an
anglophone Québécoise living in Paris and writing in English. On the
one hand, she is in a multiply-insecure position: as the "subject of an
ex-dominion," as the member of a linguistic minority within Québec,
and as a Québécoise writer faced with the "energetic confidence" and
cultural disdain of metropolitan France. On the other hand, she is still
the inheritor and user of the English language, with all its "nostalgia
for the traveller of 19th and early 20th imperialism" built into its very
syntactic structures, its secure establishment of the privileged subject
position "I."

Mediating between these positions, then, she attempts to find a narrative voice that will not privilege the narrator, but will disrupt that traditional authority. The first effect is certainly a defamiliarizing one. The reader is disconcerted, perhaps irritated, thrown off balance. It is difficult to settle into a rhythm of reading, as the short, choppy sentences continually call for readjustments as "one" tries to figure out how they relate to each other. Fairly soon, however (or at least this has been my own experience), the reader adjusts to the rhythm and learns how to read the book. And there is, in fact, despite the syntactic disruption, very little real ambiguity. Take a sample passage:

> Ordering espresso. Waiting for S. She having offered to help "program" electronic TV. Currently only capturing Belmondo types. Cigarettes in lips. Playing slot machines against white metal walls. (26)

The subject of the verbs changes continually throughout this passage, and is only once articulated ("She"). Nevertheless, these changes are not difficult to follow. It is obvious that it is the protagonist doing the ordering and the waiting, S doing the offering, the TV doing the capturing, and the Belmondo types doing the playing. Occasionally the switches can be momentarily misleading:

> Old Colette's magnificent aubergine head. Above. Sniffing. Touching. Listening. To very end. Despite pain of arthritis. Heavy immovable body. Irritating boys. Shitting below. Anyway. Standing under arcade bordering square. Staring at pastries. Looking like flat dented cooks' hats. (37)

Here the string of participial actions attributed to Colette (sniffing, touching, listening) may trick the reader at first into reading "irritating" as another in the sequence (Colette is irritating little boys). Then a double-take reveals that "irritating" is an adjective describing the boys, who in fact are paralleled to the pain and the body as objects of the preposition "despite." Similarly, a couple of lines later, the similarity between "Staring" and "Looking" may briefly suggest that both are actions of the protagonist, parallel to "Standing," until the double-take reveals that "Looking" is an adjective qualifying "pastries." Even here, however, I would suggest that the effect is little more than a stutter in the reading process; the double-take forces itself on the reader's attention, and the ambiguity is dispelled almost as soon as it is noticed.

In other words, I am inclined to question whether the syntactic disruptions of *My Paris* are indeed all that effective in dislodging the narrator, and/or the protagonist, from the subject position. Perhaps more productive is Scott's suggestion that the participles work by "extending the writing subject into its environment. And the reverse. Linking within to without." Because the participles do not express a completed action with finite borders, but rather a continuing and imprecisely defined *process*, they help to express the protagonist's absorption into her surroundings, into Paris itself. "The subject is lost in the text of the city," Scott writes, "small and Chaplinesque" (a phrase that already suggests a coherent characterization).

In Chapter 9, I argue that Scott's encounter with "the text of the city" takes place, quite literally, at the level of the street and the street name, as well as in her omnipresent intertextual encounters with Walter Benjamin and Gertrude Stein. Certainly, Paris itself—the texture of its daily life, its streets and cafés, its high fashion and its racial politics, its mundane delights and frustrations, its allure and its arrogance—emerges more strongly in *My Paris* than in many of the Montparnasse memoirs. Much as Gertrude Stein may have loved Paris, in *The Autobiography of Alice B. Toklas* it is often little more than a backdrop, a setting against which the genius of Gertrude Stein can be displayed. Stein dominates her setting effortlessly; the protagonist of *My Paris* never has that assurance or control. She is always on the verge of disappearing, like a flâneur, into the text of the city.

PART THREE --> *What Pleasure in a Name!*

THE LONG POEM OF WALKING

To wander about Paris—adorable and delicious existence! —BALZAC

Always seeking new streets to step down. As if a walk was a caress.

—GAIL SCOTT[1]

←-- 4 MISSING THE DIRECT WAY --→

IN CHAPTER THREE of *Memoirs of Montparnasse*, John Glassco gives a
bravura account of one of his early evenings in Paris in 1928. It is, to
say the least, a remarkable night. He begins at a party where he meets
the Surrealist poet Robert Desnos,[2] who recommends that he read
André Breton's *Nadja*, and to whom in turn Glassco attributes an
eloquent speech, a magnificent piece of Surrealist rhetoric (recreated,
of course, out of at best a distant memory, and then transformed by
translation) against authority: "a rebellion against the whole appa-
ratus of medicine, religion and law" (Glassco, 17). Glassco also meets
the celebrated model Kiki,[3] whom he describes memorably: "Her face
was beautiful from every angle, but I liked it best in full profile, when
it had the lineal purity of a stuffed salmon" (18). Leaving the party
with a couple of young lesbians, Daphne and Angela, Glassco is taken
to the Gypsy bar, where he is "obliged to drink a *diabolo*, a sickening
mixture of port and grenadine that I had thought was drunk by
nobody but prostitutes" (20),[4] and to dance with a lady in a monocle,
who of course takes the lead. He also encounters Daniel Mahoney,
the notorious homosexual doctor, whom he calls Maloney, and whom
Djuna Barnes, in *Nightwood*, presents definitively as Matthew

O'Connor. Glassco ends the evening in a studio on the rue Broca with Daphne and Angela, describing their erotic permutations in the delicately indelicate phrase "Our amours, which were rather outré" (22).

"We all fell asleep after midnight," the account concludes, "with the stove glowing softly and the slanted moonlight silvering the high wall of the garden outside" (22). Or at least, that *appears* to be the conclusion, in a fine romantic mode: the end of the evening, the outré lovers falling asleep, the moon shining.

But that is not, in fact, where the chapter ends. There follows a paragraph describing the two "girls" waking up to a hearty breakfast of "buttered tartines, anchovy paste, tea and apricot jam." Glassco wanders off about noon, and "in the rue de la Glacière I met a man with a flock of goats, playing a little pipe to announce that he was selling ewe's milk from the udder"—the great God Pan, no doubt, benignly surveying the aftermath of the orgies of the night before.[5] "I bought a French pastry full of yellow custard and sat on a low stone wall eating it. Paris, I thought, was an even better city than it was in the books" (22).

And again, this seems a natural conclusion, a well-rounded ending to the narrative. Indeed, the literary trope here is a common one: a comparison between the actual experience of Paris and the pre-formed expectation of Paris, as generated by literary and cultural images and stereotypes, the city "in the books." But again, it is not the actual ending of the chapter. We still have one, rather odd, paragraph to go:

> I found my way back to Montparnasse by way of the Santé prison and the Lion de Belfort, walking down the tree-lined boulevard Denfert-Rochereau as far as the Closerie des Lilas, having missed the direct way by the boulevard Raspail. The streets were dipped in warm sunshine now; it was the first day of spring. (22)

"It was the first day of spring" is, indeed, a good rhetorical period. But what are we to make of the preceding sentences? After all the extravagance of the night's events—Desnos, Kiki, the monocled lady, Dr. Mahoney, Daphne and Angela—how do we arrive at a list of street names, a mere itinerary, and an oddly stressed note on "having missed the direct way"? In what sense do these details of the Paris street system provide an adequate emotional resolution to this exquisitely calculated narrative?

There is of course a temptation to read this itinerary symbolically: it runs from the criminal (the Santé prison, with its extremely grim and forbidding rough-stone wall bordering directly on the street) to the military (the Lion de Belfort commemorates one of the few French successes in the 1870 Franco-Prussian War) to the literary (the Closerie des Lilas is a restaurant associated with both the French Symbolist poets of the 1890s and the American expatriate writers of the 1920s). But my inclination is to read it more on the literal than on the symbolic level. It is, quite simply, the way he got home. And like so many Parisian itineraries, it displays a fascination with the streets of Paris, especially with their names.

5 THE STREET MAP OF PARIS ⟶

Parisian writers always gave the street address of their characters, as though all readers knew Paris so well that only a real location in the streets would breathe life into a character, as though histories and stories themselves had taken up residence throughout the city.
(Solnit, 210)

HOW WELL DO READERS IN FACT KNOW PARIS? How many readers of Glassco would realize, without consulting a map, that he had indeed "missed the direct way by the boulevard Raspail"? How many would know which battle is commemorated by "the Lion de Belfort"?[1] When writers specify Paris street names, they always divide their audience into two: those who have been to Paris, and recognize the names, and have a whole range of public or private associations for those names; and those who have never been to Paris, for whom the names are just words, opaque to any association. However, even for those who have never been there, there must be a cloud of cultural resonance gathered around certain names—the Champs-Elysées, the Seine, the Eiffel Tower—while other, lesser-known names may evoke magic simply by their specificity, by the allure of the unknown, by their ambivalent appeal to an expertise that the reader may or may not share.

(Note here that the appeal to "fact" means that the writer must use actual street names, not fictional ones. Very seldom do writers about Paris *invent* a street name:[2] the appeal is to the richness of the existing repertory of names, and to the expertise of using them accurately.)

My point of departure, then, is this measure of Paris: street names, maps, and itineraries. Glassco does not simply say that he went from the rue Broca to Montparnasse, point A to point B: he gives a detailed route, and he lists the names of the streets he walked along. This kind of listing is a common trope in writing about Paris, as this chapter will abundantly demonstrate. My intuition is that it is *more* common in writing about Paris than it is in writing about other major European cities, though of course to prove this point would require an equally deep immersion in the literatures of London, Berlin, Barcelona, and other cities. I do believe, however, that the listing of street names and walking itineraries is particularly notable in relation to Paris, as when, for example, Adam Gopnik describes "the world's most beautiful walk—beginning at the Institut de France and moving across the pont des Arts and around the cour Carrée of the Louvre and then to the Tuileries and the Champs-Elysées" (226).[3] Or see Paul Zweig: "I walked in streets that were dingy and full of smells: the Rue Gît-le-Coeur, the Rue Xavier Primas, the Rue Maître Albert: strips of pure Zola that were grim and damp" (*Americans in Paris*, 513).[4]

This trope, ironically, is to be found everywhere in the work of a writer whom John Glassco thoroughly despised, Ernest Hemingway. The Paris chapters of *The Sun Also Rises* are full of comments like "We came out of the Tuileries into the light and crossed the Seine and then turned up the Rue des Saints Pères" (23), or "The taxi went up the hill, passed the lighted square, then on into the dark, still climbing, then levelled out onto a dark street behind St. Etienne du Mont, went smoothly down the asphalt, passed the trees and the standing bus at the Place de la Contrescarpe, then turned onto the cobbles of the Rue Mouffetard..." (33). In *A Moveable Feast* the effect multiplies:

> I walked on in the rain. I walked down past the Lycée Henri Quatre
> and the ancient church of St.-Etienne-du-Mont and the windswept

Place du Panthéon and cut in for shelter to the right and finally came
out on the lee side of the Boulevard St.-Michel and worked on down it
past the Cluny and the Boulevard St.-Germain until I came to a good
café that I knew on the Place St.-Michel. (4–5)

Perhaps the most epic of Hemingway's Parisian itineraries is the
walk shared by Jake Barnes and Bill Gorton in Chapter VIII of *The Sun*
Also Rises:

We walked along under the trees on the Quai d'Orléans side of the
island. Across the river were the broken walls of old houses that were
being torn down....
   We walked on and circled the island....We crossed to the left bank
of the Seine by the wooden foot-bridge from the Quai de Bethune, and
stopped on the bridge and looked down the river at Notre Dame....
   We crossed the bridge and walked up the Rue du Cardinal
Lemoine. It was steep walking, and we went all the way up to the
Place Contrescarpe....
   We turned to the right off the Place Contrescarpe, walking along
smooth narrow streets with high old houses on both sides. Some of the
houses jutted out toward the street. Others were cut back. We came
onto the Rue du Pot de Fer and followed it along until it brought us to
the rigid north and south of the Rue Saint Jacques and then walked
south, past Val de Grâce, set back behind the courtyard and the iron
fence, to the Boulevard du Port Royal....[5]
   We walked along Port Royal until it became Montparnasse, and
then on past the Lilas, Lavigne's, and all the little cafés, Damoy's,
crossed the street to the Rotonde, past its lights and tables to the
Select. (82–84)

J. Gerald Kennedy notes that this route "connects those parts of Paris
where Hemingway had lived and loosely follows the chronology of
his own movements" (114). Kennedy gives a long, extremely detailed,
and quite exemplary account of the Paris chapters of *The Sun Also Rises*,
tracing exactly where the characters live, where they go, and the
implications of every address. "The particulars of place," he concludes,
"seem to condense the psychic content of experience" (109).

For the English historian Richard Cobb, such lists were a fixed point of Parisian existence. "My life in France might be divided up into a series of street itineraries," he writes, explaining: "The rigid adherence to a daily itinerary gave me a sense of purpose, a feeling of security...and, above all, the sensation that I was an element in the hourly heartbeat of a great city, a unit in the flux and reflux" (9–11). Writing in 1969, Cobb could still remember the route he walked, thirty years earlier, between his lodgings and the archives where he was doing research:

> From 1936 to 1939, the itinerary was...rue Saint-André-des-Arts, rue Dauphine, Pont-Neuf, the quais place de l'Hôtel-de-Ville, under the nose of Étienne Marcel; rue Lobau, rue des Archives (right side), rue des Francs-Bourgeois, Archives Nationales (destination), returning via the pont au Change, the quai aux Fleurs, boulevard du Palais, pont Saint-Michel, place Saint-André-des-Arts. This itinerary is marked with the experience of the Front Populaire, of Weidmann, of l'Expo, of the Spanish Civil War, and Munich. (10)

Cobb's final comment here suggests that the street names function like mnemonic clues, bringing with them associations of public or private memory. Cobb's associations here are public ones, references to political and historical events. Adam Gopnik evokes a more private register when he recalls a school he went to as a boy in Montreal: "The corridors in the school were named after Parisian streets: The Champs-Elysées led the way to the principal's office, and you took the rue Royale to the cafeteria for lunch," a set of associations he could "never forget" (7). Québécois novelist Pierre Turgeon writes: "When I walk in Paris, I parade through my memory. I play the grey streets like the grooves of an old vinyl record" (68, my translation)—a vivid and memorable image.

One of the most ironic of these mnemonic itineraries is given by none other than the Baron Haussmann.[6] There is an extended passage in which he describes (very much like Richard Cobb, who would be horrified by the comparison) the walk he took every day as a student, between his lodgings and the law school. He begins at the rue

Montmartre; comes south to Les Halles; follows the "rues des Lavandières, Saint-Honoré et Saint-Denis"; crosses the Pont au Change to Cité; then passes into the maze of the Latin Quarter, "rues de la Harpe, de la Huchette, Saint-André-des-Arts et de l'Hirondelle"; and ends up, after "la rue des Maçons-Sorbonne, la place Richelieu, la rue de Cluny et la rue des Grès," at the Panthéon. But for Haussmann, the mnemonic point of recalling the route in such detail is not, as it was for Cobb or Turgeon, nostalgic: the point is to recall how many of these streets, especially on the Île de la Cité, he later changed, rebuilt, or simply destroyed: streets "que j'eus la joie de raser plus tard"! Haussmann's list is an almost perfect *anti*-itinerary of Paris: he remembers what he has had the joy of erasing.

But authors do not always list names for such specific mnemonic reasons; often, it seems as if the names are just there for their own sake. "We walked all the way to the bird market at the Place Louis Lépine, going right down through the Tuileries and past the Louvre and over the Pont au Change to the Île de la Cité" (76): that's from Rose Tremain's *The Way I Found Her*. Or in Nancy Huston's *The Mark of the Angel*:

> "Can we go for a walk? I have to talk to you."
> András grabs his coat...and they set out.
> Rue Malher. Rue des Francs Bourgeois. The entire length of the rue Turenne. Rue Béranger. The Passage Vendôme, leading to the Place de la République. They buy a bag of roasted chestnuts at the foot of the statue, then take the Rue du Faubourg du Temple as far as the Canal Saint Martin.... (133)

The effect extends even beyond the streets of Paris proper, into the named "streets" of that strange city-within-the-city, the cemetery of Père Lachaise. One of the feline protagonists of Bill Richardson's comic fantasy *Waiting for Gertrude* carefully notes: "Up and down I sallied, all along the major arteries and minor capillaries of Père-Lachaise, turning right, turning left on the chemin Gosselin and the chemin d'Ornano, the chemin Errazu and the avenue des Peupliers" (15). And, as I will comment later, many writers delight in specifying

Métro stops. (The Métro is always a subterranean, subconscious map of Paris.)

In *My Paris*, Gail Scott's narrator seems to spend almost all her time travelling around the city, sometimes by Métro, but most often on foot:

> *Walking yesterday. Down rue du Bac, Embarkment Street. Across pont Royal. Through the Tuileries garden....Heading down grand central alley. Dramatically in line with giant courtyards of Louvre. And distant Champs-Elysées....Crossing another traffic-choked avenue. In search of one of those passages. B[enjamin] calling galleries of desire. Confusing rue Croix-des-Petits Champs / Cross-of-Little-Fields Street. With rue des Petits-Champs / Little-Fields Street. As if in the country. Passing and repassing. Several armed gendarmes. Patrolling Banque de France. Making wide berth. Down other side of street. Fortunately stumbling on galérie Véro-Dodat. Vé-ro Do-dat. What pleasure in a name! (20)*[7]

What pleasure in a name. Or in this case, two names: Monsieur Véro and Monsieur Dodat. A historian can give you all the details of who they actually were, and these details are far from uninteresting,[8] but surely what Gail Scott is responding to here is simply the *sound* of the names: the trochaic pattern of long-short, long-short. That repeated D. The way the name feels in your mouth when you say it. Vé-ro Do-dat.

Such "pleasure in a name" can be found even in the magisterial prose of Henry James. In his *Autobiography*, published in 1913, he recalls staying in Paris in 1857, when he would have been fourteen years old, and walking with his brother from the family's proper Right Bank residence to the museum in the Luxembourg Gardens. "That particular walk," he writes, "was not prescribed us, yet we appear to have hugged it, across the Champs-Elysées to the river, and so over the nearest bridge and the quays of the left bank to the Rue de Seine, as if it somehow held the secret of our future." They pass the bookshops on the quais, and then "with plot thickening and emotion deepening steadily...we mounted the long, black Rue de Seine—*such a* stretch of perspective, *such* an intensity of tone as it offered in those days," until they arrive at "that comparatively short but finer and wider vista of the Rue de Tournon, which in those days more abruptly crowned the more compressed approach and served in a manner as a great outer vestibule to the [Luxembourg] Palace." "The Rue de Tournon," he concludes, "cobbled and a little grass-grown, might more or less have figured some fine old street *de province*: I cherished in short its very name" (190–91).

"What pleasure in a name!" writes Gail Scott; "I cherished...its very name," writes Henry James. The experience of Parisian streets concentrates into, becomes identified with, the *name*. The name is not only an index to the pleasure: it *is* the pleasure.[9]

The pleasure of cherishing Parisian street names is also to be found, of course, in French poetry. Among many possibilities, let me give just two contemporary examples. Jacques Roubaud, a member of the experimental group Oulipo, collects in *La forme d'une ville change plus vite, hélas, que le coeur des humains* (1999)[10] a large number of short, often whimsical poems about Paris streets and the vagaries of their naming: "Il allait un jour par la rue Madame / Un jour elle allait par la rue Monsieur" (223). Many of these poems depend on lists. For example, the Baudelairean title "L'invitation au voyage" introduces an alphabetical listing of every Paris street that consists of a place name—Abbeville, Aboukir, Ajaccio, all the way to Wagram and Washington—then concludes:

> *Et tout ça,*
> *—Avec l'Orient Express?*
> *—Non*
> *avec une simple carte orange 2 zones.* (175–77)[11]

Even more firmly in the Baudelairean tradition is Jacques Réda, whose books since *Les Ruines de Paris* (1977) contain wonderful prose poems about wandering around contemporary Paris (mostly on foot, but sometimes on motor-scooter—technologically, a modest enough vehicle for a flâneur).[12] Take, for example, this evocation of an obscure corner of Passy:

And now I turn at the bottom of the stairs and, taking the rue des
Eaux through the passage which is as steep as a black knife with its
blade becoming jagged, through the rue Dickens, where a Sunday
afternoon in Edinburgh lurks in a corner, I come to the rue Marcel-
Proust.... (82)

Here, the atmosphere of these quiet, out-of-the-way streets is
conjured not only in terms of their names (rue des Eaux) but also
(as I will discuss later) in terms of these names' literal referents: in
this case, to two major authors, Proust and Dickens. (Though quite
how Dickens, the quintessential London author, comes to evoke
Edinburgh, I do not quite understand!)

In the "First Sketches" for *The Arcades Project*, Walter Benjamin
even suggests a protocol for such walks: "A walk through Paris will
begin with an apéritif—that is, between five and six o'clock." He
suggests beginning at one of the railway stations, and lists the Gare
du Nord, the Gare de l'Est, the Gare Saint-Lazare, the Gare de Lyon.
"If you want my advice, I'd recommend the Gare Saint-Lazare. There
you have half of France and half of Europe around you; names like
Le Havre, Provence, Rome, Amsterdam, Constantinople are spread
through the street like sweet filling through a torte" (831). That is,
these names designate not only the European cities that may be the
destinations of trains leaving the Gare Saint-Lazare, but also Parisian
streets in the immediate vicinity of the station. Indexically, the names
point to the streets, the streets point to the station, the station points
to the cities, and the cities point to the names.

So important are the names that *not* noticing them can become
a sign of a character's profound depression or alienation. Such is
the case with Saffie, the protagonist of Nancy Huston's *The Mark of
the Angel*. In the early stages of the novel, she is emotionally numb,
and has almost no imaginative contact with her surroundings. Her
husband, Raphael, dispatches her to deliver a broken flute to an
instrument repairer (who, as it turns out, will become her lover and
open up her awareness of the city surroundings). Huston describes in
detail the walk she must take: "Raphael has drawn a map for her. You
go down the Rue de Seine, walk under the entryway to the Académie
and cross the Pont des Arts...." But Saffie "moves robotlike," and is

*impervious to the beauty that surrounds [her]. Here, looming up
ahead...is the grandiose Louvre, and the refined if grimy Gothic
facade of the Saint Germain d'Auxerrois Church—but Saffie doesn't
so much as glance at them....Nor is she impressed by City Hall itself,
with its turrets, its statues, its fountains, its red-white-and-blue
flags. She doesn't ask herself what historical characters and events
might have given their names to the streets she walks down next—
Pont Louis Philippe, Vieille du Temple, Roi de Sicile—they're names,
that's all. She checks them against the names on her map—yes, that's
it—and turns accordingly—left, right. (86-87)*

Here, the walk through Paris takes on negative significance. The effect
depends upon the discrepancy of awareness between Saffie's indiffer-
ence and the assumption, shared between Huston and her readers, of
the intense vitality of Parisian museums, churches, bridges, streets—
and above all, street names.

Another variation on the negative significance of a walk through
Paris is the use of an itinerary to distract attention from other things.
Mary Welsh Hemingway, Ernest's fourth wife, in her autobiography
How It Was, tells how, in October 1944, Hemingway was worried by
news that his son, Jack, had been taken prisoner. Mary, trying to
distract him, wagers that she can walk from the Ritz to the place du
Tertre in ten minutes—"I know the short cuts," she says. Hemingway
takes the bet, and follows her as she attempts the walk. She fails, but
of course she gives the route: "I walked, pushing through clusters of
other walkers in the rue Halévy to the right of the Opéra, up the rue
La Fayette, the rue Henri Monnier to the boulevard Rochechouart....I
had less than two minutes to go when I reached the bottom of the long
flight of the rue Foyatier steps" (135-36).

The point of this bet lies in its appeal to *expertise*—and this appeal
is, I would argue, one of the major motivations for writers including
such detailed itineraries and lists of street names. Paris is not a North
American city, with numbered streets and avenues, or with a grid
system that makes it easy to find routes. Paris is a city that you have
to learn your way around, and by far the best method of learning is
to walk. All the passages I have quoted so far show that the author
knows his or her way around, and they appeal to the reader's sense

of complicity with this knowledge. If the reader knows Paris, then s/he can mentally follow all of these routes, picturing every street as it is named, and realizing that, yes, Glassco *did* "miss the direct way by the boulevard Raspail." Glassco's confession of this minor failure in expertise may perhaps be a slight ironic comment on Hemingway, for whom expertise was everything. And for Hemingway, that expertise had to be continually *demonstrated*; often it seems as if he is providing a kind of Baedeker's guide for literary tourists. *A Moveable Feast* didactically instructs us that

> There were many ways of walking down to the river from the top of the rue Cardinal Lemoine. The shortest one was straight down the street but it was steep and it brought you out, after you hit the flat part and crossed the busy traffic of the beginning of the Boulevard St.-Germain, onto a dull part where there was a bleak, windy stretch of river bank with the Halle aux Vins on your right. This was not like any other Paris market but was a sort of bonded warehouse where wine was stored against the payment of taxes and was as cheerless from the outside as a military depot or a prison camp. (41)[13]

Or, more succinctly: "There was no choice at all [about writing]. There was only the choice of streets to take you back fastest to where you worked. I went up Bonaparte to Guynemer, then to the rue d'Assas, up the rue Notre-Dame-des-Champs to the Closerie des Lilas" (76).[14]

Such expertise was in some ways integral to the nineteenth-century conception of the flâneur (which I will discuss in more detail in the next chapter). Priscilla Parkhurst Ferguson, quoting Louis Huart's 1841 *Physiologie du flâneur*, writes that the flâneur "absolutely must know 'every street, every shop in Paris'...[and] is obligated to have at his fingertips all the important addresses, the best dressmaker, the best hatmaker, the bankers, magicians, and doctors. The flâneur is a living guidebook" (Tester, 31). A vividly concrete example of what such expertise might mean is given by Walter Benjamin:

> [The flâneur] stands before Notre Dame de Lorette, and his soles remember: here is the spot where in former times the cheval de

renfort—*the spare horse*—*was harnessed to the omnibus that*
climbed the Rue des Martyrs toward Montmartre. (416)

The precision of this detail appealed greatly to Benjamin: this refer-
ence is repeated several times in the accumulating Convolutes of
The Arcades Project. It was his favourite image for the expertise of the
flâneur, and it is vividly realized in the image of walking: it is the
soles of the flâneur's feet that do the remembering.

On the other hand, the flâneur must wear such knowledge lightly;
he may be an expert, but he is also an aimless walker—a stroller, a
loafer. Hemingway's "There was only the choice of streets to take you
back fastest to where you worked" is, in this sense, a most un-flâneur-
like statement. Glassco missing the direct way is more true to that
spirit.

Expertise is a form of control. If you know the city (the names of
the streets, the most convenient shortcuts, the locations of the best
shops), then you have a degree of control over your own urban expe-
rience. You take the measure of Paris. You are emphatically *not* a mere
tourist, looking for directions. But control, in its larger social and polit-
ical senses, has always been what the naming of streets is all about.

"The naming of streets," writes Priscilla Parkhurst Ferguson in
Paris as Revolution: Writing the 19th-Century City,

> *affords a crucial opportunity to affirm, or to contest, control of the
> city....Beyond identifying location, names on streets socialize space
> and celebrate cultural identity. They historicize the present and
> preserve the past. They...play politics and articulate ideologies; they
> perpetuate tradition; and they register change. In sum, street names
> offer a privileged field to examine the continual process of recording
> and interpreting the city. (15)*

Similarly, Lincoln Kerstein refers to street names as "a dictionary of
national biography, on tap for constant reference; filed for use as the
constant basis and reminder of a cohesive national culture" (*Americans
in Paris*, 372). The street map of Paris is always open to this kind of
reading.

Most obviously, those in power name streets to commemorate the ideological values of the regime and the names of its leading participants. The French monarchy named streets after generals, courtiers, ministers, mistresses, and almost every member of the royal family; many of these streets were of course renamed during the Revolution. Ferguson quotes a Revolutionary proposal to change the name of the rue des Plâtrières to the rue Rousseau, on the grounds that "It is important for sensitive hearts and ardent souls crossing this street to know that Rousseau used to live there on the fourth floor, and it scarcely matters that plaster used to be made there" (26). Richard D.E. Burton offers an entertaining account of the changing names of the place de la Concorde (62), and also stresses the negative aspect: those for whom streets were *not* named.

> *The gradual triumph of the Republic was enshrined in the naming of streets after...the heroes of the Enlightenment and the Revolution (Voltaire, Rousseau, Lavoisier, Lafayette, Mirabeau, Danton, but not, self-evidently, Robespierre and Saint-Just, who still have no Parisian streets to commemorate them)....Only a handful of Catholic-monarchical street names survived the comprehensive republicanization-cum-secularization of the city's main thoroughfares (Henri IV and Jeanne d'Arc were acceptable, but not Louis XIV, and certainly not Louis XV or Louis XVI). (270)*

Street names have frequently been changed for ideological reasons. Michel Carmona reports that "In July 1879 the Paris municipal council wished to change the names of certain streets on the grounds that they were too evocative of the empire, one such name being that of Boulevard Haussmann" (379). The attempt failed, however. (And Haussmann himself was loftily indifferent to it, writing: "An inscription can be erased. As long as Paris lives, my name will be engraved in all its stones.") Also, contrary to Burton, there *was*, at least for a short time, a place Robespierre: the place du Marché-Saint-Honoré was thus renamed in 1946; the name lasted until 1950 when, according to Eric Hazan, "the French bourgeoisie resumed control" (43) and restored the earlier name. (There is also a rue Robespierre, and a

Métro stop called Robespierre, though these are both in Montreuil, just outside the municipal boundaries of the city of Paris.) The section of the rue Broca on which Daphne and Angela had their studio is no longer the rue Broca (named after a nineteenth-century surgeon and anthropologist): after the Liberation of Paris in 1944 it was renamed the rue Léon-Maurice-Nordmann (after a lawyer shot by the Germans in 1942).

Street names may also respond to changing standards of public decency. Ferguson records that a street called "Tire-vit (Pull-Prick) had already been euphemized to Tire-boudin (Pull-Sausage) by the fourteenth century" and in the nineteenth century, in a truly bizarre intersection of sociology and history, it became the rue Marie Stuart (22–23).

Thus, Ferguson concludes, "the modern city articulates its history in the network of names that signal possession of space" (14). The naming of streets is one, very crucial way to respond to "the twin demands of a modernizing state, ideological control and administrative efficiency" (28). The increasing control exerted over the space of the city is seen not only in the naming of streets, but also, in the eighteenth and nineteenth centuries, by the drawing up of the first comprehensive and accurate street *maps* of Paris, and by the institution of systematic *numbering* of the houses on the streets.[15]

Yet at the same time, such efforts at control have only a mixed success. Even though new names are imposed, they do not always stick in popular usage. Eric Hazan, for example, claims that "no one speaks of the place Charles de Gaulle in reference to the Étoile, nor of the place André Malraux to designate the place du Théatre-Français" (174). The historical origins of names may be simply forgotten (as witness the need, in many modern street signs in Paris, to append a brief biographical note). Names sink back into what Ferguson calls "the inherent heteroglossia of the urban text" (30). Retrieving their history, and paying deliberate tribute to it, may then become another form of expertise and another appeal to complicity between author and (informed) reader.

Such expertise may extend not only to knowledge of the historical origins of the actual names, but also to knowledge of events that happened on particular streets, or of famous people who lived at specific addresses. In such cases, the street name becomes a metonymy (a rhetorical figure to which I shall return shortly) for a whole set of cultural associations. Allow me here to cite a page from my own *McAlmon's Chinese Opera*, where a series of Parisian street names are presented as a (slightly irregular) sonnet:

> *Rue Delambre*
> *Rue du Montparnasse*
> *Rue Campagne Première*
>
> *Rue Notre Dame des Champs*
> *Rue du Cardinal Lemoine*
> *Rue de Fleurus*
>
> *Rue de Vaugirard*
> *Rue du Cherche Midi*
> *Rue Rousselet*
>
> *Rue Broca*
> *Rue de la Gaité*
> *Passage d'Enfer*
>
> *Rue de l'Arrivée*
> *Rue du Départ*
> (33)

Here the first triplet consists of the addresses of famous 1920s bars: the Dingo, the Falstaff, the Jockey. The second triplet refers to writers' addresses: Joyce, Hemingway, Stein. The third cites the longest street in Montparnasse, followed by the one with the most poetic name (the street that searches for the South), followed by (discreetly) my only personal appearance in that whole book, the street on which my wife Maureen and I lived in 1975–76, and again in 1985. The fourth triplet consists of addresses mentioned by Glassco, with a conscious contrast (or equation) between gaiety and hell. The final (Shakespearean) couplet pairs the two streets (now one-way) that lead up to and away from the Gare du Montparnasse. The poem acts, then, as a metonymy for "Paris in the 20s." Such an understanding of the poem depends upon these annotations, most of which (except for my residence on rue Rousselet) are at least potentially public knowledge.

The street name is also, in many instances, a word that already carries semantic meanings and associations—as in the play (above) on gaiety and hell. In fact, the reference to hell here is a relic of a broader, and largely unacknowledged, semantic play with street names in Montparnasse bearing the name "Enfer" (hell). The Passage d'Enfer, cited by Glassco, is a tiny cul-de-sac off the boulevard Raspail, not far from the boulevard du Montparnasse. The name used to be much more broadly used in the area. Much of what is now the boulevard Saint-Michel used to be called the rue d'Enfer; and the old toll barrier on the route to Orléans was called the barrière d'Enfer. (The toll barrier stood over the main entrance to the Parisian catacombs, a detail that reinforces the allusion to hell.) But in the late nineteenth century, as the toll barrier was moved south, and as a star-shaped intersection of Haussmannian boulevards transformed the area, the place was renamed. At the centre of it was erected Bartholdi's Lion de Belfort, commemorating the heroic resistance of the citizens of Belfort to the Prussian advance in 1870; and the square itself was renamed in honour of the heroic leader of that resistance, who had died in 1879: Colonel Denfert-Rochereau. (Or, to give him his magnificent full name, Pierre Marie Philippe Aristide Denfert-Rochereau.) Thus we have the place Denfert-Rochereau, which was once the barrière d'Enfer, and the boulevard Denfert-Rochereau, which was once part of the rue d'Enfer ("I found my way back to Montparnasse by way of...the Lion de Belfort, walking down the tree-lined boulevard Denfert-Rochereau"—John Glassco, 22).

Now, d'Enfer/Denfert is a pure homophone, with no semantic significance: an accident, or a deliberate pun? Were the 1879 officials who carried out this act of renaming simply deaf, or was there a certain sly humour involved? Michel Carmona refers to "the Barrière d'Enfer (today's Place Denfert-Rochereau, with the rue d'Enfer leading down to the Seine)" (146) with a perfectly straight face, as if he had noticed nothing at all unusual in the names. The website of the 38 bus route (http:/bus38.online.fr) says bluntly that the similarity of names is only "hazard" (chance). Only the irrepressible Eric Hazan admits the possibility of "une sorte de calembour municipal" (195)—a kind of municipal pun.

But, whether intentional or not, it surely works as a pun. Belfort may have been a victory, but the 1870 war was a disaster for France, and led to the even greater "hell" of the 1871 repression of the Commune. "Enfer" is exactly the right word for these years in Parisian history. So the street name Denfert-Rochereau works on multiple levels. It does commemorate the historical man and his brave deeds; but through the pun, it also refers to an infernal reality.

At the same time, it is of course a street name (and a Métro stop, and a bus stop), with very practical purposes for giving directions, getting around the neighbourhood. That is, its meanings operate simultaneously in two directions: referring to the street itself, and referring to the person (or place, or whatever) after which the street is named. My own favourite café in Paris is the Café Bonaparte, at Saint-Germain-des-Prés; however, the reason I like it is not out of any affection for Napoleon but because it stands on the (very short) rue Guillaume Apollinaire.[16] So the name evokes for me *both* the poet (and all his associations with the heroic age of Cubism) *and* that street, where I have sat so many times, drinking a midnight cognac and waiting for the floodlights on the tower of the ancient church to be switched off. The street's name and the poet's name reinforce each other's appeal; they have for me the power of an incantation.

The naming of streets humanizes them, brings the brute facts of urban architecture into a human discourse. Balzac writes:

> In Paris there are certain streets which are in as much disrepute as any man branded with infamy can be. There are also noble streets; then there are streets which are just simply decent, and, so to speak, adolescent streets about whose morality the public has not yet formed an opinion. There are murderous streets; streets which are more aged than aged dowagers; respectable streets; streets which are always

clean, streets which are always dirty; working class, industrious
mercantile streets. In short, the streets of Paris have human qualities
and such a physiognomy as leaves us with the impressions against
which we can put up no resistance. (as quoted in Harvey, 41)

If the streets of Paris "have human qualities," then these qualities are
often registered, and inscribed, in their names.

The total repertoire of Parisian street names thus provides a kind
of cultural history, in list form, whether in terms of the political
intentions of the authorities assigning the names, or in terms of more
personal responses to the names' associations. The American jour-
nalist Stanley Karnow comments:

Unlike my native New York's monotonously numbered thorough-
fares, Paris street names were a necrology of famous and forgotten
French artists, authors, composers, scientists, politicians, diplo-
mats, marshals, admirals, clergymen and a multitude of saints, male
and female. The selection process baffled me. Monarchs, including
the guillotined Louis XVI, had not been ignored nor, strangely, had
Madame de Montespan and Madame de Maintenon, the titular
mistresses of Louis XIV. But the honor was denied Robespierre, the
architect of the Terror.[17] *Bonaparte the general was awarded a rue*
for defending France against a European coalition late in the eigh-
teenth century, yet not even an alley hallowed Napoleon the emperor,
who had transgressed the republican principles of the Revolution.
I was proud to see the numbers of American icons immortalized:
Washington, Franklin, Jefferson, Lincoln, Edgar Allan Poe, Edison,
Wilson, Pershing, Franklin D. Roosevelt and Georges [sic] Gershwin,
to cite a few [all male]. (6-7)

Jacques Roubaud systematizes this approach in a wonderful list/
poem entitled "Un peu de sociologie," which begins "158 saints, 33
saintes, / des papes, 8 cardinaux, 11 abbés, 3 abbesses, 1 chanoinesse,
1 curé" (178). And Rose Tremain gently satirizes it when her youthful
and naive protagonist, who lives on the rue Rembrandt, a historically

wonders: "I didn't know whether, long ago, Rembrandt himself had come there and said in Dutch: 'What a nice street! Please name it after me,' or whether he never set foot in it" (9).

Such reflections extend from street names to the names of Métro stations, many of which are of course named after the streets, or the street intersections, where the stops are located.[18] Walter Benjamin describes the Métro as "an underworld of names" and expands this idea into a mythological excursus which, I would suggest, might be read as a curious and unintentional commentary on Ezra Pound's "In a Station of the Métro":

The apparition of these faces in the crowd;
Petals on a wet, black bough. (35)

This labyrinth harbors in its interior not one but a dozen blind raging bulls, into whose jaws not one Theban virgin once a year but thousands of anemic young dressmakers and drowsy clerks every morning must hurl themselves....Here, underground, nothing more of the collision, the intersection, of names—that which aboveground forms the linguistic network of the city. Here each name dwells alone; hell is its demesne. (84)[19]

Colin Jones notes that "just to take the simplest journey [on the Métro] is in some senses akin to celebrating the cult of ancestors," and he takes particular delight in the unlikely pairings that occur when Métro stops are named after street intersections: "Barbès-Rochechouart, for example, conjoins the names of a nineteenth-century anarchist warrior with a seventeenth-century aristocractic abbess of Montmartre....Alma-Marceau brings together a Crimean battle and a Revolutionary hero" (435). Richard Cobb, writing of "the surrealist quality of so many Parisian itineraries," lists a whole series of Métro rides, from one stop to another, which he picks out solely for the semantic associations of their names:

Filles-du-Calvaire to Barbès-Rochechouart; Sèvres-Babylone
to Marcadet-Poissonniers; Corentin-Cariou to Corentin-
Celton; Château-Rouge to Glacière; Strasbourg-Saint-Denis to

Richelieu-Drouot; Château-d'Eau to Levallois; Porte-Brancion to Porte des Lilas; Robespierre to Jasmin; La Motte-Picquet-Grenelle to Sully-Morland; De Gaulle to Convention. (57)

"The poesy of the *Métro*," Cobb concludes, "draws heavily both on its familiarity and its banality, its ordinariness: it is hard to take FILLES DU CALVAIRE seriously, SÈVRES-BABYLONE poses no threat, SOLFERINO, CHAMBRE DES DEPUTES, as seen from below ground, are entirely unprestigious" (105). Similarly, Adam Gopnik comments:

> *The Métro ride up to the porte de Clignancourt is a joy...just for the names of the stations in northern Paris: Château Rouge, Château d'Eau—what was the Red Castle? what was the Water Tower?[20]— Poissonniers, Gare du Nord, with its lovely, thirties, Gabinish overtones. We come up, back home, at Odéon, under the statue of Danton, and a single limb of a chestnut tree hangs over the Métro stairs. (46)*

Gail Scott also explores the semantic origins of street names and takes delight in explaining them: "Rue de la Roquette. Named after two prisons. In turn named after lettuce. Once abundantly growing there" (30); "narrow market rue Mouffetard. I at first thinking named after exotic warrior sect. From somewhere. It turning out to be named after mouffette, skunk. Due to earthy nature of produce" (147). Often, Scott succeeds in emphasizing the double references of street names by the simple expedient of providing English translations—"rue de la Butte-aux-Cailles, Quail-Ridge Street" (131)—so that, for the English-speaking reader, the name is forcibly returned to its non-proper denotation. On the one hand, this tactic brings the foreign city into the realm of the familiar; "Butte-aux-Cailles" may just be an opaque name, but "Quail-Ridge" summons up a concrete image. On the other hand, it may also defamiliarize the name, for a reader who was quite familiar with "rue du Bac," but had never thought of it as "Embarkment Street."

At one point, Scott gives a whole itinerary entirely in translation, *without* the French names, thus casting the reader into an entirely new linguistic map. And it is surely no surprise that this passage ends by citing both André Breton and Walter Benjamin:

> *Sitting in café at Sèvres-Babylone. I.e. at corner of Exquisite China*
> *and Pursuit of Sensuous Pleasure....Thinking time to start wandering.*
> *From present bifurcation. Toward Hermit's Well. Stone's throw from*
> *Buffoon Street. Down Beaujolais Alley. Through Wolf's Crack or*
> *Breach. Hot Cat Road. Passage of Desire. Magenta Boulevard. Where*
> *walking* Nadja *towards Hôtel Sphinx. Little Girls' Impasse. Saint-*
> *Jacques' Ditch. B[enjamin] saying "one's" perception of Paris. Based*
> *on sensuality of names. (25-26)*

Scott's translation is one way of forcing back into the consciousness of the reader, or walker, the common meaning of proper names. Such words, writes Michel de Certeau, "slowly lose, like worn coins, the value engraved on them"—though, he adds, "their ability to signify outlives its first definition" (104). (Consider, again, the possibility of returning "Denfert" to "d'Enfer.") That is, the semantic potential of the name to some extent survives its transformation into the more limited function of designating "only" a particular urban site. Street names, de Certeau continues, "make themselves available to the diverse meanings given them by passers-by; they detach themselves from the places they were supposed to define" (104).

The temptation for the novelist, of course, is to make these "detached" names significant, to use their original semantic meanings as direct or indirect comments on the action that takes place there. (When Adam Gopnik, trying to recapture a sensation he had had in Paris in his early youth, finds himself "not far from...the avenue Marcel-Proust," he feels compelled to add "I am not making this up" [165].) Thus Lola Lemire Tostevin, in the Paris chapter of *Frog Moon*, writes:

> *[Christine's] studio is on rue Villiers de l'Isle-Adam, a name I came*
> *across last night in* Flaubert's Parrot. *Only the French would desig-*
> *nate a short street after an obscure writer. My own studio is on rue*
> *Edouard Vaillant near Levallois. Who were these men? (197)*

Tostevin's narrator does not answer her own question, but Tostevin herself surely has; and the names are indeed deeply relevant, thematically, to the surrounding narration.[21]

Glassco also produces some ironically apposite street names, which may or may not have the benefit of grounding in autobiographical fact. Mrs. Quayle, the *femme fatale* to whom Glassco is irresistibly drawn, lives on the rue Galilée, a name that suggests that her bed is indeed, for Glassco, the Promised Land. And he surely takes a mischievous delight in locating the offices of a publisher of soft-core pornographic novels about ladies' underwear on the rue des Saints-Pères, the Street of the Holy Fathers. (The irony was repeated, in somewhat different form, many years later, when the feminist publishing house Des Femmes actually did set up shop on the same street.)[22]

Names can also be punned on to ironic effect: in Canadian poet Daryl Hine's *Arrondissements*, the section on the Cinquième begins by transforming the Jardin des Plantes, the Panthéon, and the church of Val-de-Grâce into "*Jardin des Plaintes, Pandémonium, Coup de Grâce.*" Steven Smith, in "Rue Vavin. 1988," plays a similar series of bilingual variations:

> *on the street, vavin*
> va vin
> *we go on in the days' journey*
> *jour née*
> *every day*
> *severed from the night-dark rope*
> *we are born*
> *to streets we walk ride run*
> *or are rueful on*
> (88)

Here, the pun on the individual street name (go wine) extends into the bilingual puns on "journey"/the day born, and on the word "street" itself: rue/sorrow.

In André Breton's novel *Nadja*, Breton and Nadja meet in the place Dauphine,[23] then "leave the garden and lose no time getting to another bar, in the Rue Saint-Honoré, which is called Le Dauphin. Nadja remarks that we have come from the Place Dauphine to the Dauphin. (In that game which consists of finding a resemblance with some animal, people usually agree that I am a dolphin)" (89).

Such equivocations between the common sense of words (dolphin) and their use as place names (the place Dauphine or Le Dauphin bar) point towards the recurring problematic of the proper name. "The ultimate enigma is your name," writes Daryl Hine (*Arrondissements* IV). Our society's conventional notion of the proper name, especially the family surname, ties the use of the word "proper" to the idea of "property."[24] The proper name is the signal of inheritance, the name that guarantees the handing down of property from generation to generation—and especially from father to son. But a person's name is thought of as property also in the sense that it is "my own," it belongs to me. It has a unique reference, it names *only* me, it is proper(ty) to me. Common nouns and names refer to many diverse things, and thus there is always a sense that the relationship between word and thing is precarious, arbitrary, open to (mis)interpretation. But the proper noun or name refers (we would like to believe) only to one thing or person, and thus it is a signal of self-identity, of a personal *presence*— or, in the case of street names, the presence of a unique location. There is only one "place Dauphine," and in this sense the semantic reference of "dolphin" (or of "royal heir") is irrelevant. The divisions of language do not apply to the proper name; the street and its name are one.

However, as anyone who has read Jacques Derrida will realize, these assumptions prove wide open to deconstructive analysis. A name may perhaps have a unique reference, but it can never be a unique instance. The name works only by repetition, that is, by the possibility of its repetition in another context. Your personal name depends upon the possibility of some other person recognizing you by your name *again*. Like any other linguistic sign, a name has to be able to operate in the *absence* both of its referent and of its originator. Far from being a guarantee of presence, the proper name is dependent upon absence. Further: by being repeatable (not just in the sense that it *can* be repeated, but that it *must* be repeated), the proper name necessarily leaves itself open to all kinds of improper uses: forgery, mistaken identification, alias, or citation in contexts far outside the control of the name-bearer. The name is never identical with its bearer, because the name can still be cited (quoted, praised, abused, misused, given all glory or taken in vain) not only in the bearer's simple absence but in his absolute absence, his death.

The name lives on after death; and thus it is always, in some sense, a *sign* of death. Streets are named after the dead: very rarely after the living.[25] A person's name survives its bearer and lives on into the vicissitudes of its posthumous history (among which vicissitudes may indeed be its transformation into a street name). Walking through a named landscape, we walk among and along the names of the dead.

The power of naming also derives from what Priscilla Parkhurst Ferguson calls "a primal gesture of appropriation" (13). Specifically, it derives from "the biblical vision of nomination [which], with its power justified and sustained by unimpeachable authority, haunts every act of nomination" (14). Walter Benjamin was also fascinated by this aspect of the power of the proper name, as Susan Buck-Morss explains: "the idea of the 'name' refers to the God-granted, cognitive power of humans, among all natural creatures, to translate Being into language, that is, to reveal its meaning: Adam, as the first philosopher, named the creatures of Paradise" (104).

Benjamin hovers between regarding the proper name as having or not having a common reference. At times he endorses the magical, incantatory aspects of the name as pure sound: he quotes Leo Spitzer as saying, "Proper names...have an effect that is conceptually unburdened and purely acoustic" (519). It is in this aspect, perhaps, that street names could exert a fascination even for readers who are not familiar with the city they map. One might respond "purely" to their quality *as* proper names, taking on trust their various levels of reference. *Not* knowing the original streets may even be an advantage: no commonplace associations to interfere with the pure sound of the pure name. "There is a particular voluptuousness," Benjamin writes, "in the naming of streets" (517).

Yet at the same time Benjamin, like Gail Scott,[26] preserves the memories of the names' original referentiality:

...the unconquerable power in the names of streets, squares, and
theaters, a power which persists in the face of all topographic
displacement....How many street names, even today, preserve the
name of a landed proprietor who, centuries earlier, had his demesne
on their ground. The name "Château d'Eau," referring to a long-
vanished fountain, still haunts[27] various arrondissements today.
(516)

Château d'Eau is (as I noted in an earlier quotation from Gopnik)
the name of a Métro station (the last one before Gare de l'Est as you
approach it from the south), and Benjamin shares Richard Cobb's
fascination with the Métro:

How names in the city...first become potent when they issue within
the labyrinthine halls of the Métro. Troglodytic kingdoms—thus they
hover on the horizon: Solférino,[28] Italie and Rome. Concorde and
Nation. Difficult to believe that up above they all run out into one
another, that under the open sky it all draws together. (519)

For Benjamin, that is, street names transformed the city into language:
"What the big city of modern times has made of the ancient concep-
tion of the labyrinth. It has raised it, through the names of streets,
into the sphere of language" (839). And again:

What was otherwise reserved for only a very few words—a privi-
leged caste of words, the names—the city has made possible for all
words, or at least for a great many: to be elevated to the noble status
of name. And this supreme revolution in language was carried out
by what is most general: the street....Even those much-overused
names of great men, already half-congealed into concepts, here once
more pass through a filter and regain the absolute; through its street
names, the city is image of a linguistic cosmos. (840)

Other writers have utilized the metaphor of the city as a linguistic
system. Priscilla Parkhurst Ferguson writes:

To speak of the "urban text" is to do more than indulge in metaphor.
Or, rather, the metaphor makes good theoretical sense. We can read
the city because of the properties the urban text shares with other
texts....Written texts, like cities, unfold through long, and often
painful, processes of creation. In both cases the text changes. With
cities, the basic text has to change to accommodate the requirements
of new users... (15)

The metaphor is developed in very literal terms. As early as 1929, Franz Hessel wrote: "Flânerie is a kind of reading of the street, in which faces, shop fronts, shop windows, café terraces, street cars, automobiles and trees become a wealth of equally valid letters of the alphabet that together result in words, sentences and pages of an ever-new book."[29] The idea of seeing buildings as letters has sometimes been taken even more literally. Victor Hugo famously saw the façade of Notre-Dame as an enormous H, his own initial. In 1980, Michel de Certeau, all too prophetically, described the World Trade Center in New York as "the tallest letters in the world" (presumably I's); for him, they "compose[d] a gigantic rhetoric of excess in both expenditure and production" (91). According to Rebecca Solnit, "A city is a language, a repository of possibilities, and walking is the act of speaking that language, of selecting from those possibilities" (213). To walk the streets is to "read" the city: "A path is a prior interpretation of the best way to traverse a landscape, and to follow a route is to accept an interpretation" (68).

Strictly speaking, all these figures are metaphors: walking as reading, buildings as letters, street scenes as alphabets. But the street *name* literalizes the metaphor, blurs the distinction between metaphor and reality, or (perhaps the most useful way of putting it) transforms the metaphors into metonymies. The name *stands for* the street, yet it is also *part of* the street—quite literally, as street signs posted at corners. "The characteristic and appropriate trope for the city is metonymy," Ferguson writes:

For metonymic figures, in particular synecdoche, construe the
familiar sights of the cityscape that topographically and symbolically

tie its many parts: the Seine, the sewers, the catacombs, the cemetery,
and in the long term the métro are, like the printed page, networks
that bring the scattered fragments into a whole. All of these figures
reduce the city to a part, but a part that in turn contains the city. (67)

It is noteworthy that Ferguson's list here (Seine, sewers, catacombs, cemetery, Métro—to which of course we must add the street name) reads like the table of contents of *The Arcades Project*. These were the privileged sites for Benjamin's investigation of Paris, and they were all, in effect, metonymies. Metonymy has been identified by many critics, such as David Lodge and Robert Kroetsch, as a characteristic figure of postmodernism, and as an expansive, open-ended process, what Kroetsch calls "the allure of multiplicity" (117). As such, metonymy is of course the key to the (non)structure of *The Arcades Project*, to its never-ending accumulation of details and citations. As Benjamin discovered, the problem with metonymy is that one never knows where to stop. Like Ezra Pound's *Cantos*, Benjamin's *Arcades Project* is a grand-scale attempt at modernist collage that collapses into postmodernist metonymy. "I cannot make it cohere," Pound lived to confess; Benjamin (ironically because of the same political forces that Pound was embracing) failed to live to make any such confession. But his text as it survived (the name living on after death) reveals the difficulty of reducing the metonymic city to modernist coherence.

The place where the street name reveals itself most literally as part of "a linguistic cosmos" is *the map*. Indeed, the map may be seen as a metonymy of metonymies: the relation of the name on the map to the name on the street sign is the same as the relation of the name on the street sign to the reality of the street. In his novel *Paris Trance*, the English writer Geoff Dyer has two of his characters, who get lost while wandering around Paris, end up, fortuitously, outside a shop that specializes in maps. There follows a two-page rhapsody on all the various kinds of maps in the shop: historical maps, maps depicting population density, globes, Mercator or other projections, the earth seen from space, city maps that "showed every avenue and street, every cul de sac and alley." Finally, "There was even a diagram, on the wall, of the shop itself, a map of maps with a red arrow saying, 'You

Are Here'" (69). With that "map of maps," Dyer's shop enters post-modern self-reflexivity.

For Benjamin, the street map is the ideal form of the city's text.[30] He disdainfully comments: "People whose imagination does not wake at the perusal of such a text, people who would not rather dream of their Paris experiences over a map than over photos or travel notes, are beyond help" (85). The map is, in Peircean terms, an index; its semiotic function is to *point to* its referent. And it lays that referent out as a spatial system, graspable (unlike "photos or travel notes") in an instant of time. The map transforms the temporality of walking into the simultaneity of seeing.

It is this aspect of the map which has aroused a good deal of suspicion in recent theory. The map's capacity to render the everyday chaos of urban existence into a rationalized, and essentially depopulated, system is seen as a kind of betrayal. Describing an extremely detailed map of Manhattan, Geoff King (in his book *Mapping Reality: An Exploration of Cultural Cartographies*) comments:

> *The result is a map that depicts minute detail and is in one sense highly accurate but that is entirely out of keeping with the plastic experience of life in Manhattan. A bustling, crowded, noisy and poverty-ridden cityscape that generates feelings of claustrophobia in many of its inhabitants is rendered into an abstract pattern that gives a strong impression of light, space and cleanliness. (176)*

Benjamin's experience, on the contrary, would seem to suggest that maps can indeed evoke just as much passionate involvement as the realities to which they point.

The decisive characteristic of such maps is *the view from above*. Michel de Certeau begins his account of "Walking in the City" by speaking of the "voluptuous pleasure" of observing Manhattan from the top of the World Trade Center: "looking down on, totalizing the most immoderate of human texts" [i.e., Manhattan] (92). Again we see the metaphor of the city as text; and what makes the text legible is the map, the view from above:

[The observer's] elevation transfigures him into a voyeur. It puts him at a distance. It transforms the bewitching world by which one was "possessed" into a text that lies before one's eyes. It allows one to read it, to be a solar Eye, looking down like a god. The exaltation of a scopic and gnostic drive: the fiction of knowledge is related to this lust to be a viewpoint and nothing more. (92)[31]

The implications of this mapmaker's "viewpoint" include not only legibility and "voluptuous pleasure," but also power: power in terms of Foucault's panoptic surveillance, and also in military and political terms. King writes: "From the imagined bird's-eye views of Renaissance artists to the use of balloons, aircraft and satellites, a higher and higher viewpoint has been gained....The view from above has always been implicated in questions of military power" (177). The most accurate maps of Britain are called the Ordnance Survey maps— "ordnance" meaning, specifically, artillery. Just as Haussmann's boulevards supposedly opened a field of fire against revolutionary barricades on Paris streets, ordnance survey maps gave the gunners an accurate range.

The map, in these senses, is not simply a passive, more or less accurate, reflection of the territory: it imposes itself upon the territory; it even, in Baudrillard's provocative phrase, "precedes the territory." Imperialist and colonialist maps are imposed upon territorial reality, often taking little account of geographical or ethnic particularities, yet it is this imposed discourse of the map which then becomes the contested site of action and power.[32] The map becomes an instrument of political and social control. Geoff King comments:

There is and can be no such thing as a purely objective map, one that simply reproduces a pre-existing reality. Choices always have to be made about what to represent and how, and what to leave out. It is here that cartographic meaning is created. To be included on the map is to be granted the status of reality or importance. To be left off is to be denied. (16)

David H. Pinkney notes that "no accurate map of Paris existed [as late as] 1850" (5).[33] The advent of accurate maps was thus contemporaneous with the massive reshaping of the city by Haussmann, and (like the numbering of houses on streets) was an instrument of Second Empire social control. Yet it was also contemporaneous with Baudelaire's definition of the flâneur, one who walks the city in order to experience it. On the one hand, the map of Paris is still, for the flâneur, an emblem of control, that is, of expertise: the *informed* walking that knows where it is going, even if it appears to be aimlessly strolling. A good map will show you Hemingway's fastest way back to work, or exactly how Glassco missed the direct route. Yet the flâneur also *activates* the map. The map is the ultimate flâneur's text, one that he "reads" every day in the course of his activity, one that he turns into "the long poem of walking."

De Certeau notes that "The long poem of walking [la geste cheminatoire] manipulates spatial organizations, no matter how panoptic they may be: it is neither foreign to them (it can take place only within them) nor in conformity with them (it does not receive its identity from them)" (101). From this point of view, the spatial rigidity of the view-from-above map (its quality of panoptic surveillance) may be acknowledged, without its being conceded as determinative. The mapping system exists as necessary context, but variation and resistance are still possible within the system. The individual act of walking (both *le* geste and *la* geste, gesture and poem) activates the map, transforming it from a static representation to a dynamic itinerary—in de Certeau's terms, from a "map" into a "tour" (119).

And again Benjamin is the connoisseur, the virtual flâneur, of the city's map. "Couldn't an exciting film be made," he writes, "from the map of Paris? From the unfolding of its various aspects in temporal succession? From the compression of a centuries-long movement of streets, boulevards, arcades, and squares into the space of half an hour? And does the flâneur do anything different?" (83) For Benjamin, that is, the visual status of the map is not the static picture or spatial diagram, but the "temporal succession" of *film*—visual, yes, but visuality in motion.

This activation of the map is achieved by the transference of the viewpoint from a detached, panoptic view-from-above to the standpoint (or *mobile* standpoint) of the inhabitant of the city, the walker.

The map becomes, in King's words, "the traveller's subject-centred diagram of his or her own journey" (12). It becomes expressed in such terms as "you go down this street and then you turn right, take the second left beside the bakery, cross the bridge..." etc. (Compare Richard Cobb's "itinerary," quoted earlier, of how he got from his lodgings to the archives where he worked.) Such descriptions are often called "cognitive mappings,"[34] and so are highly private and individual.

André Breton, in a text called "Pont Neuf" (1950), wrote: "No doubt a highly significant map should be drawn up *for each individual* which would indicate in white the places he is prone to haunt and in black those he avoids, the rest being divided into shades of grey according to the greater or lesser degree of attraction or repulsion exerted" (quoted in Sheringham, 90). If such a map were drawn for John Glassco, or indeed for many of the 1920s American expatriates, the white section would overwhelmingly be concentrated in a very small area around Montparnasse.

Most cognitive mappings are produced as dynamic tracings of walking through the city. There is, however, one striking instance of a "private map" produced, precisely, on the basis of the panoptic view-from-above. Julien Green, living in enforced exile from Paris during the Second World War, created for himself a very remarkable image of the Parisian map:

> *Thinking about the capital all the time, I rebuilt it inside myself. I replaced its physical presence with something else, something almost supernatural; I don't know what to call it. A map of Paris pinned to the wall would hold my gaze for long periods, teaching me things almost subliminally. I made the discovery that Paris was shaped like a human brain.* (15)

Having made this irresistible identification, Green goes on to develop it playfully:

> *It tickled my fancy to suppose I had been born in the realm of the imagination and had grown up in the domain of memory; unsure*

where to situate will, reflection, and judgement, I kept moving them
from one district to another; sometimes it seemed right to me that the
capital should recall its history through the medium of the Marais,
perform its intellectual tasks with the aid of the fifth district, and
do its sums in the Stock Exchange quarter; running through it all,
however, there was the River Seine, which to my mind represented
the instinctive, unspoken part of our nature, like a great current of
vague inspirations blindly seeking an ocean in which to drown them-
selves. (19)

"Give me a map," writes Michael Ondaatje, "and I'll build you a city"
(145).

But perhaps the oddest instance of a Paris map occurs in a short
story by Mavis Gallant, "Questions and Answers" (1966). It concerns
Romanian immigrants in Paris. The two central characters, Dino
and Amalia, have established themselves in the foreign city with the
financial help of some rings and gold pieces entrusted to them by a
woman called Marie. When, years later, Marie also arrives in Paris,
she says nothing at all about the rings or the money, leaving Dino and
Amalia uneasily guilty. They are caught between their (comparatively
modest) success in the new country, and their debt (which they do not
quite wish to acknowledge) to the old. So they don't know what to do
about Marie.

Marie herself is a strange woman, never fully explained in the
story. Perhaps she is a little insane, or simply an innocent, one of life's
optimists. She abuses policemen, yet is given privileged immigrant
status. She wanders all over the city, and of course Gallant details the
route:

Now she chooses to walk along the Seine, between the ugly evening
traffic and the stone parapet above the quay. She is walking miles the
wrong way. She crosses a bridge she likes the look of, then another,
and sees a clock. It is half past six. From the left of the wooden foot-
bridge that joins Île Saint-Louis and the Île de la Cité, she looks back
and falls in love with the sight of Notre Dame. (269)[35]

Amalia's fortune-teller helpfully suggests that Marie may eventually commit suicide, but Amalia rejects the notion with scornful incredulity: "Marie kill herself? You would have to smother Marie; put the whole map of Paris over her face and hold it tight" (270).

It's an astonishing image. The map becomes the symbol of all Dino and Amalia's suppressed guilt, rage, and resentment. What they hold against Marie is not only the burden of their unacknowledged debt: it is also her apparent freedom from any of the inhibiting forces of society and property, a freedom expressed, as so often in Parisian writing, by the liberty of walking the streets. (Like Glassco, she misses her direction: "walking miles the wrong way.") So in this moment of fantasized revenge, the text of those streets—the map—becomes a weapon: panoptic surveillance, ordnance survey, the map imposed upon the territory. If not quite in the sense he intended, it's a scene worthy of a place in a Walter Benjamin movie.

<-- **6** THE FLÂNEUR -->

THERE IS NO STANDARD or satisfactory English translation for
"flâneur." Stroller, idler, loafer...none quite covers it. Indeed, it is most
often used directly, as a loan word.[1] "Flâneur" occurs as such, in its
French form, in the OED, with the earliest English citation given as
1870, and defined as "A lounger or saunterer, an idle man about town."
Colin Jones describes him as "the sentient ambler through urban
space" (278). Sheila Watson offers "Peripatetic speculators" (113). But
any definition, it seems to me, must include in some form the idea of
walking. If the experience of Paris is, as Michel de Certeau proposes,
"the long poem of walking," then the flâneur is its long poet.

The figure of the flâneur has been the object of a great deal of crit-
ical attention—see for instance the collection of essays *The Flâneur*,
edited by Keith Tester, published in 1994—yet there is still a wide
range of definitions and applications for the word. There are those
who insist on a strict definition confining it to a specific historical
place and period (Paris in the mid-nineteenth century), and there are
those who are willing to use it in a much broader sense to indicate a
continuing mode of response to urban experience. There are those
who deny that the flâneur ever existed as an actual historical

phenomenon, and there are those who, to this day, are anxious to define themselves as living, walking flâneurs. There are those who admire the flâneur as a privileged figure of the artist, and those who see him as a debased product of capitalism. There are those who see him as *necessarily* "him," and those who envisage the possibility of a flâneuse.[2] There are those for whom he is the exemplary figure of modernity; there are those for whom he is just a nuisance on the street.

In the Introduction to his collection, Keith Tester summarizes: "On the one hand, there seems to be little doubt that the *flâneur* is specific to a Parisian time and place. On the other hand, the *flâneur* is used as a figure to illuminate issues of city life irrespective of time and place" (16). And Rebecca Solnit writes: "What exactly a flâneur is has never been satisfactorily defined, but among all the versions of the flâneur as everything from a primeval slacker to a silent poet, one thing remains constant: the image of an observant and solitary man strolling about Paris" (198). I would like to situate myself in a some-what eclectic position, straddling several of these possibilities. On the one hand, I am very sympathetic to the historicist argument that the flâneur is grounded in the specific circumstances of mid-nineteenth-century Paris; but on the other hand, I do think it is useful to extend the term beyond these limits, not accepting that the flâneur died out with the advent of either the department store or the automobile (two favourite candidates for the cause of his demise). Certain attitudes of the flâneur survive as ways of responding to urban life in the twen-tieth century; in the context of this book, I will be arguing for John Glassco as a flâneur and also using the flâneur as a way of interpreting the Paris writing of Sheila Watson, Mavis Gallant, and Gail Scott.

Even walking may not be essential to the definition. There are intriguing metaphorical extensions of flânerie into activities other than actual physical walking. Susan Buck-Morss writes that "Adorno... pointed to the station-switching behavior of the radio listener as a kind of aural flânerie" (345); Zygmunt Bauman suggests video (Tester, 155); but surely the closest parallel would be surfing the Internet.[3] In my own usage, however, I still want to preserve Solnit's "strolling about Paris." Both the activity and the city remain crucial to me.

There may indeed never have been, historically, such a person as the flâneur. Flânerie, writes Rob Shields, "was...always as much mythic as it was actual. It has something of the quality of oral tradition and bizarre urban myth....[T]he *flâneur* is a mythological ideal-type found more in discourse than in everyday life" (Tester, 62, 67). Critics point to the fact that even contemporary French writers like Balzac and Baudelaire always write about the flâneur as a type, and never give names of individual examples. The story (itself possibly apocryphal) about the poet Nerval walking a lobster on a leash has been indiscriminately extended as a general characteristic of the flâneur's leisurely pace. (Sometimes it seems as if every French poet of the mid-nineteenth century was in the habit of parading crustaceans.) The flâneur was an ideal, to which individual instances could only be approximations.

Nevertheless, specific historical circumstances are necessary, even for the emergence of an ideal type. For one thing, prior to the early nineteenth century, walking around the streets of Paris was not an activity that anyone could have undertaken for pleasure. The streets were narrow, unmapped, and filthy, often with open sewers running down the centre.[4] In *Seductive Journey*, his entertaining account of American tourism in France, Harvey Levenstein quotes George Putnam, writing in 1838: "the narrow, filthy streets, with gutters in the center, and without side-walks, and the antique and irregular buildings, do not realize my notions of gay, elegant Paris"; and Levenstein himself adds: "The primitive sewage system, which did not suffer major improvements until the 1830s, continued to cause disgusting problems, and the carriages would spray the sewage in the central gutters onto pedestrians" (56).[5] One of the simplest reasons for the connection that Benjamin makes between the flâneur and the arcades is that the arcades were clean: indoor streets, along which one might walk with no danger of being splashed by mud or sewage. The earliest arcade, the Passage des Panoramas, was opened in 1800; perhaps the most elegant (and recently restored in its elegance), the Galerie Vivienne, opened in 1823. The historical period of the flâneur thus coincides with the flourishing of the arcades and with the gradual improvement of the street system. David H. Pinkney records:

"The pedestrian, who had fared so badly on many of the city's streets, could by 1869 walk safely on more than 700 miles of sidewalks" (170). Sidewalks made possible not only pleasurable strolling but also that other touchstone of Parisian civilization, the sidewalk café. And here, Walter Benjamin notes another small but essential technical advance: "With the steady increase of traffic on the streets, it was only the macadamization of the roadways that made it possible...to have a conversation on the terrace of a café without shouting in the other person's ear" (420). From the arcades to the sidewalks to the smoothly paved surfaces, the changes in Parisian streets in the mid-nineteenth century produced an urban environment in which walking on the streets could become an activity pleasurable in itself.

The historical placement of the flâneur as a firmly nineteenth-century figure does not, however, entail that he exists only in a single mode, as an unchanging type: rather, versions of the flâneur develop and shift as the century progresses. Perhaps the best historicist account is given by Priscilla Parkhurst Ferguson in *Paris as Revolution*. Ferguson notes that at the beginning of the century, the word "flâneur" was primarily pejorative, describing a lazy idler. The figure is given his first positive development in 1826, when he appears in Balzac's *Physiologie du mariage*. David Harvey argues that the flâneur in Balzac "is purposeful and active rather than motiveless and merely drifting" (56). Ferguson sees him as a "genial ambulatory philosopher," whose "conspicuous inaction comes to be taken as positive evidence of both social status and superior thought" (81, 83). But after 1848, Ferguson argues, a change sets in:

> *The debacle of 1848 and the radical disruption of urban renewal in the Second Empire [under Haussmann] turned the genial ambulatory philosopher of the July Monarchy into a key figure of loss within a larger "discourse of displacement." Baudelaire's ambivalent flâneur already illustrates a significant move from the triumphant Balzacian figure, but it is Flaubert who represents flânerie as a form of dispossession. The displacement of the flâneur within the city translated the writer's own sense of dislocation within bourgeois society. Flânerie ceased to signify freedom and autonomy; it implied instead estrangement and alienation. (81)*

The flâneur became "a figure of failure" (95), and by the end of the century, according to Ferguson, flânerie had "returned to its original sense of 'insufferable idleness,' inactivity unredeemed by creativity of any sort" (112). These developments "effectively ended the flâneur's special relationship with the city" (113).

As I have said, I am sympathetic to this approach, and to its desire to confine the definition of the flâneur to a precisely delineated and developing nineteenth-century history. But as even Ferguson acknowledges, the term does not go away; in the twentieth century (above all in Benjamin), it has flourished as a category of urban discourse. More recently, Edmund White's 2001 book on his own experiences of Paris is entitled, simply and unapologetically, *The Flâneur.*[6]

Moreover, when the term is used retrospectively, it need not be confined to the mutually exclusive stages of development that Ferguson so acutely outlines. The ahistorical twentieth-century flâneur can pick and choose between the figure's various attributes: can, as it were, create an eclectic blend of the "genial ambulatory philosopher" and the "figure of loss and alienation." For the stroller through its streets, twentieth-century Paris may have been either a sensual utopia to be observed and relished, or a fragmented waste land. Indeed, it seems to me that much of the contemporary attraction of the flâneur lies in this ambivalence: in our sense of the flâneur as an emblematic figure of *both* urban pleasure *and* urban alienation.

So here, while trying not to lose sight entirely of Ferguson's diachronic definitions, I will also attempt to assemble a synchronic figure: the flâneur, once again, as an ideal type rather than a historically specific phenomenon. I begin with what is perhaps the most famous definition, the one given by Baudelaire in "The Painter of Modern Life" (1863):

> *The crowd is his domain, just as the air is the bird's, and water that of the fish. His passion and his profession is to merge with the crowd. For the perfect idler [flâneur], for the passionate observer it becomes an immense source of enjoyment to establish his dwelling in the throng, in the ebb and flow, the bustle, the fleeting and the infinite.*

To be away from home and yet to feel at home anywhere; to see the
world, to be at the very centre of the world, and yet to be unseen of
the world, such are some of the minor pleasures of those independent,
intense and impartial spirits, who do not lend themselves easily to
linguistic definitions. The observer is a prince enjoying his incognito
wherever he goes. (399–400)

From this account, certain aspects of the flâneur can be isolated:
the mobile perspective of the walker; the leisurely pace of such
walking; the paradoxical sense of being part of the crowd and yet also
detached from it; the observer who is not himself observed, but rather
inspects the crowd like a detective or a spy; the possibility of trans-
forming these observations into literature or art. Yet what connects
all these aspects (even the sense of detachment) is the pleasure of the
activity. The word here rather blandly translated as "enjoyment" is
in the original French *jouissance*, and one is tempted to take it in its
sexual sense, as orgasm. "Pour le parfait flâneur," Baudelaire writes,
"c'est une immense jouissance."[7] The pleasure of the Paris street is,
ultimately, erotic.

To begin, then, with walking. "Paris *should* be walked," writes
Richard Cobb,

because much of it, the most secret, the most modest, the most
bizarre, the tiniest, is only discoverable by the pedestrian who is
prepared to push behind the boulevards and the long straight streets
of the Second Empire and the early confident years of the Third
Republic. It is as if a different city, made up of tiny courtyards and
diminutive houses, were prepared to reveal its unpretentious and
endearing proportions only to the walker, still clinging to early nine-
teenth-century forms of transport and the itineraries imposed by the
amount that two legs can tackle. (111)

Cobb goes on to speak of scenes "which may be spied only once in
a lifetime, thanks to the chance opening of an eighteenth-century
double-door" (111–12); and Gail Scott also refers to "walls of court-
yards. Hiding Paris's unconscious" (43). I can testify myself to exactly

this effect. One day in October 1995, I was walking along the rue des Archives in the Marais and stopped to look in at a grand street door that opened onto a lovely, rather austere courtyard. A woman walking behind me stopped abruptly and also looked in. "I've been walking down this street for ten years," she told me, "and this is the first time this door has ever been open!"

Walking thus provides a mobile perspective, open to the fortuitous possibilities of chance and improvisation. Walking is also valued for its *pace*. "I like walking," Rebecca Solnit writes, "because it is slow, and I suspect that the mind, like the feet, works at about three miles an hour. If this is so, then modern life is moving faster than the speed of thought, or thoughtfulness" (10). The pace of the flâneur thus becomes a strategy of resistance to what Ross Chambers calls "the culture of speed" (216). Increasingly as the century went on, with the enormous pace of change in Haussmann's Paris, "Flânerie...became available...for resignification, as a manifestation of resistance to the speed of progress, and hence as a site of reading and (largely implied) critique" (Chambers, 218). Benjamin picked up on this point, mythologizing the story of Nerval's lobster and turning it into a whole flock of fictional turtles: "The *flâneurs* liked to have the turtles set the pace for them. If they had had their way, progress would have been obliged to accommodate itself to this pace" (*Charles Baudelaire*, 54). Celebrating the slow pace of the stroller thus became a way of reasserting a human scale against the increasing pressures of urban traffic and the sweeping expanses of Haussmann's boulevards.

For Rebecca Solnit, the combination of walking and idling, activity and inactivity, which is implicit in the pace of strolling, and indeed in the verb *flâner* itself, is a natural one.

> [D]oing nothing is hard to do. It's best done by disguising it as doing something, and the something closest to doing nothing is walking. Walking itself is the intentional act closest to the unwilled rhythms of the body, to breathing and the beating of the heart. It strikes a delicate balance between working and idling, being and doing. It is a bodily labor that produces nothing but thoughts, experiences, arrivals. (5)

And maybe not even arrivals. For the whole point of the flâneur's walking is that it has no destination. Unlike Hemingway hurrying to work, the flâneur has nowhere to go. "I have often dreamed," says Julien Green, "of writing a book about Paris that would be like one of those long, aimless strolls on which you find none of the things you are looking for but many that you were not looking for" (11). (It is self-consciously ironic that he writes this line in precisely such a book: his wonderful, anecdotal, reminiscent, and perfectly "aimless" *Paris*.) For Green, walking in Paris is not a deliberate search but an aimless stroll: not the efficient saving of time but the almost voluptuous *wasting* of time. "Until you have wasted time in a city," he writes, "you cannot pretend to know it well" (49). It is a point he comes back to repeatedly:

> Paris, as I have said, is loath to surrender itself to people who are in a hurry; it belongs to the dreamers, to those capable of amusing them-selves in its streets without regard to time when urgent business requires their presence elsewhere; consequently their reward is to see what others will never see. (79)

Similarly, Edmund White stresses that "a specific goal or a close rationing of time is antithetical to the true spirit of the *flâneur*"—it is indeed for this reason that White concludes that "Americans are particularly ill-suited to be *flâneurs*" (39–40).

Thus, the flâneur's only aim is to be aimless, to separate his walking from any sense of purpose. "In order to engage in flânerie," writes Franz Hessel, "one must not have anything too definite in mind" (Tester, 81). The flâneur is fascinated by the urban scene around him and even acquires an extensive knowledge and expertise about it (as witness Cobb's hidden courtyards, or Benjamin's repeated story about recognizing the precise spot where the extra horse was added to help a coach up a hill)—yet he is also detached from it. "A lone walker," writes Solnit, "is both present and detached from the world around, more than an audience but less than a participant" (24).

So to the mobile perspective and the leisurely pace we must add another essential aspect of the flâneur: he walks alone.[8] "I start walking again," writes Jacques Réda, in the opening poem of *The Ruins of Paris*. "Despair does not exist for a walking man, provided he really walks without turning round all the time to chatter away to someone else, pitying himself, showing off" (13). The flâneur is not a conversationalist. Ferguson is quite insistent on this point:

> *The* flâneur *walks through the city at random and alone, a bachelor or widower....The* flâneur *is in society as he is in the city, suspended from social obligation, disengaged, disinterested, dispassionate....* Flânerie *requires the city and its crowds, yet the* flâneur *remains aloof from both. Companionship of any sort is undesirable. Another* flâneur *is only just acceptable, and female companionship is entirely out of the question. Women, it is claimed, compromise the detachment that distinguishes the true* flâneur. *In other words, women shop. (Tester, 26–27)*[9]

Solitary walking contributes to, and is a sign of, the flâneur's sense of superiority—which is, in turn, the flâneur's tactic for dealing with the alienation of modern urban experience. One reason for seeing the flâneur as an emblematic figure of modernity is that he has found a way to be "at home in this alienation" (Solnit, 199). Thus Baudelaire can become the first great poet of the modern city.

But this feeling of superiority is also problematic. Patrice Higonnet describes the flâneur as "the self-marginalized individual who rejects modernity yet understands it so well that he is able to perceive the distance that separates him from the daily experience of the masses, whom he simultaneously loves and despises" (275). Detachment from the crowd is not far from disdain for the crowd; similarly, in Baudelaire, the flâneur is not far from the dandy.[10] "The specific beauty of the dandy," Baudelaire writes in "The Painter of Modern Life," "consists particularly in that cold exterior resulting from the unshakeable determination to remain unmoved"; it is, he says, a "haughty, patrician attitude...[which] appears especially in those periods of transition when democracy has not yet become all-powerful, and when aristocracy is only partially weakened and discredited" (421–22).

It is precisely this transitional position that fascinated Benjamin. In the 1935 "Exposé" for *The Arcades Project*, talking of Baudelaire as an allegorist, he writes:

> ...the gaze of the allegorist, as it falls on the city, is the gaze of the alienated man. It is the gaze of the flâneur, whose way of life still conceals behind a mitigating nimbus the coming desolation of the big-city dweller. The flâneur still stands on the threshold—of the metropolis as of the middle class. Neither has him in its power yet. In neither is he at home. He seeks refuge in the crowd. (10)

So for Benjamin, as for Ferguson, the detachment of the flâneur was, ultimately, unsustainable; observation becomes alienation. On the one hand, Benjamin saw the flâneur himself succumbing to the forces of capitalism: "In the flâneur, the intelligentsia sets foot in the marketplace—ostensibly to look around, but in truth to find a buyer" (10). On the other hand, the increasing commodification of urban life leaves less and less for the genuine flâneur to discover, less and less of Paris uncontaminated by capitalism.[11] So Benjamin's view of the flâneur became progressively disillusioned; the figure of the flâneur became associated with figures of repression and surveillance, the spy—"He is a spy for the capitalists, on assignment in the realm of consumers" (427)—and the detective.

"Preformed in the figure of the flâneur," writes Benjamin, "is that of the detective....It suited him very well to see his indolence presented as a plausible front" (442). In *Paris and the Nineteenth Century*, Christopher Prendergast writes that the detective novel "proposes a specific form of knowledge of the urban itself, predicated on the belief that an increasingly complex and intractable urban reality can be successfully monitored and mastered" (2). A lot of Prendergast's book is based on the tension between the idea of the city as something that can be known (mapped, mastered, controlled—with Haussmann as exemplar) and the idea that the modern city is beyond knowledge, that it is too vast, complex, and multifarious for any single point of view to contain. He quotes Maxime du Camp, writing in 1883, describing Paris as "enregistré, catalogué, numéroté, surveillé, éclairé, nettoyé, dirigé, soigné, administré, arrêté, jugé, emprisonné, enterré." Prendergast concludes: "The endless reports and proliferating nomenclatures of the urban bureaucracy (from the police to the sanitary inspectors), not to mention the cataloguing descriptions and ordering plots of the novelists, suggest a massive enterprise of mapping the city as a means, both practical and symbolic, of keeping tabs on 'identities'" (2).

Much of this effort of control is analogous to the attitude of the flâneur, especially in his later, alienated mode. Ross Chambers sees the flâneur as "a class spy reporting to the bourgeoisie on the life of the exploited class...the agent of panoptic surveillance" (219).[12] The emphasis is much more on what the flâneur *sees* than on anything he might happen to (over)hear. He is "a purely visual consciousness, a walking pair of eyes" (223). Similarly, Prendergast writes of "the corresponding notion of the city as a special kind of visual field, peculiarly open to the mobile gaze and unforeseen encounter" (3). Here it might be noted that, despite the fact that Baudelaire's definition occurs in an essay on a painter, Constantine Guys, the flâneur has been discussed overwhelmingly as a literary figure. As T.J. Clark points out in his review of *The Arcades Project*, Benjamin shows remarkably little interest in the visual arts, and all his extended presentations of Paris as "the capital of the nineteenth century" somehow never manage even to mention Impressionism.

These images of the flâneur as a spy or a detective suggest that his activity of *looking* was directed towards ends of social control, and that, in thus serving (consciously or unconsciously) the emerging forces of capitalist commodification, the flâneur was contributing to his own demise, undermining the possibility of his own detachment in the positive sense (as superior observer) and succumbing to it in the negative sense (as failure and alienation). In this view, the flâneur is indeed confined to a specific period; for Benjamin, "the department store is [his] last promenade" (10), and he does not outlive his century. But Prendergast also suggests other, wider contexts, in which the gaze and attitude of the flâneur may not necessarily be so confined: "*Flânerie* as an exercise in connoisseurship, in expert 'looking,' is governed by the play, and often the mixture, of two idioms—the idiom of science and the idiom of pleasure" (135). As I have suggested, such a "play" or "mixture" is the characteristic ambivalence of the modern, ahistorical flâneur, who *chooses* a role from a repertoire of historical positions rather than being determined by any one of them. Let me close this chapter, then, by looking briefly at what Prendergast calls the "idioms" of science and pleasure.

The scientific idiom certainly includes all the efforts at control through classification; but it is also amenable to more positive interpretations. The flâneur as journalist may indeed, as Benjamin says, be selling himself in the marketplace; but the journalist is also, we may hope, capable of something like the flâneur's detachment and observational expertise. Such detachment is also an ideal for the scholar: and more than one critic has metaphorically presented Benjamin himself as a flâneur, "strolling" through the vast archives of the Bibliothèque Nationale and finding, like Julien Green, many things he was not looking for. The flâneur's observations also produce raw material for the artist; and though the two functions (making observations, and transforming these observations into works of art) are strictly speaking separate roles, they may both be occupied by the same person. Baudelaire certainly blurs the distinction when writing about Guys and, indeed, in his own practice as a poet.

The idiom of pleasure returns us to the idea of the flâneur as someone who takes *pleasure*, even "jouissance," in his walking, in his detachment, in his observations. (I think that Benjamin wanted to disapprove of the flâneur on political grounds, but was himself too sensible of the pleasures of walking the streets of Paris to be entirely capable of concealing his own complicity—as is shown in that odd phrase about the "mitigating nimbus" (10) around the flâneur.) Prendergast quotes Henry James as writing, in *Roderick Hudson* (1875), that "the prime requisite of an expert *flâneur*...[is] the simple, sensuous, confident relish of pleasure" (4). And he concludes:

> *The incarnations of the Baudelairian* flâneur *are multiple—prince, dandy, detective, connoisseur and so on—but they frequently include a staging of the poet/city relation as amorous encounter, notably in the representation of the poet's relation to the urban crowd. In*

the essay, Le Peintre de la vie moderne *and the prose poem* "Les Foules," *the city is dramatized as a scene of attraction and seduction, in which the crowd appears variously as mistress, wife and harlot, and the artist as husband, lover and client taking possession of a malleable and receptive female body. (139)*

These two "idioms" are not, of course, entirely separate from each other. In exploring the figure of the flâneur as he (or even she) occurs in Canadian writing about Paris, I will be discussing Sheila Watson in terms of a personal alienation, Mavis Gallant and Gail Scott in terms of the flâneur as detached observer of the political scene, and John Glassco in terms of the ethics of pleasure—but all of them are united by the same central experience: the flâneur's love for walking on the streets of Paris.

←-- 7 DEVIOUS ROUTES --→

Sheila Watson Walking in Paris

We went to the Embassy and walked back along the Avenue des Champs Elysées and by devious routes to the Boulevard Haussmann.

— SHEILA WATSON, Paris journal, August 26th, 1955 (91)[1]

WHEN SHEILA WATSON ARRIVED IN PARIS in the late summer of 1955, her life was at multiple points of crisis. Her husband, Wilfred, was still engaged in an unresolved relationship with another woman,[2] which had come to a head in March of that year. Although Wilfred pleaded with Sheila to join him in Paris—"it would give us both a chance," he wrote (Flahiff, 86–87)—this other relationship was far from over. The Watsons' marriage was held together, barely, and as it was to be for decades to come, mainly by Sheila's deep and devout belief in the divine bond of the sacrament.[3] Divorce was not an option, and though Sheila seriously considered legal separation, she could not go through with it. Instead, she agreed to accompany Wilfred to Paris.

Even the fellowship that made the trip possible—funds from the Royal Society of Canada—had first been considered as something that

Sheila might apply for herself. Fred Flahiff suggests that "It was very likely at her suggestion that Wilfred—and not she—applied" (87).

At this time, Wilfred's literary career had reached a spectacular high when his book *Friday's Child* had been accepted for publication by the prestigious house of Faber in London, at the explicit instigation of no less than T.S. Eliot.[4] Sheila, meanwhile, was struggling to get a few short stories published, and her manuscript for *The Double Hook*, the novel that would eventually become the defining classic of modern Canadian literature, was in the midst of a long succession of rejections and revisions. (She continued to work on it throughout the year in Paris.) In 1955, there could have been no doubt in either of their minds about which member of the household was enjoying the more successful or significant literary career.

The result was that Sheila largely saw her role as that of the enabler—not quite to the self-effacing extent of Alice B. Toklas in relation to Gertrude Stein, but not entirely dissimilar. Almost every morning, it seems, she left the apartment on rue Vignon and walked around Paris, leaving Wilfred at home to write. The diaries are not always completely clear about who went on these walks. Sometimes they use the pronoun "we," but this usage seems to refer more often to the accompaniment of their landlady, Madame Gouzien, than to Wilfred. He did often accompany her to theatres and concerts, and sometimes to museums and galleries, but rarely, as far as I can tell, on her undirected walks, her "peripatetic speculations."[5] The reason for this self-imposed flânerie was, quite simply, to leave him alone and let him work. The journal never quite states this motivation in so many words, but the implication is clear. Wilfred, the poet anointed by T.S. Eliot, would stay at his comfortable desk and continue to produce significant work; Sheila, the as yet unsuccessful novelist, would wander the streets and scribble in her diary. The irony, of course, is not only that Sheila's novels would ultimately prove more significant than Wilfred's poetry, but also that her Paris journal is a much livelier and profounder document than anything Wilfred produced that winter.[6]

Sheila Watson was thus a flâneur—or a flâneuse—mostly by compulsion, driven by the dynamics of her domestic situation. This consideration already indicates that I am adopting a very broad definition of "flâneur," rather than any of the more narrow, historicist versions discussed in the previous chapter. The ideal flâneur *chooses* his role, out of the luxury of being able to indulge it; he is not forced into it by a recalcitrant partner. Nor, normally, is he a she.

Under the pressure of this unusual necessity, Sheila Watson became a true flâneur, a connoisseur of the Paris streets. The apartment was on the rue Vignon, close to the Opéra and the Church of the Madeleine, so her wandering was mainly (though not exclusively) on the Right Bank. While some of her walking was certainly directed (she went to art shows at specific galleries, she haunted bookstores), much of it seems to have been at random: wherever her feet might take her, just to stay out of the apartment as long as possible. (As winter closes in, she worries that "the time might come when I would be less free to wander at large" [112].) Under these unique circumstances, and in her own utterly individual way, she relived and recast the essential characteristics of flânerie: the detailed knowledge of the Paris streets; the quality of being an observer of, but not a participant in, the life of those streets; a deep-seated sense of being alone but not lonely; and the capacity to transform this experience into art, to move from walking to writing, from being a flâneur to being an *écrivain*.

One primary characteristic of the flâneur is, therefore, immediately apparent in Watson: the delight in street names, in detailed itineraries, the kind of obsession with urban topography that I have discussed in Chapter 5. Street names permeate Watson's journal as much as they do any other Parisian text:[7]

In the afternoon we walked down the rue Royale, through the Place de la Concorde and through the gardens of the Petit Palace and the Grand Palace....Between the ave. Montaigne and the Champs Elysées is an attractive street, rue Jean Gujon—on the east side of ave. Fr. D. Roosevelt it becomes the av. de Selves. On it there is an Armenian chapel and a small Church of Our Lady of Consolation.... (93)

After I crossed the bridge, I walked along the two Gds Augustins[8] to the rue Gît-le-Coeur,[9] along the rue St. André [des] Arts to the

Carrefour de Buci, down the rue Mazarine to the rue Guenegaud.
(117)

Just after lunch I set out in the rain for Montmartre—up the rue
Lafayette into the rue Lafitte, through the Sq. St. George and up
the rue Notre-Dame de Lorette to the rue Pigalle, along the Bd.
Rochechouart to the rue des Martyrs, to the rue Antoinette, across
the rue [des 3] Frères and up the rue Chappe and across the rue St.
Eleuthère to the Sacré Coeur. (120)

This latter is a heroic itinerary,[10] especially in the rain! The obses-
sive detailing of the route (largely uphill) might perhaps be read as
implying a reproach against Wilfred—look what I went through,
just to leave you in peace—but by and large I believe that any note of
blame or self-pity is absent from the journal. The street names are
listed for their own inherent fascination. Sheila's walking may have
been motivated by the desire to get away from the apartment, but that
does not mean that she did not also enjoy it, even relish it.

Watson responds vividly and sensitively not only to the names of
the streets but also to the particularities of their atmosphere. She sees
them as having an intense individuality, for which she (as a student of
classical Modernism) uses the Gerard Manley Hopkins term "inscape."
Walking one night to the theatre (to see the *Oresteia*), she notes:

Still the sky was not black—the street lights shone up through the
green and terra-cotta brown of the leaves. The bit of street beside the
black wall of the Palais has its inscape: on rainy days when the leaves
are wet underfoot—on windy days when the leaves twist on the pave-
ment and the sky is pigeon blue—or on still days when everything is
drawn up into the arch of the black boughs. (105)[11]

Later, she observes that "Paris rain too has its own inscape" (108); and
then, disagreeing subtly but decisively with Wilfred, she writes:

W says the Seine is a dull, stagnant river. He can't really have looked
at it. It is not like the Fraser—it is not like the North Saskatchewan

certainly, but it has its own necessity, its own inscape. Today I walked
on the quais on the river banks. When a boat passed, the water was
cut with blue—the greyed blue which can be seen so often roofing the
Place Vendôme. (128)

Here, the intensity of feeling in the landscape (or riverscape)—that
intensity of utter individuality and self-presence for which Hopkins
coined the term "inscape"—transcends any distinction between the
natural and the man-made. The river's inscape is the colour by which
the open-air place Vendôme is "roofed." Hopkins finally gets his explicit
name-check recognition when Sheila buys a hyacinth from an Italian
baker:

I think of Hopkins and how well he understood the fragile and
gleaming beauty of things—and their strength, too, for I carried the
delicate plant back in my basket with the bread and the artichokes
and the sausages—and the pink flowers glow remote and contained
now in the pale fold of the leaves. (137)

So for Watson, the streets have a unique life, inscape and instress,[12]
that the attentive walker, the peripatetic speculator, can respond to.
Like the classic flâneur, she is an acute observer but not a participant:
on the street, but always slightly apart from it, as is demonstrated in
this passage:

On the left side where the rue de Rome meets the Bd. Batignolles
is a curious dungeon-like building called the Collège Chaptal. In a
narrow passage just past the Hébertot there are a number of work-
shops—men working in wood—a cobbler in a shop no bigger than a
cupboard—four women ironing clothes with flat irons—the wooden
clack of pigeons' wings as the birds settled precariously on the narrow
windowsills—the smell of sawdust—the uneven thrust of cobble
stones against the soles of the feet. I sat in a café at the corner of the
avenue de Villiers and the rue Lévis for a while reading and drinking
a cup of café noir express. (119)

The detailed observation of the cobbler and the four women ironing is balanced by the detachment of someone who can afford to sit and read and drink coffee.

At times, Watson turns her attention to the more historical implications of these addresses. The rue de l'Hirondelle is a tiny street leading from the rue Gît-le-Coeur into the place Saint-Michel; Watson notes that it was the residence of Ambrose Paré , a sixteenth-century physician who published an influential study of deformed babies. She also notes that the exact site no longer exists: his house was on "the part of [the street] that was cut off by the construction of the Place Saint-Michel" (117): it was a victim of Haussmannization. Watson then combines these two associations—the dead children and the vanished house—and adds the extraordinary comment: "When one is very much alone, ghost hunting becomes a family affair" (118).

That is, the solitariness of the flâneur does not lead to an escape from the family, but directly back into it. The names are all ghosts; you walk, always, the streets of the dead. The ghost whom Sheila most wants to leave behind is, precisely, Wilfred. On September 26, she makes a very conscious effort to exorcise him for good: "W turns his face to Calgary and to his vision [to the woman who is his other lover]. There is nothing more to say—and I write his name here for the last time" (101). This resolve lasts for just over one month. There is no reference to "W" until October 27, and even then, though "W" again resumes a regular appearance in the journal, it is mainly as casual references to experiences they have shared (concerts, art shows), seldom to any detailed consideration of their relationship. Sheila Watson lived the experience of Parisian flânerie essentially alone.

Solitude is a central characteristic of the flâneur. Although Watson is occasionally accompanied by her landlady, the journal lays little stress on this relationship. The dominant feeling conveyed is one of being alone. Early in the winter (September 19) she records an experience of visiting a museum when she (a woman alone) meets another woman (also alone), who says to her: "Paris is the one city where a person can be completely alone yet not lonely."[13] To this proposition, Watson gives a somewhat tentative assent: "For the moment I felt inclined to agree with her" (98). But a month later, October 21, she is more decisive: "more and more I want to be alone—freed for a moment from the burden of feeling the need to excuse myself for being what I am—indeed for existing at all" (114). A few months later, on January 14, she writes: "what I feel I must feel alone. The only safety...[is] to walk as many hours as the street has corners" (136).

Much of what Sheila feels about solitude, about walking alone, and about her continuing isolation from Wilfred is summed up in a remarkable entry from very late in her Paris stay, July 22, 1956:

> At four o'clock this morning I was wakened by the incessant ringing of the telephone. Then Mme Gouzien knocked on the door to say the Mlle [Wilfred's young friend] was calling W "du Canada."
>
> Light had just begun to creep through the shutters. I smoked a couple of cigarettes, then turned off the light and lay watching the light through the slits.
>
> W's objections to the privileges of "the rich" with respect to books, music and university educations applies [sic] equally to an "inter-subjectivity" which is preserved in special delivery, telegraph and transAtlantic telephone.
>
> It is a dull day—misty and threatening rain.
>
> Figaro outraged by the statements of Tito, Nasser, and Nehru....
>
> Tonight I feel like a person who has walked too far to the final judgement—or simply walked too far. (159)

The pain of the relationship is registered in several ways. First there is the classical modernist image, à la Pound, whereby the emotional mood is displaced to the physical surround: the light barred by slitted shutters, the cigarettes, the misty day threatening rain. Second, there is the bitter identification of the ways in which Wilfred's academic terminology (derived, already, from McLuhan's theories of media) disguises infidelity as "intersubjectivity." Thirdly, these personal references are expanded by a rare allusion to the political situation.[14] The "outrage" of the right-wing newspaper *Figaro* matches, it is implied, the hypocrisy of Wilfred's "objections to privilege." The situation leaves Sheila alone, in the early hours of morning, smoking as she watches the barred light.

The final image equates the ultimate teleology of the theological Last Judgement with the secular image of someone who has simply walked too far—as if all the past winter of avoidance, of walking alone, has amounted to an error of excess. It poses a challenge to flânerie as such: is it possible to walk *too far*?

If we are to reclaim any hope from the bleakness of this July 22 entry, then we must seek it in passages of her Paris journal that reaffirm the position of the artist (and, ultimately, of the artist as walker, the flâneur as écrivain). Certainly, the whole journal bears testimony to Sheila Watson's intense involvement in the cultural life of the city of Paris. If her walks have any destinations, they are bookstores, galleries, museums, theatres, concert halls. In one key episode, recorded at length in the journal (January 18), she is at La Hune bookstore in Saint-Germain (still, fifty years later, the best bookstore in Paris) when Jean Cocteau visits. She observes him closely: "in a steel grey coat—or rather a charcoal black—cut like a doctor's gown, with great folds over the shoulders and a sort of pleat falling from an elegant tailor's arrow in the middle of the back" (137-38). She also notes the effects of celebrity—"His presence filled the whole room— and he knew that it did"—from which she herself of course (as witness the length of the journal entry) is not at all exempt. "When he left, people who had politely gone about their business while he was there, twittered to one another and turned to watch him go— lifting his hands and shaking the folds of his new coat and stepping delicately over puddles because it had begun to rain." This would not, however, be a Sheila Watson moment without the addition of a final comment, which is simultaneously unexpected, illuminating, farfetched yet apposite, self-deprecating yet endlessly suggestive: "I don't know why but I thought of Mrs. Dalloway" (138).

While she may preserve an ironic edge on the spectacle of Cocteau's celebrity, she is by no means apart from the existentialist worldview of the 1950s Parisian intelligentsia, and from its key concept of "absurdity":

Our life, S[imone] W[eil] says, is an impossibility and absurdity. Everything that we want is contradicted by the conditions or consequences that are attached to it. It is because we ourselves are contradictions, being creatures being God and infinitely different from God....

It is across the absurdity of the world, conceived of and suffered as an absurdity, not only that man finds "the Kingdom which is not of this world" but also that the artist finds his world of discourse. (141)

And where does the artist find this "world of discourse"? This immediate journal entry (February 5) offers two possibilities, but a third may also be found. The first suggests the circus (many years before any trace of Bakhtin's "carnivalesque" was available in the West):

The circus becomes the symbol of life for the writer—for me at least. There is no message—there is the impossible—and men lifting it like a weight or jumping through it like a hoop—or trying to tame it: torn faces, falls from the tight rope—spectacular manipulations—tigers bowing humbly before men—clowns drooling. (141)

A second manner in which the artist might find the world of discourse refers to Professor Salter, her mentor at the University of Alberta, who was always, for Sheila Watson, the reader who most needed to be convinced about The Double Hook. Continuing directly on from the passage just quoted:

That is what Mr. Salter didn't understand about The Double Hook. He thought that my people were stripped of society—conceived of as progressive. I meant that they were stripped of their bridges or centre, roots, traditions.... (141)[15]

But these concepts of the artist—as a drooling circus clown, as a builder of bridges—may be extended to a third possibility: the walker, the flâneur. When Sheila attempts to guarantee her position in France as an accredited alien (the same official process that will, forty years later, cause such paranoia for Gail Scott), she encounters "a curious little man in charge of the outer office" of "the minister of foreign affairs" (82). This punctilious official

knew what an "écrivain" was—not someone attached to a school—
not someone studying under a master—but a man who lived in the
city, who went here and there, peered into this corner and that—
walked about looking, looking. (113)

Here, for one glorious moment, the flâneur is given official state recognition as an écrivain: the wanderer who "walked about looking, looking" could be admitted, on that basis alone, to the citizenship of the Republic. (Even if she was a Canadian writer who knew (unlike her husband) that the Seine had a different inscape than the North Saskatchewan.) On December 23, she "walked the circle of the rue de Viarmes," and came out at the Church of Saint-Germain l'Auxerrois. "Apart from the noise made by two men chipping in the entrance," she wrote, the church "was quiet and undisturbed. In the late afternoon the windows above the high altar burn like flames. I had no time to speak to the gargoyles" (130–31). But surely they had time to speak to her.

8 MAVIS GALLANT ON THE STREETS OF MAY 68

<-- **8** MAVIS GALLANT ON THE

STREETS OF MAY 68 -->

MAVIS GALLANT lived through the events[1] of May 1968 in Paris, and I want to propose that her stance and attitude during this critical time were in several ways highly reminiscent of the flâneur. She was both a resident and a foreigner; a sympathetic but detached observer; present at the heart of the action yet also absent from it. Like Walter Benjamin, she experienced revolutionary Paris as a kind of waking dream. Above all, she walked. She walked, on the riot-scarred streets of Paris, and then she wrote, and then she walked again.

Her writing was done initially, she tells us, without thought of publication. "I simply followed events as they occurred from day to day, keeping track of conversations and things observed. If *The New Yorker* had not asked to see the record, I might never have bothered to type my notes and put them into order" (*Paris Notebooks*, 3). But she did publish them, in two long articles in *The New Yorker* in September 1968, and then again, in slightly revised form, in *Paris Notebooks* (1986). The journal form is visible in some syntactic shorthand—such as a tendency to omit the pronoun "I" in front of verbs or to jot down lists of notes rather than construct elaborate sentences—and also in the immediacy and commitment of her encounter with events.

Obviously, someone writing a journal doesn't know what's going to happen next, or how events are going to turn out (and that whole month of May, as the very existence of the French state hung in the balance, was an *extreme* instance of not knowing how events were going to turn out). Later fiction, written at more leisure, can afford a more distanced tone. Gallant's short stories often adopt a retrospective time scheme, looking back at events in a non-chronological sequence, thus enabling Gallant's characteristic authorial stance of irony. The few references to May 68 in Gallant's later fiction do indeed adopt this ironic tone. For example, in "A Painful Affair," published in 1981, Henri Grippes, the French littérateur who appears in several sardonic stories, has the misfortune to see his "long-awaited autobiographical novel" published in Paris on May 9, 1968:

> *His stoic gloom as he watched students flinging the whole of the first edition onto a bonfire blazing as high as a second-story window. Grippes's publisher, crouched in his shabby office just around the corner, had already hung on his wall the photograph of some hairy author he hoped would pass for Engels.* (Selected Stories, 836)

Here, everything is in place for Gallant's polished, ironic black humour: the precision of the verb "crouched" or the adjective "hairy"; the delicious equivocation of "hoped would pass for," snidely commenting on both the cravenness of the publisher and the ignorance of the students. This is Gallant at her acerbic and aphoristic best. But such a stance is not available to the woman writing in her journal:

> *Get dressed, go out as far as Carrefour Raspail. All confusion....The courage of these kids! Don't get too near. See what is obviously innocent bystander hit on the ear by a policeman....All night, shouts, cries, harsh slogans chanted, police cars, ambulances, cars going up and down my one-way street, running feet.* (Paris Notebooks, 10)

Despite her admonition to herself,[2] this writer is "getting near." And in the syntax of that last sentence, one of Canada's most elegant prose styles becomes a random list of jotted notes. In her 1986 "Introduction" to *Paris Notebooks*, Gallant attempts to re-establish her distance: "Now, eighteen years after the events, even the 'I' of the journals seems like a stranger" (4).[3] But the May Notebooks tell another story, and—much as I admire Gallant's more accomplished fiction—in many ways they seem to me the best thing she has ever written.

This interaction between distance and nearness, between ironic detachment and passionate involvement, is a central feature not only of the status of the writing as journal, as "Notebook" rather than finished product, but also of the whole position Gallant occupies vis-à-vis the political events around her. And in many ways it is the flâneur's position: in the crowd but not of it; alienated, but somehow at home in his (her) alienation; detached, but acutely observant; as Priscilla Parkhurst Ferguson puts it, "At once on the street and above the fray, immersed in yet not absorbed by the city" (80); or in Rebecca Solnit's phrase, "more than an audience but less than a participant" (24).

Like all expatriates, Mavis Gallant occupies an equivocal position in France. Though a long-time resident of Paris, she is still a Canadian; moreover, born in Montreal, she occupies a doubly-equivocal position in relation to issues of nationality and language. One of the most ironic moments in the May Notebooks comes when she gets into an argument with a "red-hot-Gaullist friend" who is complaining bitterly about the student leader Daniel Cohn-Bendit being German. "'How would you, a Canadian, feel if some foreigner went to Canada and tried to interfere?'" "'Some foreigner did,'" Gallant laconically replies, and though she notes that the point was missed by her Gaullist friend, it is certainly not lost on the Canadian reader (24).[4] The presence (or absence) of de Gaulle dominates the Notebooks, as it dominated the political events of the month. (Much space is devoted to analysis of his use of the word "chienlit."[5]) De Gaulle speaks directly to Gallant's sense of being, or not being, at home in Paris:

Why is it that when de G. speaks I always feel like a foreigner? If I had ordinarily felt like a foreigner in France, I would not have stayed here more than a weekend. But whenever he manifests himself, something

about the way he thinks, the things he says, and the reactions he
arouses in people—even in friends—always leaves me thinking:
Thank God I am not a refugee; I can pack up and leave whenever
I like. (90)[6]

Here is the detachment of the flâneur: looking at the crowd, he
still knows that he is not part of it, that he can "pack up and leave
whenever I like" (a privilege that is, of course, as much a question of
economics as it is of citizenship). "I'm not French and these aren't
my children," Gallant insists at an earlier point in the Notebooks
(17). When, later, she observes a Gaullist crowd, "They sing the
'Marseillaise,' which would move a stone, but for the first time I
feel a foreigner; I don't join in" (76).

Of course, she adds, balancing as always, "I didn't sing the
'Internationale' with the students" either. The flâneur doesn't take
sides. In many ways, it's clear that Gallant sympathizes with the
students, but her sympathy is never mushy or sentimental; it never
blinds her to the very real limitations, not to mention idiocies, of their
positions. Her account of a meeting at the School for Photography
(37–39) provides a devastating exposé of the inadequacies of the
French educational system and of the mind-numbing inertia and
entrenched stupidity of its Establishment. On the other hand, she is
wickedly funny in her description of one of the interminable debates
at the occupied Sorbonne, when a professorial friend outlines to the
students an ideal undergraduate curriculum of major and minor
subjects, which he attributes to the University of Peking:

When he sits down, I say, "But that is the American university
system." He replies, "I know, but I couldn't possibly say that. They
would never have accepted it. It had to be from Peking." (63)

Similarly, an early entry (May 11), balances, in successive para-
graphs, severe doubts about intimidation tactics used by the students
("Too much like post-Occupation") against scorn for "elderly profes-
sors suddenly on the side of the students. If they thought these reforms
were essential, why the hell didn't they do something about it before
the kids were driven to use paving stones?" (13).

In the long run, however, it must be admitted that Gallant does not maintain an ideal flâneur's neutrality. Just as Ross Chambers argues that the Baudelairean flâneur was forced into an identification with the marginal and excluded of nineteenth-century society, so Gallant, almost inevitably, identifies with the losers even before they have lost, even before de Gaulle stumbles back into power and the ideals of May 68 retreat into nostalgia and a romantic sense of tragic loss. Looking back in the 1986 Introduction, she writes: "The collective hallucination was that life can change, quite suddenly, and for the better. It still strikes me as a noble desire" (2-3).

Her use of the word "hallucination" here suggests another connection to the figure of the flâneur, especially as used by Walter Benjamin. For Benjamin saw the flâneur's territory as being, essentially, a dreamworld: "Dream houses of the collective: arcades, winter gardens, panoramas, factories, wax museums, casinos, railroad stations" (405). These are the privileged sites of *The Arcades Project*, the sites in which the emerging bourgeoisie is dreaming its future. (And for Benjamin politically, unlike the Surrealists, the important moment was not the dream itself but the awakening: hence his obsessive interest in the opening passage of Proust.) Through these sites moves the flâneur. In the arcades, T.J. Clark summarizes,

> "The domestic interior moves outside," but even more, the street, the exterior, becomes the place where we live—where we linger all day on a permanent, generalised threshold between public and private spheres, "neither on the outside nor truly in the open," in a space belonging to everyone and no one. We linger, we drift, we fantasise. "Existence in these spaces flows...without accent like the events in dreams. Flânerie is the rhythm of this slumber." The proper inhabitant of the arcade is the stroller. For only the stroller is wordless and thoughtless enough to become the means by which the arcades dream their dream—of intimacy, equality, homelessness, return to a deep prehistory. (6)[7]

This set of associations—of the flâneur moving through the streets as if through a dream—is strongly present in Gallant's *Paris Notebooks*. At times her use of the word "dream" is quite casual—the political

events of May 68 are so unbelievable that they seem like a dream—
but the image is repeated so often that it becomes far more than casual.
The "nightmare news" (*Paris Notebooks*, 12) of May 11 may be such a
casual image, but the line between reality and dream increasingly
blurs. On May 22, she has a "Dream image (but real) of middle-aged
men shuffling up in alphabetical order to vote" (32). By the 24th, she
writes: "This morning I had trouble remembering whether the news
was real or I'd dreamed it. Last thing I heard (or dreamed) was 'Small
groups setting fire to trash in Les Halles'" (39). By the next day, the
doubt has vanished: "Fell asleep and went on dreaming the news"
(43). The news is now unequivocally the product of the dream.

She records specific dreams in which the whole landscape of the
city, even its identity, has altered: "Dream: City besieged, strikebound.
Rivers of people in the streets. Have to meet someone (who?), and
walk *à contre-courant*. Faces all strange to me, but distinct. Everyone
very polite. City not Paris" (54). Again there is the position of the
flâneur, walking through the streets but walking *against the flow*,
maintaining detachment. Again her sympathy is divided: the faces in
the crowd are "strange," yet "polite." (Perhaps the joke here is that it
is precisely this politeness that proves that the city cannot be Paris!)

And Gallant is not the only one dreaming. As in Benjamin, the
dream has become collective:

> *Everyone reports strange dreams and nightmares. [A friend] dreamed
> his rooms were broken into and everything destroyed—books all
> over the floor, furniture burned, etc. In dream, was astonished—
> who could possibly have it in for him this way? Suddenly (in dream)
> thought: Of course, it was the Anarchists. Nothing personal. (66)*

The repetition of the word "dream" here (four times in five lines) has
an obsessive quality. In this world where one dreams the news, the
boundaries between the public and the private have broken down. The
destruction of the streets invades the home, the library. All events find
their dream-rationale in ideology. There is "nothing personal" left.

Even at the end of the Notebooks, after Gaullist "order" has been
restored, people cannot wake from their dream. Gallant talks with the
wife of a local shopkeeper:

She says that she dreams about "the events"—that she is with the
Minister of Social Affairs or the Minister of the Interior, and that they
go on and on talking about the situation, and that in her dream it
keeps her from sleeping: "I wake up as if I hadn't slept at all." (94–95)

The dream, then, that is conscious of itself: where one dreams that one
is dreaming, or one dreams that one is waking. "When I awoke like
this, and my mind struggled in an unsuccessful attempt to discover
where I was, everything would be moving round me through the dark-
ness: things, places, years": the opening pages of *A la recherche du temps
perdu*, carefully copied out by Walter Benjamin into Convolute K of *The
Arcades Project*: "Dream City and Dream House, Dreams of the Future"
(403). "We are all living in a future," Gallant concludes, "in something
that has not taken place" (*Paris Notebooks*, 58).

Yet the events of May 68 did take place, and the place that they
took was the street. As an observer of these events, Gallant had to be
in the streets, and it is in this respect that her Notebooks most clearly
evoke the figure of the flâneur—defined above all by *walking*—and
resonate with the whole topos of the *street name*, as I have earlier
outlined it. Gallant's instinctive response to the sound of commo-
tion outside her windows is: "Get dressed, go out as far as Carrefour
Raspail." That is, she proposes to walk, on the contested streets, to a
specifically named location. While she admires "The courage of these
kids!" facing the CRS riot police, her position is not without some
danger to herself: "Decide not to tell anyone, as friends would have
fit" (10). Yet the urge becomes compulsive: "Impulse to walk all over
Paris, as if the city were about to disappear" (69).[8]

In many ways the city *is* disappearing. Gallant's accounts often
seem like reports from a flâneur walking through a war zone: "The
ripped streets around the Luxembourg Station....The Rue Royer-
Collard, where I used to live, looks bombed" (12). She observes that
"the Boulevard Saint-Germain has something desolate, ruined about
it....Grilles up from around the trees, stop signs and one-way signs
lying in the gutter, traffic lights smashed" (40). The trees are cut
down: "Great sections of the Rue des Écoles torn up" (41). Along the
Seine, "Keep turning my ankles—so many holes in the ground, and
so many stray wood, stone, and iron *things*" (41). In the middle of a

familiar square, she finds "a hole like a bomb crater....Enormous truck on its side. Charred cars pushed half on each other" (44).

The effect is one of total dislocation. The city is disappearing; the streets are no longer streets. "How quickly a street becomes mud and garbage! I cannot identify this new ground I am walking on" (44). Like Proust awakening, she scarcely knows where she is. The city as war zone takes on the quality, already described, of a dream:

> Walk in morning rain to Luxembourg Gardens, on an impulse I cannot define. To see uninjured trees? Gates are shut, chained, and padlocked. Behind them the silent trees. Walk all the way around, past the Senate, past the occupied Odéon—its curb a hedge of spilled garbage. This is the fringe of the battleground: more and more spilled ordures, a blackened car still running, another car looking as if it has been kicked and punched. Something dreamlike [my emphasis] about the locked secret garden: green on green, chestnut petals all over the filthy pavement; behind the iron-spike fence a Sisley in the rain, a Corot with the sun gone. A fountain jet still playing. The final unreality—three workmen and a small bright-orange jeeplike thing for transporting rakes and shovels. I believe—I do believe—they were about to sweep the paths and rake the gravel. (43)

In the midst of all this walking, there persists, of course, the iconicity of Paris street names. No more than any of the authors cited in Chapter 5 can Gallant resist the allure of an itinerary: "Walk miles out of my way, just to walk. Down the Boulevard des Invalides, Rue de Grenelle, Boulevard de la Tour-Maubourg, along the Quai d'Orsay a short distance, the Pont Alexandre III" (75). Walking just to walk, the aimless stroll of the flâneur. But the very familiarity of these names only increases the horror: "The Rue Royer-Collard, where I used to live, looks bombed" (10). Or consider what Gallant herself calls, in a by now familiar image, "a conversation in a dream":

> We are walking up the Boulevard de la Tour-Maubourg. I say, "Do you think there will be a civil war?" "It is possible," he says politely. (77)

Surely the dreamlike quality here, the sense of utter unreality, resides not just in the evenly toned contemplation of the possibility of civil war, not just in the politeness of the conversation, but even more in the fact that this contemplation takes place on the stuffy, respectable, 7th arrondissement boulevard de la Tour-Maubourg. The irony resides in the banality of that *naming*.

At times, Gallant deliberately manipulates this effect. On the very first page of the Notebooks, she speaks of a "police charge, outside the Balzar Brasserie" (9). The Balzar is a fine old Parisian brasserie, where the waiters wear ankle-length white aprons and maintain an old-fashioned formality of service. It is much-beloved of Left Bank intellectuals, and when it was bought by a fast-food chain in the mid-1990s, a vigorous campaign was fought to ensure that its character would not change.[9] But the point here is that the Brasserie Balzar is separated from the north façade of the Sorbonne by the width of one shopfront (a Pharmacie) and one narrow street, less than twenty metres. Any police charge outside the Balzar is, necessarily, a police charge outside the Sorbonne. But consider the changed effect if Gallant had in fact written that. A police charge outside the Sorbonne is, in times of political unrest, almost to be expected, part of the normal order of things;[10] a police charge outside the Balzar is an invasion of violence into an order of comfortable familiarity.

Gallant the flâneur's ultimate experience of the streets of Paris in May 68 occurs during the massive demonstration (estimated at times at the improbable figure of three million participants) on May 13.

On the Boulevard du Montparnasse, not a traffic policeman in sight. Students (I suppose they are) direct traffic. From about the Rue de Montparnasse on, considerable crowd collected on pavements. Reach intersection Saint-Michel-Montparnasse a little after five: Marchers pouring by, red flags, black flags....In the middle of the road, small island for pedestrians. Make my way over to traffic island between a wave of Anarchists and a ripple of North Vietnam supporters. Stand on step of traffic island, which means standing with one foot in front of the other, heel to toe, and hang onto borne with arm straight back from the shoulder. Remain in this position, with only minor shifts, until a quarter to nine. (15)

The passage continues for several more pages, describing the passing crowds: the "mixture of students and workers"; the woman who "had been a Gaullist all her life until last Friday"; the young man who asks for the shouting of slogans to be muted as the demonstration passes a hospital; the politicians; the film stars ("all the New Wave"); the Anarchists and Communists; the exaggerated estimates of the crowd's size; the rumours of police violence—"I am convinced," concludes Gallant, "that I have seen something remarkable" (15-18).

Surely this is the flâneur's definitive position (ironically, because of its immobility): on a traffic island in the middle of the boulevard, she is quite literally, in Ferguson's words, "At once on the street and above the fray" (80). She is in the crowd, but not part of it; in the centre of the street, but not moving; observing, close-up and first-hand, and yet not participating; detached and ironic, yet also sympathetic and involved. Almost four hours she stands there, arm hooked around the *borne* (milestone, limit, marker of boundaries: the measure of Paris), positioned at the intersection of Montparnasse and Saint-Michel. "Only the meeting of two different street *names*," writes Benjamin, "makes for the magic of the 'corner'" (840). So let that be the final image of Mavis Gallant in May 68. Flâneur on her traffic island. The magic of the corner.

←-- 9 "LOVING WALKING HERE" -->

Gail Scott's Paris

MANY OF THE ASPECTS of the flâneur as I have defined or adapted them in relation to Mavis Gallant—the "impulse to walk all over Paris"; the ambivalence of being a Canadian citizen, especially a Québécoise, resident in France; the balance of detachment and involvement; the acute yet always slightly distanced observation of the French political scene—recur in Gail Scott's *My Paris* (1999). The title itself is a fine equivocation. On the one hand, it modestly declines to be definitive: this is not "the" Paris but only "my" Paris, one person's subjective and limited view. On the other hand, it almost arrogantly asserts possession: I have a privileged relation to the city, Paris belongs to me.[1]

Scott stayed in Paris for six months in 1993, as "part of an exchange programme between La Société des Gens de Lettres (the French writers' union—founded by Balzac) and the Union des écrivain(e)s québécois....La Société provided the studio, whose occupant changed every six months, and L'Union provided a subsistence grant" (details kindly provided, in correspondence, by Gail Scott). She never feels entirely at ease with this arrangement, though it affords her the opportunity to be a flâneur in one of the senses defined by Priscilla Parkhurst

Ferguson, that is, someone who enjoys "ambles through the city streets that offer the fortunate individual the delights of the cityscape and the perhaps even greater pleasures of suspended social obligation" (80). Scott's whole book can be seen as an extended dialogue between her delight in the cityscape and her deep uneasiness about any suspending of social obligation.

This uneasiness is shown by her consistent reference to the process by which she was awarded this position, which was in fact a juried competition, as a "lottery"—as if to emphasize that her winning it was a question of sheer chance, not merit: as if she were, in the most literal sense of Ferguson's words, nothing more than a "fortunate individual." In an early draft, published in *Contemporary Verse*, she describes herself as "A Québécoise or Canadian.[2] Parachuted into an art-deco studio in Paris. Having won a contest. A very swank studio. Not the kind she wanted" (14). In the finished novel, she consistently describes it as her "leisure lottery studio." Moreover, she suspects that her anglophone background is a source of embarrassment for her sponsoring body. When she meets the "male leisure lottery director," and explains to him that her family tree is "Only little French. Also English. Irish. Huron. Fairly typical mix," he is left "Staring nonplussed" (28). All through the book, she never uses the word "Canada," but rather the circumlocution "chez nous"—which, especially in its French form, raises all kinds of questions about who is or is not included in a "we" that is also "no us."

In other words, Scott is a professional flâneur, a *subsidized* flâneur, paid by the Québec government to do nothing but live in Paris for six months, walk around the city, and write a book. It's an uneasy, innately paradoxical situation. Early on, she describes herself[3] as "Maybe already less a traveller. Than a sort of flâneur," but immediately qualifies the definition by worrying: "Though Benjamin saying flâneur already hawking observations" (14).[4] The uneasiness here is clearly a doubt as to whether her subsidized status compromises her integrity, or whether the subsidy, by freeing her from the need to earn a living, might not in fact give her (if only for a limited time) the ideal disinterestedness of the flâneur: distance, detachment, the freedom to stroll in the city.

Early on, she isn't sure even of that. She describes herself as "exhausted," so "Clearly not flâneur. In later 19th-century sense of industriously strolling" (15). But she is being unfair to herself here. It is clear from the book that she does move around the city a great deal. (I have already cited, in Chapter 5, some of her quite extensive itineraries.) Almost every day's entry describes some place she has gone, and in the course of her six months she covers a great deal of Paris. Often, admittedly, she uses the Métro,[5] but a good deal of the time she is walking, and walking through the usual litany of street names: "Strolling to Pont-Neuf....Leaning over bridge. Taking in sunset....Then strolling back again. Walking up Rennes...hurrying down curved white Grenelle" (33). Section 81 describes an extended walk with her friend S along the Canal Saint-Martin: "Retracing steps southward. S trotting quicker. Past La Villette basin. Canal Saint-Martin. Across Seine to student quarter. Left foot blistering. Right to S's street in Montparnasse" (104–05). These are not negligible walks; the blister is earned. She roams the Right Bank, in search of the remaining Walter Benjamin arcades: "Yesterday visiting *three* of those old commercial passages or arcades. B calling Ur-forms of 20th" (137). "Continuing up Rennes," she writes at another point. "Dodging little Saabs and Renaults. Loving walking here" (125). *Loving walking here*— it is the ultimate credo of the Parisian flâneur.

It is also, of course, for any woman walking alone in a major late-twentieth-century city, an exposure to risk. Scott is acutely aware of the danger implicit for a woman like her friend F, whom she visits at her apartment near the Bastille:

> *After which she walking me back. To left bank. Then walking back to right bank again. Another 50 minutes. Albeit past midnight. Walking all over Paris. Any time of night. (30)*

The male flâneur still has a freedom that the flâneuse cannot with complete confidence claim. Scott approaches this apprehension through her project for a "little book" about "murdered women wanderers" (21).[6] This project becomes one of the continuing *leitmotifs* of *My Paris*, as Scott fails to sell it to a succession of publishers.

She treats the topic with a kind of bitter humour, manifested in the increasingly drastic abbreviations of the name: "Bk of Murdered Women" (47); "Bk of Murder'd Wom'n" (59); "Bk of Md'd Wm'n" (79); "Bk of MW" (81); finally reaching the logical absolute "BMW" (88). The connection to the luxury automobile is made explicit on pages 114–15, when the initials BMW appear on two successive pages, in reference to the book and then to the car. The BMW, stud car symbol of masculine display, is an exact metonymy for all the reasons why a single woman might worry about "Walking all over Paris. Any time of night."

Another danger in walking the streets, less fatal but for many people no less serious, is the risk of being stopped by the police and asked for one's papers. For Scott is not, strictly speaking, a legal resident of Paris. "True I don't have the proper papers. Too late to the consulate for a visa. Permitting me to stay" (11). At the three-month mark, she takes a quick trip to London, so that she can return to France with a new re-entry date stamped on her passport. (John Glassco and Graeme Taylor, facing the same predicament, took a trip to Luxembourg with Robert McAlmon. But as Glassco reports, "we were feeling so well that we quite forgot the original reason for the trip. We never acquired our *cartes d'identité*, and after that we never needed them" [65].) In all probability Scott never needed hers either, but her uneasiness on the topic produces a slightly paranoid edge to every sighting of a policeman on the street: "Several armed gendarmes. Patrolling Banque de France. Making wide berth. Down other side of street" (20); "Several cops. Checking Africans stepping off trains. Therefore I crossing to café opposite. Pretending to phone" (100–01). She refuses to sign a petition in support of a cause she supports, because it would require giving an address (140). She gets very nervous—"Paranoia rising"—when a woman in a café photographs her twice (91).

Her friends consistently laugh at her anxiety and discount her fears. When she sees "Two cops hanging out. In front of Saint-Germain-des-Prés" beginning to follow her and her friend Z, she whispers "Don't make eye contact....Notwithstanding Dunquerque stamp in passport. She [Z] smiling mockingly" (149). Her friends know, cynically but realistically, that as a white female she has little chance of being challenged. S tells her of an incident in the Métro, when she saw a "Plump young white American with brushcut" sitting on a bench between a "young African" and a "veiled woman." A cop comes by and demands identity papers from both the latter; "Not a word to brushcut" (75). Similarly, another friend, R, actually does apply to the préfecture:

> For purpose of securing carte de séjour, work permit. Where he immediately ordered. Into expeditious line. Rapidly outflanking those—mostly from "south"—in non-expeditious queue. Who waiting there for hours....Why bother—official declaring. When R asking how to go about. Applying for proper papers. But I was told I need them. R protesting. Oui, logiquement, mais vous êtes canadien; yes in principle, but you are Canadian. (95)[7]

So Scott's apprehensions about her own legal status are, in practical terms, groundless. But the grain of truth they contain, coupled with her own sense of guilt at her privilege of race and skin colour,[8] leads her to an acute awareness of the extent to which the French authorities are cracking down on immigrants. Immigrants—all those euphemistically described as being from "the south"—had become, in mid-1990s Paris (and increasingly since then), the major instance of the marginalized and peripheral urban class with whom, Ross Chambers claims, the flâneur is driven to identification. And again it is on the streets of Paris (and its park benches, Métro stations) that the drama is played out, as Scott records, again and again, incidents of policemen stopping immigrants to ask for their papers.

Scott's observations, her meticulous recording of the stories she hears, are just as detached and acerbic as Mavis Gallant's commentaries on May 68. At regular intervals, *My Paris* documents the casualties (relying mostly on reports in *Le Monde*). An Algerian professor is expelled, shortly before his doctoral defence, but not his French-born wife and children (30). An African walking by the Seine is stopped and asked for his papers; although they are in order, he has only a photocopy on him; panicking, he jumps into the river and drowns

(49). A famous Kenyan athlete also jumps into the Seine, this time to save a would-be suicide: "One month later Kenyan receiving *two* letters from préfecture. One citing bravery. The other inviting him. To leave country" (75). A singer from Zaïre is refused asylum, though his wife has been murdered and his daughter raped, the French authorities "esteeming family having no good reason. For needing refuge" (105). (Somewhere in behind all these stories lies the shadow of Walter Benjamin, evoked on page 50, committing suicide while attempting to cross the Spanish border with inadequate papers.)

So Scott is placed, in relation to this issue, in the ambivalent position of detachment and sympathy. She observes the situation, but there is nothing she can do about it politically (she can't vote for any French party that might alter immigration policy). She feels involved, since her own papers are irregular, but at the same time this "involvement" is absurdly and embarrassingly minimal in comparison to the life-and-death tragedies she records. She can bear witness, as the flâneur always does, but is that enough?

The same issues are repeated, on a wider scale, with reference to Bosnia. The six months Scott spent in Paris were among the worst phases in the bloody disintegration of the former Yugoslavia, and that awareness is never distant from the narrative. Again the sense of detachment and helplessness is combined with a horrified feeling of closeness: this is a European war, a European atrocity, happening only a few hundred miles away from Paris. Scott registers this dilemma in a gesture of very black and bitter humour: she intersperses her narrative, usually in a single sentence at the end of a section, with a weather report: "Raining in Sarajevo," etc.[9] It's as if Bosnia were close enough to Paris that they might experience the same weather systems, though everything else is so horrifically different. The weather reports seem like evasions, deliberately hiding (behind fog, rain, snow) the other events that might be described; yet in their very avoidance they become, through their accumulation as the book goes on, deeply expressive.

Her attitude towards the social, political, and historical realities around her is, then, the familiar balance of the flâneur: as she describes it in a deliberate evocation of Baudelaire, "Neither too distanced. Nor spleenish" (114). Such a role is also seen as "requiring frequent changing. Of position or angle" (114). Scott negotiates back and forth between all these changing positions: a Canadian citizen, supported by a separatist government, resident in Paris, but without legal papers; the occupant of a "leisure lottery studio," but constantly moving around the streets, one eye open for the nineteenth-century arcades of Walter Benjamin, the other eye open for the cops. It is raining in Sarajevo, but in Paris she cannot even sign a petition. She is surrounded by friends and visitors, is harassed by an archetypal Parisian concierge, and walks every day in the crowded streets; yet she is also essentially solitary. *My Paris* recounts no extended personal relationship or intimacy, and the protagonist is most often in dialogue only with herself. The book is a continuous record of an acutely observing consciousness, but the flâneur, as always, walks alone.

10 JOHN GLASSCO AND THE ETHICS OF PLEASURE

A MAJOR PART of what bothers Gail Scott about her status in Paris is the idea of living at *leisure*—as is shown in her repeated deprecation of her accommodations as a "leisure lottery studio." She is being paid to do nothing, which is an offence against every work ethic, Puritan or otherwise. "In feudal society," wrote Benjamin, "the leisure of the poet is a recognized privilege. It is only in bourgeois society that the poet becomes an idler" (802). "Idler," along with "loafer," is one of the commonest attempts to find an English translation for "flâneur," and it carries a distinctly pejorative tone. The flâneur, if he was to spend his days strolling the streets, had to be a man of leisure, free of any worry about earning a living; but this independence always opened him up to the criticism that he was an unproductive parasite upon society. Walking itself could be seen as a suspect activity. Rebecca Solnit writes:

> *The history of both urban and rural walking is a history of freedom and of the definition of pleasure. But rural walking has found a moral*

imperative in the love of nature that has allowed it to defend and open up the countryside. Urban walking has always been a shadier business, easily turning into soliciting, cruising, promenading, shopping, rioting, protesting, skulking, loitering, and other activities that, however enjoyable, hardly have the high moral tone of nature appreciation. (173–74)

These accusations against the nineteenth-century flâneur were frequently repeated against the 1920s expatriates. The highly favourable exchange rate pre-1929 gave many of these young Americans, for the first time in their lives, the independence of means to indulge themselves in leisure, and unfavourable portrayals presented them as doing nothing but lounging around the cafés of Montparnasse. Their sexual or alcoholic irregularities, though much commented on, were only the more obvious manifestations of their fundamental sin: doing nothing.

Many of them (including John Glassco) were quite content to accept the criticism, and even to attempt to transform leisure and laziness into virtues. Others' reactions were more uptight and defensive. Hemingway, for instance, indignantly dissociated himself from the idleness of his compatriots, insisting that he went to the cafés *to work*, that a café table was the best place for him to write. (This is what he had in mind in his statement, quoted earlier, about "the choice of streets to take you back fastest to where you worked": the itinerary he gives there finishes, not at his apartment, but at the Montparnasse café the Closerie des Lilas.) Similarly, Morley Callaghan insisted that "the Paris streets were my workshop. While loafing along the streets ideas for the stories would grow in my head" (147). Here, "loafing" and "workshop" are closely and defensively juxtaposed.

But a certain problematics of pleasure had been deeply ingrained in American attitudes towards Paris long before the 1920s. "For two centuries," writes Adam Gopnik, "Paris has been attached for Americans to an idea of happiness" (*Americans in Paris*, xiii). It is Thomas Gold Appleton, a Bostonian who visited Paris in 1839, who is credited with the famous phrase "Good Americans, when they die, go to Paris" (Levenstein, 72). Norma Evenson comments:

Only thus, one assumes, might a life sternly disciplined by Puritan morality and relentlessly dedicated to utilitarian toil be appropriately rewarded. Certainly, the concrete imagery of broad, tree-lined boulevards, the shops, cafés, and theaters, the good food and wine of this earthly city might easily eclipse a nebulous vision of celestial pearly gates and golden stairs. Rich Americans, of course, did not have to wait until they were dead to see the City of Light. (1)

For American travellers throughout the nineteenth century, "gay Paris" was the absolute epitome of pleasure. In *Seductive Journey*, his definitive history of American tourism in France, Harvey Levenstein gives 1845 as his earliest citation for this phrase, and notes that "Diarists also used the terms *gay* and *gaiety* as code words for carnal pleasure" (77). "Carnal" here primarily means sexual pleasure (though "gay" does not yet connote homosexual), but not exclusively so. Food was also a major consideration; French cooking was, Levenstein reports, a "major revelation" (39) for most early-nineteenth-century American travellers. For Christopher Prendergast:

> *...the gastronomic topos is not just a matter of neutral description. It is also a constitutive element, a discourse, specifically the discourse of pleasure. Pleasure is very far from being a "repressed" category in nineteenth-century representations of the city. On the contrary, the capacity of the city to supply all manner of pleasures is often at the heart of its perceived* raison d'être....*The gastronomic theme is at once a privileged form of, and a metonymy for, this inexhaustible capacity....In a great deal of the relevant literature, Paris is not simply a treasure-house of gustatory delights; the gustatory itself comes to act as a metaphor for the experience of Paris: Paris is above all there to be "tasted." (20)*

The fullest treatment, historically, of this "gastronomic topos" is given in Rebecca L. Spang's *The Invention of the Restaurant: Paris and Modern Gastronomic Culture*. Even in relation to gastronomy, we find, the walking of Parisian streets, and the specialized knowledge of their names, are an integral part of flânerie. Spang cites the splendidly named Alexandre Balthasar Laurent Grimod de la Reynière and his *Almanach des gourmands* (first appearing in 1803), noting that he outlined "nutritive strolls" or "nourishing promenades" around Paris, in which the novice gastronomer might be "instructed to follow the rue Traversière to the rue de Richelieu (via the Cour de Saint Guillaume) and turn right" in search of the best sources of culinary delight (153–54). Here, the long poem of walking and the voluptuousness of street names join each other in the expertise of the gourmet.

In any form, culinary or sexual, the discourse of pleasure always has to be balanced against discourses of justification. Just as Hemingway felt the need to justify the time he spent in cafés as *work*, so the pleasures of touring Paris had to be defended on grounds of cultural self-improvement. Levenstein's history begins from "the eighteenth-century American idea that travel should not be undertaken merely for pleasure" (4); rather, the experience of Parisian culture and taste was an essential part of the education of a gentleman. Levenstein traces, in fascinating detail, the gradual progress of this idea *down* the social scale. In the early nineteenth century: "Since it was universally acknowledged that culture was in greater supply in Europe than in the New World, a trip there to imbibe it could thus either reinforce an upper-class claim to cultural attainment or, for the nouveaux riches, represent an important step in staking one out" (27). But as the century progressed, the upper classes became more interested in a conspicuous display of leisure, and in the pursuit of pleasure for its own sake. "Now cultural uplift fell by the wayside. Pursuing it became the mark of tourists in the class below" (139). That is, as trans-Atlantic travel costs fell, and as more and more Americans became able to afford a trip to Europe, "cultural tourism" became the rationale for the lower classes (exemplified in the ferociously organized package tours that whisked visitors around a dozen monuments and museums per day). Of course, as this idea descended the social scale, so too (one step above) did its opposite; the twentieth century "[brought] both the upper-middle and middle classes around to the upper-class view of France as primarily a venue for recreational tourism" (175). Increasingly, the idea that the pleasures of Parisian life had to be justified on grounds of cultural self-improvement became marginalized (though, as criticisms of the 1920s expatriates show, it never entirely disappeared).

The 1920s expatriates were thus the inheritors of a long cultural process. In preferring the cafés of the Quarter to the cultural guide-book sites, they were adopting what had originally been the first stage of the aristocratic shift away from self-improvement and towards the conspicuous display of leisure. Many of them, indeed, seldom strayed more than a hundred metres away from the Dôme; Paris was for them a small village called Montparnasse. John Glassco and his friend Graeme Taylor did walk farther afield, but they too declared off limits anything that smacked of museums or monuments: "we absolutely refused to enter the Louvre. Once, having made a mistake in the mazes of the subway, we surfaced at the Invalides and were so appalled by the sight of Napoleon's tomb that we fled back down the steps" (24).

While foreign tourists with money to spend were the most conspicuous examples of the problematics of leisure, the issue was also widely discussed in France itself, especially around the turn of the century. In *Pleasures of the Belle Epoque*, Charles Rearick discusses the enormous rise, in late nineteenth-century France, of leisure activities such as sports and theatres, along with the "prodigious quantity of alcohol consumed" in Paris.[1] He quotes numerous expressions of social concern and of the need to inculcate or reinforce a strong work ethic among "the new industrial workers and the urban poor" (28). But he also notes the presence of several influential "crusaders for pleasure" (32), prominent among them Paul Lafargue, who, although a doctor by training, was himself a gentleman of leisure, being the heir to a large fortune. (He was also the son-in-law of Karl Marx, and inherited yet more money from Engels.[2]) In 1883, Lafargue published a declaration on *le droit à la paresse*—the right to be lazy. Rearick summarizes its arguments thus:

> "*The right to be lazy*"—le droit à la paresse—*was the title of a caustically witty tract by Lafargue published in the year of Marx's death. No one in the belle époque delivered a more forceful and biting attack on the work ethic and the misery of workers in capitalist industry.*

"The unbridled work to which [the proletariat]...has given itself up
since the beginning of the century is the most terrible scourge that
has ever struck humanity," charged Lafargue. It was "the cause of
every intellectual degeneration, every organic deformation," the
source of "all individual and social miseries"....Not only were workers
killing themselves by overwork, but they were also "vegetating in
abstinence," refraining from claiming the fruits of their labour....
Lafargue insisted that work be prohibited or at least reduced to three
hours a day. In "the regime of laziness" the capitalists would be
rescued from the "work of overconsumption and waste with which
they have been overwhelmed," and the proletarians would be free to
return to their "natural instincts" and to practice the "virtues of lazi-
ness"....After three hours work, everyone in Lafargue's utopia could
"loaf and carouse the rest of the day and the night." (33–34)

"Basic to flânerie," writes Benjamin, "is the idea that the fruits of idle-
ness are more precious than the fruits of labour" (453).

This whole argument bears striking similarities to certain passages
in John Glassco's *Memoirs of Montparnasse*. Even if he was actu-
ally writing in the 1960s, Glassco situated himself in the 1920s, and
so could be seen as responding to a debate that was, in these terms,
current in French culture; and, even if he scarcely needed to go
outside of Montreal, or indeed his father's home, to encounter a
Puritan work ethic, it was also very prevalent (and challenged) in
France. There is even a further similarity: just as Glassco's hedonism
brought him to "a bad end," facing death in a Montreal hospital, so
Lafargue ended miserably; his fortune exhausted, in 1911 he killed
both himself and his wife (Laura, the daughter of Marx).

In discussing the "pleasures of the Belle Époque," Rearick pays
particular attention to the celebration of Bastille Day. July 14 was not
in fact observed as a public holiday in post-Revolutionary France
until 1880; neither monarchist nor Bonapartist regimes particu-
larly wanted to commemorate such a loaded event, or to celebrate the
overthrow of an established government. Even the Third Republic
"adopted the Bastille fête only with reluctance, as a token concession
to the strengthening Left" (5). Further, Rearick argues, the initial cele-
bration in 1880 was organized at very short notice, and so allowed for

a good deal of spontaneous invention; in later years, as it hardened into an annual institution, it became less genuinely joyful. Rearick describes some of these 1880 celebrations:

> In the cities they dedicated statues of a classical woman, nicknamed Marianne, who symbolized the Republic; in the villages, they paid homage to busts of the Republic, busts in some cases carried through the bourg like saints' effigies and then enshrined in the town hall.... In Ars (Île de Ré), for example, "an artist of our little village made a statue for the public square," reported the mayor to the prefect in July 1881. Communal officials marched there on July 14 to "pay homage to the Republic." Awaiting the cortege was a group of little children dressed in tricolor robes and liberty caps, and one of them—"a charming little girl"—"made some patriotic remarks ringing with emotion," according to the mayor's report. (10–11)

Again there is a parallel in *Memoirs of Montparnasse*; indeed, Glassco's account of Bastille Day is a cheerfully obscene burlesque of the kind of ceremony Rearick describes:

> The whole city was seething with celebration. Everywhere people were dancing in the streets, and many of the women, like Arlette, had taken off their clothes; the effect was medieval....
> "What a good idea it was to capture the Bastille in July," murmured Diana, who was sitting on my lap, "rather than in December"....
> As we returned down the avenue [from the Arc de Triomphe] a parade came out from the rue de Presbourg. About a hundred students, led by a makeshift band of drums and tin trumpets, were pulling a float bearing a gigantic movable phallus;[3] worked by ropes, its head was slowly rising and falling. The crowd shrieked with joy as it moved slowly into the glare and crawled down the avenue. We fell in behind this symbol of the Third Republic. (90)

Rearick's commentary suggests just how seriously such a "symbol" might be understood in relation to the Third Republic; but for Glassco, the political reference is a throwaway piece of sarcasm (and, indeed, one of his very few directly political comments). Unlike Gallant and Scott, Glassco pays very little attention to the political climate of the city in which he lives; he is far too intent on having a good time.

"I'm lucky to be here," he announces early on, "in this city that I love more and more every day. What do I mean to do with my youth, my life? Why, I'm going to enjoy myself" (3). The unabashed pursuit of pleasure is the central motif of Glassco's book, even though he never quite has the economic independence to indulge in it as fully as he would like. There is certainly a major focus on sexual pleasure, but what Christopher Prendergast calls "the gastronomic topos" is not neglected. Glassco lovingly details the menus of many of his restaurant meals; and, looking back from the privation of his Montreal hospital bed, he laments: *"Lobsters boiled in butter, portugaise oysters, tender little octopuses in black sauce, how your memory haunts me in this abode of corned-beef hash and Jell-O!"* (97).

Unlike Hemingway (a phrase which, in reference to John Glassco, is more or less redundant), he has no qualms at all about neglecting his writing in favour of a life of leisure. Finding the excuse that he is still "too close to the events [he] was relating," he "closed [his] scribbler with a sense of relief and went for a walk" (58)—walking, here as elsewhere, being an exemplary sign of leisure. More explicitly: "telling myself once again that I could always return to the toilsome life of art, I chose once more the primrose path of present enjoyment. The important thing in life was to have a good time" (121). Glassco, that is, embraces as a virtue precisely the accusation that the expatriate so-called "writers" were in fact not working at all, but simply wasting their time. He vaguely floats around Montparnasse the idea that he is writing his autobiography, and then lives on that reputation for as long as he can without producing any more than the drafts of a couple of early chapters and a few Surrealist poems. Especially when we consider the *Memoirs* from the standpoint of the 1960s, as a conscious response to Hemingway's *A Moveable Feast* (1964), Callaghan's *That Summer in Paris* (1963), and Kay Boyle's reworking of *Being Geniuses Together* (1968), the challenge could not be clearer. Hemingway goes to cafés to write, Glassco to drink; Callaghan sees the streets as his workshop, Glassco sees them as his playground—in which, again, he takes pride in "missing the direct way."

But though Glassco talks about his own "flippancy, hedonism and conceit" (xxxi), he is also perfectly serious about his commitment to pleasure—in his own way, just as serious (and probably far less self-deluding) than Hemingway in his commitment to work. Glassco's philosophical justification of hedonism reaches its most eloquent climax in a passage of which, I think, Paul Lafargue would have been proud:

> *The next two months passed very pleasantly. As we were not impelled by ambition, envy, avarice or pride, none of us did anything at all: we remained sunk in greed, sloth and sensuality—the three most amiable vices in the catalogue [of the Seven Deadly Sins], and those which promote so much content and social ease that I could never see what they were doing in it at all, and have often thought they should be replaced by jealousy, exploitation, and cruelty, which are much worse sins for everyone involved. I do not think the life we led...was in any sense wicked for all its irregularity. It did no harm to anyone—and far from misusing our time, we were really turning it to the best account for our own sakes and the world's as well; for I am persuaded half of man's miseries result from an insufficiency of leisure, gormandise and sexual gratification during the years from seventeen to twenty. This is what makes so many people tyrannical, bitter, foolish, grasping and ill-natured once they have come to years of discretion and understand they have wasted their irreplaceable years in the pursuit of education, security, reputation, or advancement. (122–23)*

What one might expect, conventionally, would be that such attitudes would get their come-uppance, and that the more mature voice of age and experience would disown them. Glassco certainly seems to set his narrative up for such a gesture: his self-indulgence ruins his health and leaves him fighting for his life in a Montreal hospital bed. The scenario is not quite as drastic as Lafargue's murder/suicide, but it is still serious, and potentially fatal. The hospital is the setting (supposedly) for the retrospective passages that Glassco inserted in the narrative (setting them off in italics at the suggestion of his editor, William Toye). But in fact, the italics passages explicitly refuse to perform the conventional role. The "older" Glassco may be sadder than the young, but no wiser. For example, the passage quoted above is immediately followed by the comment: "*I realize that such remarks do not come with much authority from one whose pursuit of pleasure has led him to a hospital bed, but on the other hand I do not think my own want of moderation, and my bad luck, should altogether vitiate these arguments in favour of a youth of wine and roses*" (123). The italicized passages reject all the conventional arguments to the effect that one learns from experience and suffering: "*I have not yet been taught anything but the pointlessness of suffering and feel no deepening of my spiritual apprehensions*" (59).

As I discuss in more detail in Part Two, the stance of the hospital-bed narrator is a complex one, not least because it is fictitious. (Glassco wrote none of these passages—neither the original eulogy of pleasure nor the italicized commentary—in the Montreal hospital. All of them were written thirty years later.) While the figure of the dying, writing youth was intended to elicit readers' sympathy, it also enables a particularly devious twist of rhetorical argument. The initial statement—pleasure is more important and beneficial than "the pursuit of education"—may seem deliberately outrageous and overstated. If so, we are led to believe that a more mature perspective will modify it: that is, we are predisposed to accept what the italicized commentary is surely going to say. But then along comes the "more mature perspective" and endorses the original argument, and we find that we have been trapped into agreeing with it in advance. Through this rhetorical twist, Glassco somewhat underhandedly reinforces his argument in favour of "a youth of wine and roses."

There is another, more indirect sense in which it is appropriate that this whole debate should find a particularly strong focus in the city of Paris—and that is the possible parallel to the Greek myth of the Judgement of Paris. The connections between the city's name and the mythological Trojan prince have always been rather tenuous, but nonetheless persistent. Colin Jones notes that "From the twelfth century a myth of origins developed which attributed Paris's foundation to the survivors from the sack of Troy" (31). There is no direct etymological link—the ancient tribe of the Parisii have no connection to Troy—and the tendency, among the expatriates at least, to gender the city as female (itself a topos of the discourse of pleasure) discourages any identification with a male hero.

For the male expatriates, in the words of Samuel Putnam's title (1947), *Paris Was Our Mistress*. For the female expatriates, in the words of Andrea Weiss's title (1995), *Paris Was a Woman*. But for the French themselves, the matter is not so simple. For the most part, Paris is thought of as male, both in terms of its monopoly on social and political power, and of course grammatically—*le* Paris. However, Patrice Higonnet notes that "its name was for many centuries considered to be a feminine noun," and that it was "not until around the sixteenth century" that the masculine form began to take over. Baudelaire and Marx, writes Higonnet, both "continued to refer to the city indifferently as masculine or feminine" (21–22).

A male Paris offers a route back to the Trojan prince, and to the judgement he is called upon to make. Paris had to award the prize apple to one of three goddesses: Hera, Athene, and Aphrodite. Hera is conventionally understood to represent power, and Athene wisdom, while Aphrodite stands for beauty and sensual pleasure. In choosing Aphrodite, Paris makes exactly the same choice as John Glassco. Pleasure wins out over wisdom—at least until power, in the shape of Mrs. Quayle, takes its revenge.[4]

Glassco himself does not allude directly to the mythological story. Indeed, evocations of it in Parisian art and literature are rather rare.[5] Robert Delaunay did include figures of the three goddesses in his vast allegorical painting *La Ville de Paris* (1912), but rather pointedly excludes any representation of Paris himself. A more interesting reference occurs in Louis Aragon's *Paris Peasant*. Aragon quotes a rather abstruse passage from Hegel on sexual identity, then comments: "For me, this remark reveals the true meaning of the story about Paris: no doubt, only Venus among all her rivals seemed woman to him, and so he threw her the apple. But what would he have done here? In the Passage de l'Opéra, so many female strollers of all kinds submit themselves to the judgement of Hegel..." (48).

Aragon's ironic comment returns us, then, to pleasure on the streets of Paris. The Judgement of Paris is replayed in the Passage de l'Opéra, one of the old arcades demolished by Haussmannization, and described by Aragon in a brilliant piece of writing that was to prove the direct inspiration for Walter Benjamin's *Arcades Project*. For both Aragon and Benjamin, one of the key aspects of the arcades was that their upper levels were occupied by prostitutes.[6] "The arcade is a street of lascivious commerce only," wrote Benjamin; "it is wholly adapted to arousing desires" (42). Indeed, one of Benjamin's favourite arcades was actually called the Passage du Désir.

John Glassco entered fully into this "lascivious commerce," supporting himself at various times by writing pornographic novels, posing for nude pictures, and acting as a gigolo in an exclusive male brothel. His pursuit of hedonism was by no means confined to abstract philosophical statements. And, while all of these dubious professions place him metaphorically "on the streets," he also spent a good deal of time quite literally on the Parisian streets. Chapter 4 began by noting that, for Glassco, the detailed enumeration of a street itinerary served as the last word in an extended account of an evening's sensual pleasures. And, like so many of the writers cited in Chapter 5, Glassco cannot resist the allure of an evocative roll call of Parisian street names:

> Soon Graeme and I simply spent the warm sunny days of spring wandering about the odd and archaic parts of Paris—the rue Mouffetard, the Place de la Contrescarpe, the rue des Tanneries, the Halle aux Vins, the rue de la Gaîté, the Alésia district and the little network of streets around the Place St. Michel—the rue Galande, the Passage des Hirondelles, the rue de la Huchette, and the churches of Saint-Séverin and Saint-Julien-le-Pauvre. (24)

Indeed, Glassco's closest communion with the city of Paris occurs in the context of an extended walk. He begins on the Île Saint-Louis, and of course he tells us exactly how he got there: "I arrived by the rue de l'Archevêque[7] and crossed by the little Pont Saint-Louis, went around the Quai Bourbon and through the heart of the island by the rue des Deux-Ponts, coming back to the sun-drenched Quai d'Orléans" (177). There he sits and daydreams, picking out the house where he might live some day if only he were wealthy enough: a "small Louis XV hôtel" with a view of "the back of Notre Dame—so much finer than the front."[8] At this point, a brief italicized passage cuts in, contrasting *"my dream of life in Paris in November 1929"* with the gloomy hospital-bed view of *"a strip of soot-covered Montreal snow"* (177–78). Strolling back towards Saint-Michel, Glassco begins to feel that "the city had swallowed me and I now made part of it. It was an experience of possession so stately and vivid that I walked along in a dream of absolute subservience to stone and river and sky" (178). This feeling is perhaps the ultimate goal and vindication of the Parisian flâneur. Although the flâneur is so often depicted as ironic and distanced, standing back from the crowd and its spectacle, I would also contend that the flâneur *loves* the streets of Paris ("loving walking here," as Gail Scott says); that the flâneur's pride is eventually to be "swallowed" by the greatness of the city; and that indeed he "walk[s] along in a dream of absolute subservience."

Glassco's walk continues. He sits in the small park of the Vert Galant, "at the very prow of la Cité," well-equipped with "a half-baguette of bread, a small sausage and a bottle of ordinaire," and muses on philosophical problems (178). As night falls, he decides (having been evicted from his hotel) to sleep under the bridge, the Pont Neuf.[9] The place he chooses is disputed by a clochard, who indignantly accuses him of being "not a man of Paris," whereas he (the clochard) is "the man of the Pont Neuf." "So am I, for tonight," Glassco retorts (180). Thus, Glassco's sense of possession by Paris, of being "made part of it," is immediately challenged and reasserted. Not just walking on the streets, but sleeping on them, becomes his ultimate mark of ownership.

Waking the next morning:

I got up and went down on the tow-path, standing over the water and looking right across to Saint-Germain-l'Auxerrois.[10] The Pont Neuf still strode on its solid arches to the Cité, as it had for three hundred years and would keep on doing while civilization and consciousness lasted. I looked at the Seine and the island in a kind of rapture. This morning I felt for the first time fully implicated in the Paris of Villon, Nerval and Baudelaire, in an existence that would have been meaningless without the city. (181)

From this point on, *Memoirs of Montparnasse* descends into bathetic anti-climax. But this walk, this night, this morning, represent its true climax, the flâneur's epiphany. On the streets of Paris, missing the direct way, John Glassco is, finally and fleetingly, at home.

PART FOUR --> *Parisian Sites*

11 A WALK WITH GERTRUDE STEIN

←-- **11**   A WALK WITH GERTRUDE STEIN -->→

I BEGIN WITH A DIGRESSION. This chapter is mainly about certain sites in Gertrude Stein's Paris, especially the famous walk between her home on the rue de Fleurus and Picasso's studio at the Bateau-Lavoir. It will end with a digression, too: a gesture towards Stein's final destination (not on that direct route) in the cemetery of Père Lachaise. But first, I want to offer some pages about Gertrude Stein's most famous (or infamous) utterance.

"Rose is a rose is a rose is a rose."

--→ ONE OF STEIN'S earliest biographers, John Malcolm Brinnin, prefaces his book with this anecdote:

> When in the course of a conversation I told him that I was writing a book about Gertrude Stein, my friend Erv Harmon, one of the last great comics on the dwindling stages of the burlesque circuit, seemed suddenly thoughtful. "Well—" he said finally—"I can go along with those first two roses of hers all right...but when she gets to that third rose she loses me." (xiii)

Brinnin's book, which came out in 1959, is entitled *The Third Rose*.

So why is it that the second rose is acceptable, but the third rose becomes problematic? (Not to mention the fourth.) What is it in this phrase that has attracted such compulsive attention, not only from Stein herself, but from other writers alluding to it, repeating it, parodying it, transforming it?

It appears first in a poem called "Sacred Emily," written in 1913, and published in *Geography and Plays* (1922):

> *Night town.*
> *Night town a glass.*
> *Color mahogany.*
> *Color mahogany center.*
> *Rose is a rose is a rose is a rose.*
> *Loveliness extreme.*
> *Extra gaiters.*
> *Loveliness extreme.*
> *Sweetest ice-cream.*
> (187)

Three preliminary things to note. Firstly, it is only through the retrospective of the phrase's subsequent notoriety that it stands out here. In this initial context, it is given no more stress (and indeed less repetition) than the phrases surrounding it. Only later does this single line leap out at the reader. Secondly, its context is one of dark eroticism. The lines stress "Loveliness extreme," and associate such beauty with blackness ("Night town...Color mahogany") and sweetness to the tongue. Can the Melanctha of *Three Lives* be far removed from this "mahogany center"? And thirdly, the positioning of "Rose" at the beginning of a line and of a sentence allows, through conventional punctuation and capitalization, for one of the phrase's central syntactical ambiguities: is "Rose" a verb, past tense of "rise"; or is it a common noun, a flower; or is it a proper noun, a woman's name?

The phrase recurs, in a similar way, in "Lifting Belly," Stein's extraordinary long erotic poem, written in 1915–17 but not published until after her death (in *Bee Time Vine*, 1953, and in *The Yale Gertrude Stein*, 1980):

Lifting belly exactly.
Why can lifting belly please me.
Lifting belly can please me because it is an occupation I enjoy.
Rose is a rose is a rose is a rose.
In print on top.
What can you do.
I can answer my question.
(35)

Again, the line stands out only in retrospect: there is no other refer-
ence to it in a fifty-page poem. Again, the context is fully erotic.
Again, the capitalization of the first word of every line obscures the
distinction between past-tense verb, noun, and proper name.[1]

At some point, however, the line did detach itself and become a
kind of emblem for Stein: her signature, the phrase by which she was
best known to the world. It also began to appear as a circle, printed all
in capital letters, as it was embossed on the cover of the first edition
of *The Autobiography of Alice B. Toklas*—though here there is still a
period after the final rose: "ROSE IS A ROSE IS A ROSE IS A ROSE."
Later, the circle would drop the period and add the connecting "A," so
that there was no longer any way of knowing where it began: neither
"Rose is a" nor "A rose is." In this format it appeared on Stein's letter-
head notepaper and on porcelain plates, and on the dedication page of
The World Is Round, Stein's 1939 children's book about a girl called Rose.
This Rose literalizes the circularity of the phrase by carving it around
a tree:

> *So she took out her pen-knife, she did not have a glass pen she did*
> *not have a feather from a hen she did not have ink she had nothing*
> *pink, she would just stand on her chair and around and around*
> *and around even if there was a very little sound she would carve on*
> *the tree Rose is a Rose is a Rose is a Rose until it went all the way*
> *round. Suppose she said it would not go around but she knew that it*
> *would go around. So she began. (76)*[2]

The first assertion of "Rose is a rose" is, then, one of identity. I am
what I am, the thing is what the thing is. There is a solid core of self,

which can be known and asserted, and which remains immutable in the face of shifting circumstances. It appeals to blunt common-sense realism: calling a rose a rose is like calling a spade a spade. No matter what fancy linguistic theories you spin around it, a rose is still a rose.

At the personal level, the assertion of identity is equally blunt: I have my own identity, I am I, and that's it. Such a position accords with Stein's notorious egotism, and may be asserted all the more forcefully at times when such certainty is open to challenge,[3] yet it is also always grounded in a sense of the self as the sense of the other— Alice. The circular emblem on the private notepaper was another assertion to the world of the two women's intimate relationship: coded, yet all but openly coded. The erotic context of the phrase's initial appearances persists, even in a children's book, and far more in that "autobiography" in which the one speaks in the voice of the other.

That apparent split, in the narrative stance of *The Autobiography of Alice B. Toklas*, in fact does little to disrupt the sense of a unified identity; in the end, it still stands firmly in the Cartesian tradition that grounds identity in assured self-knowledge: *cogito, ergo sum.* Stein is a Stein is a Stein is a Stein. The repetition's insistence is not just metaphorical but also quite literal. The phrase may be about Stein's sense of identity, but it also *is* about flowers. "In that line," Stein later claimed, "the rose is red for the first time in English poetry for a hundred years."[4] By making the language real (through insistent repetition), she also makes the flower real.

But "making the language real" entails the further, more problematical step of grounding identity not just in the self, but in the *name*. For Rose in *The World Is Round*, the name opens up troublesome questions:

> Rose was her name and would she have been Rose if her name had not been Rose. She used to think and then she used to think again. Would she have been Rose if her name had not been Rose and would she have been Rose if she had been a twin. (8)

In one sense, Rose here is replaying one of the most famous debates in English literature:

What's in a name? That which we call a rose
By any other name would smell as sweet.
(Romeo and Juliet, II, ii, 43–44)

These lines assert a division between the name and the thing named; the thing (the flower) has an essential existence in the physical world (its scent[5]) independent of the word used to designate it. The lines are often quoted as if, unproblematically, they represent Shakespeare's opinion on the matter. But it is also possible to argue quite the opposite: that they are the words of a fictional character in a dramatic situation, and that Shakespeare designs them in order to show how wrong that character is. Juliet desperately *wants* there to be a split between thing and name, between Romeo and "Montague." It is for her, quite literally, a matter of life and death. She lives in a political world where names and things are not separated: she *is* Capulet, he *is* Montague, and that reality will kill them both. Her wish to ignore or dissolve this linkage is a sign that, in the flush of adolescent love, she is immature, idealistic, and fatally naive—which is why Shakespeare assigns to her lines that the whole context of the play shows to be patently untrue.

So the relation between identity and name already seems a bit queasy, and it is opened up further by the introduction of the third rose. "A rose is a rose" is barely acceptable as a tautology, or as a statement of the obvious given emphasis for rhetorical reasons. But the third rose throws the word into the field of linguistic play and indeterminacy. The syntax suddenly becomes fluid. The second rose is both the completion of one syntactic unit—"a rose is *a rose*"—and the beginning of a new one—"*a rose* is a rose." In the circular form, syntactic closure is denied altogether: the phrase becomes self-perpetuating; there is no full stop.

And the more often it is repeated, the more it becomes subject to the possibilities of linguistic play and chance—most obviously, the pun. I recall here a story by the great English comedian Frank Muir[6]:

It is not well known that Julius Caesar, apart from being a victorious general, was also an avid gardener. His particular passion was roses. At his villa in Rome, he cultivated a rare strain of deep red rose, of which he was inordinately proud. His great rival, the orator Cicero, was also a breeder, but he specialized in white.

One time when Caesar was away on a campaign, subjugating the Britons or the Gauls, disaster struck his garden in Rome. An errant goat invaded the garden, and consumed a whole row of young plants. The slave in charge of the garden, panic-stricken, resorted to desperate measures. Late at night, he crept over the wall into Cicero's garden and dug up a dozen young bushes, which he replanted in place of the ones consumed by the goat.

The plan worked well enough—the transplants flourished—but there was a problem. They came up white. All the slave could do was wait in trepidation until Caesar returned from subjugating Gaul.

On his first night home, Caesar of course went to inspect his garden. He returned with a deep frown on his brow, and summoned the unfortunate slave, who prostrated himself at Caesar's feet. Looking down at the wretch, Caesar observed coldly:

"Our roses arose. Is a row Cicero's?"

Such an exquisite result is only the extreme case of what happens when words themselves—their sounds, their phonemes—are treated not as transparent ciphers on their way towards meaning, but as physical entities in their own right, with properties that may not always be reined in by the imperious demands of a singular definition. One way to achieve such a change is certainly repetition. (Take any word, and repeat it over and over, until sense begins to give way to sound.) Stein felt that way about this phrase:

When I said. A rose is a rose is a rose is a rose. And then later made it into a ring I made poetry and what did I do I caressed completely caressed and addressed a noun. (Lectures in America, 231)

Paradoxically, this "caressing" of a noun involves the possibility of turning it into a verb: "a rose" = "arose." So in Stein's phrase, grammatical distinctions begin to break down. Noun becomes verb; substance becomes action. Similarly, present tense becomes past tense: "is a rose" = "is arose." The continuous state of being is equated to a limited past action. Post-structuralist critics (to whom Stein's work has greatly appealed) would describe this process as "deconstruction"; Stein describes it as "caressing." In the circle, "rose" is never far from "eros."

Despite its apparent simplicity, then, Stein's phrase is difficult, resistant to being pinned down to any one meaning. While it may seem to be a straightforward assertion of identity, its linguistic form slips and slides into multiple ambiguities. The more fixed and iconic it becomes (as on letterhead notepaper), the more elusive its precise meaning appears.

So its appeal has extended beyond Stein herself, to other writers interested in one or another of its multiple possibilities.[7] Here, I will single out only the Scottish poet, gardener, and artist Ian Hamilton Finlay. Finlay seized upon two coincidences: that between the name Gertrude Stein and the name Gertrude Jekyll,[8] and that between "rose" as garden flower and the use of the same word to designate the spraying device attached to the spout of a watering can. The resulting phrase—"A rose is a rose is a rose is a rose: Gertrude Jekyll"—appeared in many forms: as a poem-card; as an inscription on a ceramic tile; painted around the watering can in Finlay's own garden at Stonypath. But in one pamphlet, it appeared in juxtaposition to another transformation. Finlay had long been interested in the pre-Socratic Greek philosophers, especially Heraclitus.[9] One of the central maxims of Heraclitus concerns an arrow's flight: how at any given moment it is in one place, thus problematizing the whole notion of progression, of the continuity of time. What is movement, if any attempt to define it denies it? Present tense/past tense. "Is a rose / is arose." Or, in Finlay's formulation:

A ROSE IS A ROSE IS A ROSE
Gertrude Jekyll
ARROWS ARE ARROWS ARE ARROWS
Heraclitus

Practically every afternoon Gertrude Stein went to Montmartre,
posed and then later wandered down the hill usually walking across
Paris to the rue de Fleurus. She then formed the habit which has never
left her of walking around Paris, now accompanied by the dog, in
those days alone. And Saturday evenings the Picassos walked home
with her and dined and then there was Saturday evening.
—The Autobiography of Alice B. Toklas (60)

THIS STORY—of Gertrude Stein walking back and forth between her home at 27 rue de Fleurus and Picasso's studio at the Bateau-Lavoir on the rue Ravignan—is one of the most familiar aspects of the Parisian expatriate legend. But its very familiarity obscures a couple of obvious questions: To get between these two sites, what route would she follow? And how long would it take her? On a Monday afternoon in October 1995, ninety years later, I set out to do some practical research.

I started at 27 rue de Fleurus about 1 o'clock in the afternoon, having walked through the Luxembourg Gardens (always a favourite haunt of Stein's) from boulevard Saint-Michel. But immediately I cheated, taking advantage of a possibility that would not have been available to Stein in 1906: that is, I decided to go uphill by Métro. Stein sometimes avoided the uphill walk by taking a horse-drawn omnibus. One such route did run from the carrefour de l'Odéon to the place Blanche—reasonably close at both ends.

There is, now, a direct Métro line with stops very close to both Stein's apartment and Picasso's studio. From rue de Fleurus, you need only walk down to the boulevard Raspail and turn the corner past the headquarters of the Alliance Française (the school where I myself learned whatever I know of the French language), to arrive at the station stop Notre-Dame-des-Champs on the Métro line 12 from Mairie d'Issy to Porte de la Chapelle; seventeen minutes later, you arrive at the Abbesses stop, which still has a fine Guimard-designed entrance and is just two minutes' walk from the Bateau-Lavoir.

But in 1906, this Métro line did not yet exist—and neither, for that matter, did the boulevard Raspail. For many tourists now, Paris has the air of a historic city that has somehow "always" existed; but for

Stein, it was a city in process of constant change, still undergoing the upheavals initiated by Haussmann fifty years earlier. In her book *Paris France* (1940), Stein wrote:

> From 1900 to 1930, Paris did change a lot. They always told me that America changed but it really did not change as much as Paris did in those years that is the Paris that one can see, but then there is no remembering what it looked like before and even no remembering what it looks like now.
>
> We none of us lived in old parts of Paris then. We lived in the rue de Fleurus just a hundred year old quarter, a great many of us lived around there and on the boulevard Raspail which was not even cut through then and when it was cut through all the rats and animals came underneath our house and we had to have one of the vermin catchers of Paris come and clean us out.... (15)

Construction of the boulevard Raspail had begun as early as 1866, but was not completed until 1913; the Métro line linking Montparnasse and Montmartre was begun in 1905, but was not fully connected to the Paris system until 1930 (Evenson, 21, 109). It was known as the "Nord-Sud" line, and as such gave its name to Pierre Reverdy's literary magazine, *Nord-Sud*, which was explicitly intended to link the divided camps of the old bohemia in Montmartre and the new avant-garde of Montparnasse in the years following the First World War.

This motif of constant change was to continue throughout my walk. Practically every major site I passed on the way would have changed, drastically, since Stein passed it in 1906. Walking in Paris is always like that: you need to see, and appreciate, the layers of the city's history. There is no point in holding on to any one conception of Paris; for better or worse, it changes and renews itself. From Haussmann's boulevards to Mitterrand's "grands projets," the physical landscape of Paris is a text of contestation and debate; in few cities in the world is architecture so personal, or so political.

So, in the days before Nord-Sud, Stein would have either taken the autobus, or else walked uphill, and I was content to let her. I took the Métro to Abbesses and began my own peregrination at the site of the

Bateau-Lavoir, so-called because the tumbledown buildings reminded some observers of the laundry-boats that used to ply their trade on the Seine. Unsurprisingly, it no longer exists. On the place Emile Goudeau, one display window offers a selection of historic photos of those cheap, ramshackle buildings in which Picasso lived and painted, as did, at various stages, Juan Gris, Max Jacob, Kees Van Dongen, André Salmon, Pierre Reverdy, and Pierre Mac Orlan. On the far side, visible only from the small square down below, off the rue Burq, the untidy jumble of south-facing windows has been replaced by a series of smart, modern, studio apartments. Although by no means at the top of the Butte Montmartre, they must still be high enough to command a spectacular view over the city of Paris—which at times seems, from Montmartre, a quite distant and separate place. At night, its lights twinkle in the distance like a foreign city.

I imagined Stein setting out to walk home after a visit to Picasso: not alone, as she would have been in the early days, but as she might have been a couple of years later, in the devoted company of Alice B. Toklas. Alice, I said to myself, shall we go home? Yes Gertrude, I replied. From 13 rue Ravignan (the official address of the building, though it stands on the small, tree-shaded place Emile Goudeau), a flight of stairs leads down to the rue Ravignan proper. This stretch is the only really *steep* section of the walk; since the Bateau-Lavoir is on the south side of the Butte, Gertrude and Alice would not have had to face the more precipitous streets near the summit, nor the truly fearsome staircases on the north side. The rue Ravignan runs down to the rue des Abbesses, which in turn leads to the rue des Martyrs. (A certain religious motif runs through a good many of the street names on this route.)

In planning my own way, I had consulted maps and attempted to establish the most direct route between the two locations. It is of course possible, even likely, that Stein would have taken all kinds of detours, and, on a couple of occasions, I too strayed out of the most direct line in order to walk through more pleasant surroundings. But for the most part, I took the shortest route that I could see.[10] For the most part, that is, I declined to follow John Glassco's example of missing the direct way, opting instead for the expertise of the flâneur, or at least of the map-reader.

The rue des Martyrs is a straight, broad street that drops directly down from the slopes of Montmartre. It is not particularly steep, but I imagine that the gradient would certainly make itself felt to those going up! Going up, they would also have in front of them, framed at the end of the street, the spectacle of the white gleaming domes of Sacré-Coeur. (For reasons both aesthetic and political, Sacré-Coeur is a building I detest, so I was just as glad to have it at my back and not have to look at it.) The rue des Martyrs crosses the boulevard de Clichy just at the point where it turns slightly north and becomes the boulevard de Rochechouart; one street to the right is the place Pigalle. Even in Stein's time, the Pigalle area of Montmartre was largely disreputable; nowadays, it is the centre of the sleaziest sex trade in Paris. But, coming down rue des Martyrs in the early hours of the afternoon, I saw none of that and continued south until the rue des Martyrs ends at the rather severe bulk of the church of Notre-Dame-de-Lorette.

This is the location vividly memorialized by Walter Benjamin when he wrote of the flâneur:

> Wouldn't he, then, have necessarily felt the steep slope behind the church of Notre Dame de Lorette rise all the more insistently under his soles if he realized: here, at one time, after Paris had gotten its first omnibuses, the cheval de renfort was harnessed to the coach to reinforce the other two horses. (417)

Would Stein, like Benjamin, have been interested in such an arcane point of lore? And would she have known, as he did, that the street prostitutes of this area were called by the slang term *lorettes*?[11]

Here I took a slight detour, shifting a couple of blocks east in order to walk down the rue Drouot. It's an interesting street, filled with dealers in stamps and old books. Gloomy windows display discreet samples of postage stamps from around the world, whose rarity it is left to the discerning collector to judge. One book store featured in its window, opened to the title page, a first edition of Captain Bligh's account of the mutiny on board His Majesty's ship *The Bounty*. At 9 rue Drouot, you pass the Hôtel des Ventes, the leading auction house in France, though again, what you see today is not the building that was there in 1906.

The rue Drouot reaches the Grands Boulevards at a complicated interchange, where the boulevard Haussmann changes into the boulevard Montmartre, with the boulevard des Italiens coming in at an angle. This effect would not have been fully apparent to Stein; the boulevard Haussmann was among the last completed of the great sweeping thoroughfares planned by the man after whom it was named. Indeed, construction of the boulevard Haussmann was not finished until the 1920s, long after Picasso had moved away from Montmartre, and long after Gertrude's walks would have taken her in this direction. By that time, the Passage de l'Opéra had been destroyed, and Surrealism had risen from its ruins.

South of this intersection, the rue Drouot becomes the rue Richelieu, though the venerable restaurant at the corner still bears the name Drouot. Just off to the left is the Bourse, the Paris Stock Exchange, housed in the neo-classical façade that attempts to give it the dignity of a temple. And then there looms up, dominating the whole left side of the street, the long and imposing bulk of the Bibliothèque Nationale. From the outside, it looks like a rather grim storehouse, with nothing to indicate the interior grace of the vaulted ceiling of the Reading Room, designed by the architect Henri Labrouste. But would Stein, I wonder, ever have gone inside? Her interest in the classics of the French language was somewhat intermittent,[12] and though she read widely, it was not in a scholarly fashion. I can quite imagine Gertrude and Alice passing the library by without giving it much of a thought.

At the end of the library, the most direct route would be to continue down the rue Richelieu (the route taken, now, by the 39 bus), past a charming statue of Molière. But at the rue des Petits-Champs, I turned left. My main reason for doing so was to pass through the gardens of the Palais-Royal, but first I made a brief stop at an institution that most definitely was not present in Gertrude's time: Willi's Wine Bar. In the midst of institutional Paris, a block from the National

Library and the Stock Exchange, Willi's is not only an English invasion, but an invasion into the heart of French culture: wine. Owned and run by a young Englishman with a passion for French wine, Willi's is still a curious bastion of Englishness in the heart of Paris; as I took a break from my walk and sat sipping a glass at the bar, I heard all around me the accents of the English public schools (one man shifting into fluent French as he took a call on his cell phone).

There are in fact many possibilities in this area for detours from Gertrude and Alice's direct route home. Around here is the greatest concentration of the arcades, or passages: the glassed-in shopping streets, built in the nineteenth century, which became the predecessors of the department stores and shopping malls of more developed consumer cultures. Twenty years after Stein's walks, the arcades would become the focus of Walter Benjamin's huge and ultimately unfinished study of Paris as the capital of the nineteenth century. At that time, the arcades had largely fallen into disuse and disrepair, but some of them have since been restored and revivified. A few blocks to the west of Willi's, the Passage Choiseul is today a long, narrow, and very busy commercial street, featuring several stores specializing in art supplies: paints, brushes, and fine papers. Just to the east is the most elaborately restored of the arcades, the elegant Galerie Vivienne, with its fine mosaic floors, its spacious courtyards, and the retro splendour of the restaurant Le Grand Colbert.

For my own route, however, I turned south through the gardens of the Palais-Royal. One enters the gardens beneath the apartment where Colette spent the last years of her life. John Russell comments:

> Perhaps it is above all of Colette that we should think when ambling around the Palais Royal. The latter part of her long and immensely fertile life was lived in an upstairs apartment at 6, Rue de Beaujolais....Even when she could no longer get to the Grand Véfour she wanted a detailed rundown on the day's menu and would comment upon it in growly Burgundian tones. (198)

Although Colette and Stein knew each other, they were not close friends; still, the route seemed appropriate. The walk so far had been entirely urban, on streets that are closely built-up and often rather gloomy; the gardens, which are among the loveliest public spaces in Paris, would make a pleasant change. The arcades of the Palais-Royal were, at some stages in their history, sites of vice and dalliance, and at other times of revolutionary fervour, as in the famous insurrectionary address delivered here by Camille Desmoulins in 1789. Now it is a park in which people sit to catch what is left of the late October sun, and distinguished women in formal dresses walk their dogs (in later years, Alice and Gertrude might well have brought Basket here). In the Cour d'Honneur, youths on skateboards and rollerblades weave between the witty columns of Daniel Buren's sculptures.

I emerged from the Palais-Royal by way of the theatre of the Comédie Française. Again, I am left wondering whether Stein's great love for drama extended to classic performances of Molière or Racine, Hugo or Corneille. (Even for someone like me, with limited French, the purity of diction of classically trained actors is fully comprehensible.) Here, where the avenue de l'Opéra encounters the rue de Rivoli, is one of the most jammed and complex traffic interchanges of Paris; even in the days of horse-drawn carriages, a decade before Gertrude began to navigate the Ford she called Godiva, it must have been a site of congestion and invective. One escapes from it through the archways of the Louvre, into the place du Carrousel.

As recently as 1870, this space would have been formally closed off, to the west, by the Palais des Tuileries. The palace's destruction in the revolution of 1871 opened the (slightly off-kilter) prospect through the Tuileries Gardens, past the place de la Concorde, and down the Champs-Elysées to the Arc de Triomphe: the grand east–west axis of historic and triumphalist Paris. In Stein's time, this heroic vista must still have had the air of novelty—and was, of course, as yet unmarred by the distant highrises of La Défense. To the left, the courtyard of the Louvre is occupied now by Pei's Pyramid, of which I cannot but think that Stein would have approved. It would surely have appealed to her sense of the modern, paradoxically combined with the ancient. The pyramid shape echoes not only the Egyptian antiquities of the surrounding museum, but also the strange mixture of the mystical and the rational that characterized the French Revolution; it would have been the ideal site for one of Robespierre's Festivals, his wildly irrational celebrations of Reason. Today, tourists delight in taking photographs that shoot the decorum of seventeenth-century stone through the open construction of twentieth-century glass. It is not a bad analogy for Gertrude Stein's prose.[13]

Leaving the Louvre, might Gertrude and Alice not have experienced the same sense of relief as I do, seeing the Seine? Were they not, like me, essentially creatures of the Left Bank? I feel uneasy anywhere to the north of the Seine. Paris at times seems to be not so much a city as a collection of villages, neighbourhoods, *endroits*—and mine have always been to the south of the Seine, in Saint-Michel, in Saint-Germain, along the rue de Sèvres, towards Montparnasse. Crossing the river here, and looking to my left towards the tip of Île de la Cité, and beyond that to the twin towers of Notre-Dame, I feel that I am coming home.

And again, the choices divide. In retrospect, I feel that I took the wrong choice here. The best way would be to cross the Seine and jog decisively left before taking the rue Bonaparte, right up through Saint-Germain-des-Prés, past the place Saint-Sulpice, until it turns into the rue Guynemer along the side of the Luxembourg Gardens, and turn into rue de Fleurus by the gate that leads out of the gardens there. If I were ever to do this walk again, that is definitely the route I would take—missing the direct way.

But on this occasion, I stuck to a slightly more direct route, tempted by the name: the rue des Saints-Pères. Not only does this saintly name nicely echo the rue des Martyrs at the beginning of the route, it also offers an irony that I like to believe Gertrude and Alice would have found irresistible. On the one hand, their own lesbian relationship must have offered (privately) a deeply ironic comment on the Street of the Holy Fathers; on the other hand, there was a sense in which Stein would have regarded herself and Picasso, quite unironically, as the "Saints Pères" of modern art. (A similar irony must surely have struck the feminist publishing house Des Femmes in the 1970s when it established its first premises on the rue des Saints-Pères, before later moving to a more neutral address on the rue de Seine.) As for today's ironies, I was pleased to notice, on the rue des Saints-Pères, as a kind of counterpoint to Captain Bligh on the rue

Drouot, a shop window exhibiting for sale a volume on *La Vie et Les Crimes de Robespierre*.

This route crosses the rue de Sèvres at the carrefour de Croix-Rouge, and then leads to the rue Cassette, a thoroughly dull and undistinguished street that eventually reaches the rue de Fleurus. And so we are home, Alice. Yes, Gertrude, home.

And I look at my watch.

The total walk (not counting my pit-stop at Willi's Wine Bar) had taken me just over one and a half hours. I had been walking at a steady pace: not loitering (except perhaps in Palais-Royal) and not hurrying either. In 1906, Gertrude and Alice were healthy young women, accustomed to walking long distances; one should not jump to conclusions about their pace. (Though Gertrude was always inclined to do things in a somewhat placid manner.) Let me assume that they walked slightly more slowly than I—especially when going uphill. Say it was a two-hour walk for them, a four-hour round trip. Four hours out of each day, as Stein walked up to Picasso's studio to sit for that famous portrait (and also, to bring him the latest episodes of the Katzenjammer Kids comics from American newspapers). And for "the Picassos"—Pablo and Fernande—after those famous "evenings" at rue de Fleurus, another two hours home, across the deserted streets of midnight Paris: through the quiet shadows of Saint-Germain, across the moonlit Seine, through the deserted courtyards of the Louvre, past the sleeping money of La Bourse, into the early-morning revelry of Pigalle, up the slope of the rue des Martyrs, back to the staircase off the rue Ravignan, and into the quiet studio, where the jagged figures of *Les Demoiselles d'Avignon* stared accusingly out from the wall at 2 A.M....

--> I UNDERTOOK ONE OTHER PILGRIMAGE in the Paris of Gertrude Stein: to her grave in the cemetery of Père Lachaise. It does not fall on any direct route between the Bateau-Lavoir and the rue de Fleurus. Indeed, it's not a part of Paris that I would associate with Stein at all, except for her grave. I'm surprised that she is not buried in the Cemetery Montparnasse, so much closer to her regular, as it were, haunts. Père Lachaise is huge, a veritable bourgeois necropolis.

Even equipped with a guidebook and a map, I walked right by the stone and had to retrace my steps to find it.

Graveyard tourism is one of the oddest forms of homage. Perhaps one is moved by a reductively materialist view: here, and here only, is all that remains of the famous dead. The physical site itself carries an almost fetishistic power. (I once saw a young man pick up a handful of dust from Jim Morrison's grave and place it in his pocket.) Yet there is also the metaphysical sense: whatever remains of spirit, of presence, may best be addressed here. Graves are for the benefit not of the dead, but of the living.

The stone is plain and simple; on top of it, people have left small stones (*Stein*) and single stems of roses. Most of the roses were withered; I left a fresh blossom, deep red, to last for another few days, having bought it at one of the many flower shops located, conveniently, just outside the cemetery gates.

The inscription is equally simple: the name at the top, place and date of birth and death at the bottom. No lines, no quotation from her writing. Even so, this brief text contrives to contain two errors. The effect is summed up, wittily but seriously, by the feline narrator of Bill Richardson's *Waiting for Gertrude*:

> *The flat top of the stone was peppered, as it always is, with pebbles, placed there in accordance with the Jewish tradition of leaving a stone in remembrance. I studied, as I have many thousands of times before, the carved summation of my Allegheny gal's living and dying, which provides enduring evidence that, however short the text, a good proofreader should always be engaged:*
>
> Gertrude Stein Allfghany 3 February 1874—Paris 29 July 1946
>
> *There are two significant errors. July 27, not 29, was the day of her passing....And Allfghany will never be found in any atlas or gazetteer.* (41)

No proofreader, however, could have coped with the effect of the design, which must have been foreseen by whoever designed it:

Gertrude herself; or Alice, who must surely have approved it. One line at the top, one line at the bottom, the space in between forbidding intrusion. There is no room at all for any other inscription on this side of the stone. So Alice had to take her place, with the modesty that always became her, in the subsidiary role that she chose, and cherished, in death as in life: her name and dates are carved on the same stone as Gertrude's, but on the back.

←-- 12 WRESTLING WITH THE ANGEL -->

Djuna Barnes and Saint-Sulpice

WHEN THE AMERICAN NOVELIST, poet and journalist Djuna
Barnes first arrived in Paris, in April 1921, she headed directly for two
landmarks, two measures of Paris. Her biographer Philip Herring
reports that, having come in by train to the Gare Saint-Lazare, Barnes
then "went straight to the Hôtel Jacob...down the street from Natalie
Barney's at 20, rue Jacob, and thereafter walked to Notre-Dame
Cathedral" (132). Notre-Dame is a very literal "measure of Paris":
it is the point from which all distances on road maps of France are
calculated. If a signpost in a rural village tells you that you are 973
kilometres from Paris, it means that you are 973 kilometres from the
Cathedral of Our Lady. 20 rue Jacob was another kind of measure,
another kind of madonna; here for several decades Barney, the
wealthy American writer and patron of the arts, conducted the most
influential lesbian and literary salon in Paris. It is an enduring irony
that she should have done so on a street named Jacob: the founder of
Israel, the ultimate patriarch.

Barnes's address at the Hôtel Jacob was followed by one at a
pension on the rue de Grenelle; a room at 2 rue Perronet; and a flat at

173 boulevard Saint-Germain. By 1927, she was established in an apartment at 9 rue Saint-Romain, farther down rue de Sèvres—a street that has also been host, over the years, to both Mina Loy and Mavis Gallant.

But Barnes's devotion to Paris grew slowly; her first instinct was resistance. She brought with her all the practised skepticism of a New York journalist, prepared to resist the lures of history and romance, Notre-Dame or lesbian salon. Herring writes:

> A skeptic as always, Barnes looked for authenticity amid unfamiliar surroundings, and for the first three weeks she disliked Paris....She was absolutely determined to be unimpressed, to keep her nose in the air, to see her surroundings only as a source for amusing observations. The mood did not last long, for Paris was destined to become Barnes's favorite city, a place that would generate intense nostalgia. (132)

One aspect of that eventual nostalgia is to be found in her novel *Nightwood* (1937),[1] in its careful and loving evocation of particular settings in Paris. *Nightwood* is a novel of immense psychological complexity and imagistic richness, one of the pinnacles of modernist fiction. In this chapter, I wish only to comment on one thread of its intricate tapestry: the role played by specific Parisian sites—mostly ecclesiastical.

The Parisian settings of *Nightwood* are, for the most part, carefully specified, and they cluster around the area of the church of Saint-Sulpice—albeit with a certain amount of retrospection. Herring quotes a letter by Barnes

> describing her deep attachment to the Parisian neighbourhoods of *Nightwood, which for a time after the novel's publication became her geographical center: "I want to live...in the Hotel Recamier—where, in my book, Robin lived—tho Thelma never put her foot, in reality, over its steps—I haunt the Place St. Sulpice now, because I've made it in my book into my life—as if my life had really been there." (217)*

Saint-Sulpice, then, is as much an idealized setting, fantasized in memory, as a real one.

The huge church of Saint-Sulpice, with its oddly mismatched towers, is one of the most dominating in Paris. It was constructed from the mid-seventeenth to the mid-eighteenth century; the façade was designed in 1732 by an Italian theatre and stage designer called Giovanni Servandoni. Ecclesiastical buildings on the site date back, however, for many centuries. Sulpice himself is one of the dullest saints in the canon, having lived a life remarkable only for its utter lack of saintly drama. Born in 570 A.D., he felt from a young age the calling to priesthood. But his parents objected, and, rather than displaying any heroic defiance, he quietly went along with their wishes and worked as a manager of their agricultural estates for forty years. Only in placid middle age did Sulpice become a priest, and then a bishop, applying his managerial skills to the dioceses of central France. He died in 647 A.D. and was canonized as a tribute to filial piety and sheer mute patience.

To this day, the area around Saint-Sulpice has a pious character: religious bookshops, and small stores selling rosaries, candles, statues of the Virgin, and other objects of devotion. Barnes describes the Doctor "buying holy pictures and *petits Jésus* in the *boutique* displaying vestments and flowering candles" (29).

The church has had a chequered history. It was, for instance, the site for the baptisms of both the Marquis de Sade and Baudelaire. Victor Hugo was married here, and so (under protest of the curé) was the Revolutionary leader Camille Desmoulins. Saint-Sulpice has extensive connections to the French Revolution: the first priest to refuse to vow acceptance of the temporizing agreement between the Church and the Revolutionary government did so from its pulpit. Later, Robespierre attempted to use it as a centre for the cult of Reason. Above the central door of the front façade is an inscription that reads: "Le peuple François reconnaît l'Etre Suprême et l'immortalité de l'âme (The French people recognize the Supreme Being and the immortality of the soul)"—a nicely nuanced phrasing, in which the religious is subordinated to the secular, and the existence of a Supreme Being is made to seem dependent on the recognition by "le peuple françois." Unfortunately (or fortunately, depending on your point of view) this inscription was not carved in stone; rather, it was painted on wood. The church has made no attempt to erase it, but has let time run its course. By the early twenty-first century, the words are almost entirely illegible.

Saint-Sulpice has, however, been considerably more active in combating a more recent intrusion of unorthodoxy. It relates to one of the most striking features of the church: its *gnomon astronomikon*, a device intended to determine the exact date of the equinoxes (and hence of Easter). It consists of a meridian line set in brass on the floor of the church, running to an eleven-metre-high obelisk; sunlight coming through a carefully placed window will hit the top of the brass line on the winter solstice. The *gnomon* was commissioned in 1727 by Languet de Gercy, priest of Saint-Sulpice, and constructed by an English astronomer, Henry Sully.

The *gnomon* has long been subject to mystical, occult, and esoteric interpretations, often connected to theories about the Templars, Mary Magdalene, and the so-called "Priory of Sion." These fringe ideas suddenly became mainstream with the publication of Dan Brown's *The Da Vinci Code*, which sets a couple of sensational scenes in Saint-Sulpice. Faced with an influx of credulous tourists, the church fought back. It refused permission for any scenes of the movie version to be filmed on site (unlike the Louvre, which co-operated enthusiastically), and beside the *gnomon*, it put up a firmly debunking notice (in English, as well as in French), as follows:

> The "meridian" line materialized by a brass inlay in the pavement of this church is part of a scientific instrument built here during the 18th century. This was done in full agreement with Church authorities by the astronomers in charge of the newly-established Paris Observatory. They used it for defining various parameters of the earth's orbit. Similar arrangements have been made, for the sake of convenience, in other large churches like the Bologna cathedral where Pope Gregory XIII had preparatory studies made for the enactment of the present "Gregorian" calendar. Contrary to fanciful allegations in a recent best-selling novel, this is not a vestige of a pagan temple. No such temple ever existed in this place. It was never called a "Rose-Line." It does not coincide with the meridian traced through the middle of the Paris Observatory which serves as a reference for maps where longitudes are measured in degrees East or West of Paris. No mystical notion can

be derived from this instrument of astronomy except to acknowledge
that God the Creator is the master of time. Please also note that the
letters "P" and "S" in the small round windows at both ends of the
transept refer to Peter and Sulpice, the patron saints of the church, not
to an imaginary "Priory of Sion."

The *gnomon*, then, is another "measure of Paris," not unlike the defini-
tive "metre" on the rue de Vaugirard, only a couple of hundred metres
away.

Directly across the square from the church is the Mairie of the 6th
Arrondissement, which in turn gives its name to the café on the north
side of the Square, the Café de la Mairie du VIème, where Barnes's
Doctor, Matthew O'Connor, spends much of his time.[2] The Doctor's
lodgings, we are told, are on the rue Servandoni, named for the
designer of the church: a grey and narrow street with a slight twist
in it that leads from the south side of the church to the Luxembourg
Gardens. Inhabitants of this street have ranged from the feminist
Revolutionary Olympe de Gouges to, more recently, Roland Barthes.
Between the rue Servandoni and the Café de la Mairie du VIème,
tucked discreetly into the southeast corner of the square, is the Hôtel
Récamier, where in the novel Robin Vote is first discovered. (These
locations are all still there; the devotee of *Nightwood* can still stay at
the Hôtel Récamier, have a drink at the Café de la Mairie du VIème, or
follow a lonely path down the rue Servandoni.)

This group of settings, then, is highly localized; much of the
Parisian action of *Nightwood* takes place under the shadow of Saint-
Sulpice. But there is little direct description of the church in the
novel; other churches feature more prominently. I shall return to
Saint-Sulpice later; but first, I would like to examine some of these
other ecclesiastical locations.

--> AN EARLY PASSAGE in *Nightwood* describes the "wandering" of
Robin Vote. It takes place early in her troubled marriage to Felix, at
the beginning of her pregnancy. The "wandering" is of course meta-
phorical, and it becomes one of the key images associated with Robin;
but it is also quite literal:

strangely aware of some lost land in herself, she took to going out;
wandering the countryside; to train travel, to other cities, alone and
engrossed. Once, not having returned for three days, and Felix nearly
beside himself with terror, she walked in late at night and said that
she had been half-way to Berlin. (45)

Then, "Suddenly she took the Catholic vow"—and her wandering
changes its character. Now the places she goes to are all within Paris,
and are all religious:

Many churches saw her: St. Julien le Pauvre, the church of St.
Germain des Prés, Ste. Clothilde. Even on the cold tiles of the Russian
church, in which there is no pew, she knelt alone, lost and conspicuous,
her broad shoulders above her neighbours, her feet large and as
earthly as the feet of a monk.

She strayed into the rue Picpus, into the gardens of the convent of
L'Adoration Perpétuelle. She talked to the nuns and they, feeling that
they were looking at someone who would never be able to ask for, or
receive, mercy, blessed her in their hearts and gave her a sprig of rose
from the bush. They showed her where Jean Valjean had kept his rakes,
and where the bright little ladies of the pension came to quilt their
covers; and Robin smiled, taking the spray, and looked down at the
tomb of Lafayette and thought her unpeopled thoughts. Kneeling in
the chapel, which was never without a nun going over her beads,
Robin, trying to bring her mind to this abrupt necessity, found herself
worrying about her height. Was she still growing? (46)

The specificity with which Barnes lists the names of the churches
Robin goes to suggests that she had particular associations in
mind. Why *these* churches, out of all the hundreds in Paris? What
do they have in common, or alternatively, what are their unique
characteristics?

The two that have the most in common are Saint-Julien-le-Pauvre
and Saint-Germain-des-Prés. They are among the oldest churches in
Paris. The earliest building on the site of Saint-Germain dates from
the year 542 A.D. Parts of the present church go back to the eleventh

century, though it was extensively restored in the nineteenth. Saint-Julien-le-Pauvre was built between 1165 and 1220; since 1889 it has been a Greek Orthodox Church—not, strictly speaking, the "Russian church" that Barnes refers to—with dim and faded icons on the walls and an iconostasis at the eastern end. Both churches have an air of history about them, a sense of immemorial time, which might well have appealed to Robin. Saint-Julien is a small church, very intimate in feeling; although much larger, Saint-Germain has a similar ambience. Describing Barnes's early impressions of Paris, Herring notes that "as she was 'a lonely creature by preference,' Nôtre-Dame left her 'comparatively untouched'; she preferred the 'less aloof' church of Saint-Germain-des-Prés" (132). Both churches are also attractively situated, within easy walking distance of the Saint-Sulpice quarter.[3] In the 1920s, the area around Saint-Germain had not yet become the intellectual centre it would be thirty years later—it would have been more associated with the Parisian high society depicted by Proust—but it is still an attractive, central location. Saint-Julien-le-Pauvre is on the edge of the Latin Quarter, near the Seine, with a view across to Notre-Dame; it is quite lovely.

Sainte-Clothilde is quite different. From the point of view of the 1920s, it is quite a modern church, built in the mid-1800s; of its neo-Gothic architecture, Norval White notes "It has the symmetrical perfection achieved only in academic revivals" (106). Its interior is large, empty, and cold. Standing inside its vacant spaces, I could feel no affinity with the other churches on Barnes's list. Its location is also without apparent attraction, buried in the heart of the 7th arrondissement, surrounded by streets occupied by government ministries with high walls and forbidding gates. In these streets one searches in vain for a bookshop, an art gallery, or even a cozy café. Nothing, that is, in the history or the physical appearance of Sainte-Clothilde offers any reason why it might have attracted either Robin or her author. Its inclusion on the list remains to me a mystery.

Perhaps, however, the key to these churches is to be found in their names. All of them, in one way or another, are associated with legends of discord between husbands and wives, parents and children—matters with a direct import on the situation of Robin at this point in the novel. Most extreme, in this respect, is the legend of Saint-Julien-le-Pauvre. "Julian the Hospitalier...was a nobleman who through a mistake of identity killed his own father and mother. To expiate his unwitting crime he went with his wife to live by a ford across a river, where they gave help to travellers and built a refuge for poor people" (Attwater, 206–07). Saint Germain, who founded the monastery in which he is buried, was bishop of Paris in the mid-sixth-century; the *Penguin Dictionary of Saints* records that "Saint Radegund appealed [to him] successfully for protection against her brutal husband, Chlotar I" (Attwater, 152). As for Sainte Clothilde, accounts vary. The *Encyclopaedia Britannica* notes that "Clotilda was tireless in urging her husband to renounce his idols and acknowledge the true God" (V, 944), whereas the *Penguin Dictionary of Saints* records only that "after a long widowhood made miserable by the atrocious behaviour of her sons, [she] died in 545, and she too is revered as a saint in France" (Attwater, 89). So: one saint who killed his own parents; one who protected a wife from attacks by her husband; one whose life was made miserable by her sons. It's quite a record of domestic felicity for Robin to contemplate.

The Convent of the Perpetual Adoration of the Virgin Mary, on the rue de Picpus,[4] takes Robin farther afield. The rue de Picpus leads south from the place de la Nation; to get there from Saint-Sulpice today requires one change on the Métro, though there is a direct bus line (the 86), along the once-Revolutionary rue du Faubourg Saint-Antoine. John Russell describes it as "the tranquil rue de Picpus" (184), but perhaps he is thinking of the convent garden rather than of the street itself, which today is occupied mainly by auto garages and condominium-style highrise developments. The convent, however, still exists as such; on the right-hand side of the courtyard rises a high wall of sober windows. When I went into the chapel, one afternoon in October 1995, there were indeed, as Barnes says, two nuns in the front rows, absorbed in a devotion that absolutely excluded any intruding tourists.

Nowadays, the convent is best remembered for the adjoining garden and cemetery. In the summer of 1794, at the height of the Revolutionary Terror, mass executions were carried out in the place de la Nation, and the grounds of the nearby convent provided a convenient (if enforced) location for a discreet, unpublicized mass burial. On the two days designated by the Revolutionary calendar as the 26 Prairiale and the 9 Thermidor de l'An II of the Republic, 1,306 people were guillotined in the place de la Nation. Their bodies were brought to the Cimitière de Picpus, where they were stripped of their clothes and valuables (the due of the executioners), and buried in a common grave. In post-Revolutionary days, the Picpus cemetery was strictly reserved for those whose relatives or ancestors had died in the Revolution; it is for this reason that, as Barnes records, Lafayette is buried here—his grave now a site of American patriotic pilgrimage. The American general Pershing came here, after the First World War, to proclaim: "Lafayette, we have returned!"; the grave is adorned with plaques and memorials from the Daughters of the American Revolution.

The Picpus Convent was also, as Barnes noted, the refuge for Victor Hugo's hero Jean Valjean, but here the interplay between fiction and history becomes rather complex. Hugo gives an extended history of the Convent and the Order of the Perpetual Adoration (*Les Misérables*, Part Two, Book Six), but it is largely fictionalized,[5] and bears little relation to the real Picpus. For one thing, since Hugo's plot requires that Jean Valjean be smuggled *out of* the convent in a coffin, his fictional Picpus cannot itself include a cemetery. Thus, Hugo also has to omit any reference to the events of 1794. So, when the nuns "showed [Robin] where Jean Valjean had kept his rakes," they are talking about a fictional character, in a fictional situation, as if he had been real (and they are doing so, of course, *to* another fictional character—Robin Vote).

The Picpus Cemetery today is one of those miraculous quiet places, within the bustle of urban Paris, where time seems to stand still, and where history lives. On the day that I visited, I shared the tour with a small group of people whose ancestors, members of the Parlement de Toulouse, had died in the 1794 executions. The caretaker seemed touched by their presence and gave us a more than usually detailed commentary. The names of the dead are all recorded, in two huge wall-size plaques in the chapel.[6]

Djuna Barnes makes no mention of the Revolutionary connotations of the Picpus cemetery. Yet it is worth noting that one other of the churches she mentions—Saint-Germain—is also associated with the Terror. The monastery attached to Saint-Germain was the site for the massacre of 318 priests in September 1792. Can it really be a coincidence that two out of the four churches mentioned by Barnes were the locations of extreme Revolutionary violence?

Seeking solace, Robin Vote seems to have been drawn to churches that all have a direct link to the history of Paris, from its earliest legendary foundations to its recent Revolutionary past. While Sainte-Clothilde remains, in many ways, the odd-one-out in the list Barnes provides, there remains enough of a symbolic coherence to support the notion that these place names were not chosen at random, but represent a deliberate significance that can still be read in the geography of Paris today.

⇢ BUT LET ME RETURN to the area around Saint-Sulpice. I wrote earlier about the infamous *gnomon* as a "measure of Paris." Another type of measurement was attempted, at this location, by the Oulipo writer Georges Perec, in his book *Tentative D'Epuisement D'un Lieu Parisien* (1975). The Oulipo group of experimental writers delighted in setting themselves arbitrary limits, severely restricted forms within which to produce their works.[7] In this short book, Perec sets out to offer a complete inventory of ordinary objects passing by him as he sits at the Café de la Mairie du VIème for several hours on successive days. He largely ignores the historic monuments, such as Saint-Sulpice itself, and concentrates on "what we don't usually notice, what is not remarkable, what has no importance: what passes when nothing passes, except time, people, cars, and clouds" (12; my translation). Since he is sitting near a bus stop serving four lines, buses feature largely in his account (identified by their line numbers):

> Passage of a driving-school car, of a 96, of a 63, of a florist's van, blue, which parks alongside the mortician's van, and from which someone takes out a funeral wreath.
> In a magnificent formation, the pigeons make a circuit of the square and return to rest on the gutter of the Mairie.

There are five taxis at the taxi-stop.

An 87 passes, a 63 passes.

The bell of Saint-Sulpice begins to ring (doubtless, the tocsin).

Three children being taken to school. Another apple-green Citroën.

Again the pigeons make a circuit of the square.

A 96 passes, stops at the bus-stop (Saint-Sulpice section); Geneviève
    Serreau gets off, heading for the rue des Canettes; I call her by
    knocking on the window and she comes to say hello to me.

A 70 passes.

The tocsin ends.

A young girl eats a half-coconut.

A man with a pipe and a black bag.

A 70 passes.

A 63 passes.

It's five past two.

An 87 passes.

(24–25, my translation)

And so on, for about sixty pages. The effect is oddly hypnotic; the repetition of ordinary events, punctuated by the regular recurrence of the bus numbers,[8] evokes the "daily commerce" of the street. (I take this phrase from Leonard Cohen, who attempted something very similar in *Death of a Lady's Man* [173–74].) It is a form of "measure," but drawn out to the extent that measure turns against itself, becoming almost its own parody. It is *épuisement*: exhaustion, both in the sense that it exhausts the possibilities of the scene, and in the sense that it is exhausting to read (and, presumably, to write). At the same time, it is only a *tentative*, an attempt (with the English sense of "tentative" also present): Perec's sixty pages certainly do not say everything that could be said about the place Saint-Sulpice.

A different measure of the scene is given by Etel Adnan in her book *Paris When It's Naked* (1993). Adnan was born in Lebanon, of a Syrian father and a Greek mother; she has lived, studied, and written in France and in the US. She is the author of many books (fiction, poetry, essays), in English, French, and Arabic. *Paris When It's Naked* is one of the most delightful books I have read about the city. It is a lyrical evocation of the whole of Paris, but especially of Saint-Sulpice.[9] "I come back home by some narrow streets," she writes (she lives on rue Madame), "cross Place Saint-Sulpice, and I do it slowly because I love water on water, and it's raining on the flowing fountains" (8). As a great lover of Djuna Barnes, she is naturally drawn to the café:

> Between the Police and the Church (who always lived on good terms with each other), I hurry, regularly, and, at last, I reach the fountain, do my best not to slow my pace near the massive Saint-Sulpice, quickly buy the paper, start to read it on the sidewalk and enter the Café de la Mairie du VIème arrondissement which is part of legends and posterity. You know why. It is the café immortalized by Djuna Barnes, and I dream of her, I say hello to her, every time I enter the café, which is at least once a day. Djuna Barnes. She lived by this fountain, she looked at those maple trees, wrote on these tables, cried on this sidewalk, loved under this weather. (14–15)

The café, and Djuna, becomes one of the recurring leitmotifs of the book:

> I go and sit in the Café de la Mairie du VIème arrondissement, smell fried eggs, beer and lemonade, absorb the smoke of the clients, drink a thick coffee, read a stuffy paper like Le Monde, and, oh yes! and think of Djuna Barnes. (38–39)
>
> ...
>
> It's time for a break at the Café de la Mairie. It won't give much comfort, though. Such a messy place. But it has energy. Little amounts of money circulate constantly, and there's good draft beer, the smell of fries coming out of the kitchen. It's crowded, rather unfriendly. But it's home, in a special way. The garçons are as grumbly as stepmothers. But when a customer trips over a chair,[10] they show good care, shake their heads, enter long conversations. In the summer the terrace is under wonderful shades. I not only evoke Djuna Barnes, yes, always, and remember her as she was sitting in her New York studio, on Patchin Place, living in the penumbra of her fame, but do also my daily trivial meditations. (96)

These are lovely and moving meditations, not at all "trivial." But if Adnan is drawn to the café because of Djuna Barnes, she is also drawn to the church itself, by an equally strong magnet: Delacroix. For the ultimate glory of the Church of Saint-Sulpice is to be found in the Chapel of the Angels—the first chapel on your right as you enter the church—the brooding, dim, intense mural by Eugène Delacroix, completed in 1861. *Jacob Wrestling with the Angel*. Adnan writes:

I think the fountain stops at night, too (not out of its own free will). The pigeons sleep on the shoulders of stone (and famous) cardinals. I will not disturb them with my thoughts. Jacob, nearby, fights his angel, day and night, like me. He does it not in the desert, but in Saint-Sulpice, a good place to look for angels. And in Delacroix's painting God watches in the form of an omnipresent tree. (33)

Two vast trees indeed loom over the action of Delacroix's mural. To the left, the wrestling match itself: Jacob, all muscular force, pushing against the imperturbable Angel. To the right, seemingly oblivious, Jacob's company, the people of Israel, pass by, and file into a steep valley on the upper left. In the front centre, casually laid on the ground, Jacob's spear and cloak and a yellow straw hat with a jaunty brim: a charming still life sketch that, legend has it, Delacroix painted in a mere thirty minutes. The painting seems dark in the dim light of the chapel; the contemporary visitor can switch on a timed spotlight.

Adnan returns repeatedly to this image:

Walking in that bustle, and the difficulty, something else inhabits me, the knowledge that in the massive Church of Saint-Sulpice legions of angels reside, some visible, some not. I go there, often, regularly, and plunge into Delacroix's secretive world. The itinerary he followed from Place de Furstemberg to the church, the last years of his life, had been mine too when I lived on Rue Jacob under some linden trees. You enter the Chapel of the Holy Angels. It's an obscure place, very obscure, and your steps are uncertain....Jacob is still wrestling with his Angel. I'm at the bottom of the painting, then I'm in a forest, a valley, it could be Yosemite which in Delacroix's days was barely known to Europe, it

has oak trees. Spiritual fights are secret and Jacob's men are running away, terrified, knowing that the battle is not carried on at the ordinary level of things. Jacob and the Angel are also embraced in a dance, their bodies glued in the confrontation of the Will against Love.
(54–55)

Here Adnan again evokes Natalie Barney, as a Muse not only for herself but for Djuna Barnes. The itinerary is (as usual) important. In the last years of his life, Delacroix moved to a studio in the place Furstemberg (one of the loveliest and most delicate small squares in Paris), so as to be closer to his continuing labour on the walls of Saint-Sulpice. It is just around the corner from the rue Jacob: one might even speculate (though there is no evidence for such a supposition) that the painter chose it for its proximity not only to the church but also to a street called Jacob. So Etel Adnan, in her later itinerary, moves from Natalie Barney on the rue Jacob, to Delacroix in the place Furstemberg, to Djuna Barnes at the Café de la Mairie, to Jacob himself, on the wall of Saint-Sulpice.

Jacob, wrestling with his ambiguous Angel. The Angel in *Genesis* (32: 24–32) is unambiguously male—indeed, in the King James version, he is not referred to as an "angel" at all, but simply as a "man." "And Jacob was left alone; and there wrestled a man with him until the breaking of the day" (32: 24). Yet Delacroix's Angel, with long, curly, golden locks and loose-fitting dress, looks at least ambivalently female. There is an erotic thrust to Jacob's assault, as he longs to be taken under her wing.[11] The line of Jacob's spear, which he has left lying on the ground, points directly between her legs. She (or he, as I must Biblically say) accepts his assault, as the immovable object accepts the irresistible force. In *Genesis*, the Angel wins the fight only by exerting his supernatural force (like a superhero in a comic book): "And when he saw that he prevailed not against him, he touched the hollow of his thigh: and the hollow of Jacob's thigh was out of joint" (32: 25).

The wound is placed in the thigh: symbolically and euphemistically. It is the mythological wound of castration, as suffered by Oedipus, or by the Fisher King—yet in this case, the wound is the sign of victory. By suffering it, Jacob has "won" the wrestling match: the Angel tells him "thou...hast prevailed" (31:28). He has "won" not by any unambiguous wrestling takedown, but by sheer persistence, struggling "until the breaking of the day" (31: 24). Through this persistence, he has compelled the Angel to resort to his supernatural power—in effect, to cheat. The wound that might otherwise destroy his fertility (castration, "in the thigh") paradoxically transforms him into a patriarch, the ultimate Father of his people: a transformation that is accomplished by the changing of his name—the alias as destiny. "Thy name shall be called no more Jacob, but Israel....And he halted upon his thigh" (32: 28, 31).

The story of Jacob thus involves profound questions of paternity and inheritance, naming and foundation. The Biblical Jacob has tricked his way into the inheritance of Abraham.[12] Delacroix himself was haunted by speculations that he was the unacknowledged illegitimate son of the French statesman Talleyrand.[13] The painting has an intensity that speaks, and continues to speak, to the emotional depth of these issues. Jacob continues to wrestle in a dark wood that is both literal and metaphorical. In Adnan's words, "an omnipresent tree." In Dante's words, "una selva oscura." In Djuna Barnes's words, "a night wood." All gathered together by Delacroix, on the wall of the Chapel of the Angels, at Saint-Sulpice.

←-- 13   19 RUE ROUSSELET --→

IN ALL OF PARIS, the single street that means the most to me—the street I lived on, the street I still dream about—is the rue Rousselet.

Rue Rousselet is a fairly short street in the 7th arrondissement, running between the rue de Sèvres and the rue Oudinot, about halfway between Montparnasse and Les Invalides. If you approach it from the general direction of Saint-Germain-des-Prés, you would walk down rue de Sèvres from the intersection called Sèvres-Babylone (translated by Gail Scott as "corner of Exquisite China and Pursuit of Sensuous Pleasure" [25]), site of a rather grandiose hotel, the Lutetia-Concorde, which has an unfortunate reputation as the major Gestapo hangout in the years of the Occupation. As you walk down rue de Sèvres, on your left is the chapel that contains the shrunken relics of Saint Vincent de Paul; on your right is the Laennec Hospital, memorably described by down-and-out George Orwell; ahead of you is a blank brick wall on which a "Du—Du bon—Dubonnet" painted advertisement has been steadily fading over several decades.

You pass the Vaneau Métro station,[1] which has a fine art nouveau lettering announcement of its name and a curious fountain with an

Egyptian-style sculpture of a man with two water-jugs. A few more paces and you enter one of those wonderful Parisian mini-neighbourhoods, in which all the necessities of life—a bakery, several butchers (one of them specializing in horsemeat, another providing the most sublime calf's liver I have ever tasted), a wonderful cheese shop, a cheap restaurant, an expensive restaurant, two other bakeries, a post office, an incredibly cramped "supermarket," a tailor, a newsagent, an incandescent patisserie (Peltier's), a corner bar (Le Rousselet), a laundry, and at least two wine shops[2]—are all available within a hundred-metre radius. Off to your left is the rue Saint-Romain, on which at various times both Djuna Barnes and Mavis Gallant had addresses. Then off to your right runs rue Rousselet.

It's a narrow, not particularly distinguished street. On the right there used to be a photographer's shop, which I think I single-handedly kept in business in 1985. (Since then, certainly, it's disappeared.) Also on the right is a very small Moroccan restaurant, existing as two rooms at the end of a narrow passageway, which seems always to have been there but was finally up for sale (due to the owner's retirement) in the summer of 2003. Another restaurant, on the left side of the street, has gone through many different incarnations, few of them successful. There was a small book-binding business in one building, re-covering old books in appropriate leather. But for the most part it's a quiet, dull, residential street.

The second half of the street, on the left as you walk away from the rue de Sèvres, is lined by a long high wall, which protects a private garden. I was never quite sure who owned this garden—a convent, or a hospital. At ground level, it's never open to the public, and the wall shuts off all views. You have to get up at least to the third (or in French usage, second) storey to see over that wall, and then there is a sudden, clear, and unexpected view, in the distance, of the Eiffel Tower.

At the end of the street is the T-junction corner of rue Oudinot. To the left are the extensive offices of the Ministry for Overseas Territories, whose responsibilities include the almost-Canadian islands of Saint Pierre and Miquelon. To the right, as Oudinot runs down to Vaneau, there used to be a tiny shop (more stationery than bookstore), where I bought my copy of Marguerite Duras' L'Amant in 1976.

Walking back down Rousselet, from Oudinot towards Sèvres, you
are directly facing the soaring height of the Tour Montparnasse,
perfectly framed by the lower buildings at the end of the street.
By the time I first saw it, in 1975, it was already a fact of the land-
scape. Indeed, it was a landmark, something by which to find my
way home. To this day, I resent its intrusion on the skyline of, say, the
Luxembourg Gardens, but I find great nostalgic comfort in its looming
presence at the end of rue Rousselet.

My wife Maureen and I lived on rue Rousselet twice: from
September 1975 till June 1976, and again from January till June 1985.

Both times at #19, though in different apartments. On both occasions, the rental was arranged by an international organization that provided accommodations for visiting university professors and graduate students. Especially in that first year, our lives were enriched by the other renters in the building: Terry from Texas, Madelyn from Boston, Katie from Toronto. Our respective landladies, Mesdames Warnier and Vincens, had dealt with the agency for years, and I think that both of them, widows living on their own, enjoyed the regular turnover of intelligent young people they could talk to.

The façade of #19 was, to put it mildly, undistinguished. The rest of the street (on the non-walled side) had a generalized, post-Haussmann, five-storey-plus-attics conformity. #19 had obviously been rebuilt, or resurfaced, some time in the mid-century; it had a bland concrete facing, slightly set back from the frontage line of other buildings on the street, and no romantic Mansard attics. What faced onto the street was a flat, anonymous, five-storey concrete fronting. You passed through a narrow entrance (always open in our day but now protected by a keypad-coded lock), and came into a tiny courtyard, in which there was one quite elegant apartment with a first-floor studio, then, separately, a garage with a single cramped room above it. The whole set-up was as intimate, and yet as anonymous, as the set of Hitchcock's *Rear Window*.

The garage was occupied, in 1975, by a family of Cambodian refugees. With the discretion of (possibly illegal) immigrants, they were perfectly invisible. It was impossible to tell how many people were actually living there, though it was certainly a lot; nor did we ever learn who, among the other occupants of the building, was renting the space to them. The studio apartment, however, was audibly occupied by a concert pianist, Christian Ivaldi. At the time, we only succeeded in finding one record by him, an LP of Beethoven song transcriptions, but he performed quite regularly for French radio, and his open-window practice sessions were always a pleasure.[3]

On the street side, the top floor was occupied by a family called Niépce—direct descendants of Nicéphore Niépce (1765–1833), who in 1816 pioneered a process called "héliogravure," and who thus is the main French candidate for the honour of having invented photography.

Janine Niépce was still a photographer (see below), but I regret to say that we never established any contact with this potentially fascinating family. The next floor down housed a dour family with a Germanic name (which I have forgotten), whom we vaguely associated with banking, and who seemed to have no contact with anyone else in the building. For all I know, they are still, anonymously, there.

Our main contacts were with the proprietors of the first and second floors. On the first floor lived Madame Germaine Warnier, who was our landlady in 1975-76. She also owned, and rented, the small (very small) flat at the back of the ground floor, which had in previous times been the concierge's lodge. For a year, we huddled in that one-room-and-kitchen apartment, which had been painted a dingy orange for the sake of Madame Warnier's son, who had spent a year as a volunteer worker in Africa. It is unlikely that this orange could ever have enticed him home, and towards the end of our time there, Maureen persuaded Madame Warnier to allow her to repaint it in a more luminous white.

Madame Warnier had distinguished family connections. She was a distant descendant of the mid-nineteenth-century painter Johan Barthold Jongkind, and she had several of his maritime landscapes hanging on her walls. She was also a niece, several times removed, of Jean Cocteau, and could still remember, as a child, sitting on Uncle Jean's knee—until such time as her family decided that Jean Cocteau's knee was not an entirely respectable place for a young girl to be. In addition to the apartment on rue Rousselet, she maintained a house in the country, where she increasingly spent more of her time. But in Paris, she would frequently go swimming, and Maureen accompanied her.

Even more interesting was Madame Antoinette Vincens, who owned the flat on the second floor. (Terry and Katie stayed there in 1975-76; Maureen and I inherited it ten years later.) The flat itself consisted of two large rooms, living room and bedroom, both of which had windows facing onto the interior courtyard (and thus with a perfect angle on Christian Ivaldi's piano), plus a cramped kitchen that also included the bathtub. Whereas Madame Warnier was quite large, hale, and healthy, Madame Vincens was small, stooped, and shrunken. Indeed, she seemed to get smaller over the years.

I continued to visit her until the late 1990s, and every time I saw her she seemed to have become smaller, more hunched over, more contained within herself. She would welcome me into her apartment (with its wonderful view, across the rue Rousselet wall, of the Eiffel Tower) and offer me Schweppes and dry biscuits; I would bring lemon tarts from Peltier's on rue de Sèvres.

Madame Warnier spoke very little English, but Madame Vincens was, when she chose to be, quite fluent. She read authors like Edith Wharton in the original. But she also insisted that Maureen and I speak French with her, and she was never slow to correct our mistakes. I remember one time when Maureen was sick, and I told Madame Vincens that I had gone to get some medicine for her to swallow: only I said "médecin" instead of "médecine," so it sounded as if Maureen was swallowing a doctor! But Maureen spent a lot of time talking with her; and years later, Madame Vincens said to me, quite simply, "Maureen me manque—sa voix, son sourire" ("I miss Maureen—her voice, her smile").

Madame Vincens also had distinguished relations. Her family was Swiss; there was some obscure connection, which I never got clear, with Madame de Staël. With her husband, who was a banker, she had spent a good deal of the 1930s in Indochina, in French colonial cities like Hanoi. (In fact, though she never said so, she shared some of the same background as Marguerite Duras.) She returned to France in 1940; her husband spent the war with the Free French in North Africa then died, suddenly, two days after he came home. She had lived in Paris ever since.[4]

Her maiden name was Mademoiselle de Bonstetten. It was under this name that she received, between 1924 and 1926, a series of letters, written in French, by the great German poet Rainer Maria Rilke. He wrote them to her at the instigation of mutual friends, at a time when she was going through a period of great personal sorrow, and he was dying; they never met. In 1977, she authorized a small press edition of these letters (his side of the correspondence only; she had burned hers), under the title *Lettres d'autour d'un jardin*, published by La Délirante. In 1989, in my poetry book *Dunino*, I published a few extracts from this correspondence in English translation. In republishing them here, I must note that (1) I am taking these translations out of their context as an integral part of my poem "The Dunino Elegies," and returning them, as it were, to their original context as letters from a distinguished German poet to a young Swiss correspondent; and (2) that the French original letters were written as prose, which I have here rendered as a loose free verse. So here is Mademoiselle de Bonstetten, fifty years before I knew her on the rue Rousselet, as the recipient of Rainer Maria Rilke's letters on gardening:

Sometimes my garden seems to me
a hospital of flowers, so, if you come,
you will scarcely diverge from your vocation
of being with the sick....

[She was at the time working as a nurse.]

Oh come, chère Mademoiselle,
and give my flowers some ideas.
It has always seemed to me
that they think only of emptiness
for want of an education.

[And from another letter:]

Regard these shivering anemones,
come up too soon, along with a few
pious primroses, small in size
and slovenly clad: they constitute
the meagre morning Mass of spring
here in the Valais. We lack those rains
so gentle, out of other climes, which bring
an almost-forgotten caress as they fall
in long lines like a fluent writing,
love letters between earth and sky.
Here, when the clouds grow dark, it is hail
and snow which come from the mountains, breaking

the promises of spring. Even the rain
is clumsy here, the sky only sketches
a few broken lines on the air, taking no pleasure,
like a schoolboy with broken fingers.
.....

And when, a few days later, the sun
comes back, he's a brutal dictator:
he pulls the flowers up out of the earth
and shows them no mercy; hits them with heat
they're too young to withstand. The chestnut trees
are forced to open their leaves right now!
without a moment's tenderness. One day
he orders wisteria into bloom, the next the lilac;
and lilac, wisteria rush to obey,
flinging on their finery. It's only the vine
to which, they say, the Valaisian sun
addresses himself politely: all the rest
he treats like amateurs, like dilettantes,
he roughs them up. Even the streams
run only to the vine: you can't convince them
of any other thirst on the arid plain.

[And finally, in October 1926, two months before his death:]

We only travel from
one Angel to another: but
considering the scale and distances
that angels are accustomed to, for us
it sometimes seems a little far to go.

And then, thirty years after Rilke, she met Borduas.

Paul-Emile Borduas, principal signatory of the 1948 *Refus Global* manifesto, and, along with Jean-Paul Riopelle, the greatest Québécois painter of the twentieth century, came to Paris in August 1955, and lived there until his death in February 1960. He lived in a small apartment on the ground floor, at the street side, of 19 rue Rousselet.

It is not an attractive location: at street level, opposite the garden wall, facing west, it cannot have had good light for a painter. When Maureen and I lived there in the 70s, it served as offices for an accountant; during the 90s, it was occupied by a publishing firm bringing out very specialized local guidebooks. The last time I was in Paris, it was completely anonymous: no indication at all of who was living or working there. But this is the apartment in which Borduas lived for almost five years, where he painted those majestic late canvases in which the white surface rips apart to reveal the black void beyond, and it was here that he died. In the National Film Board's documentary film on Borduas, the first shot shows the doorway of 19 rue Rousselet draped in formal black mourning. In François-Marc Gagnon's definitive book on Borduas,[5] there is a photograph of his studio—taken by none other than Janine Niépce, from the fourth floor.

Quite recently, a plaque has been mounted on the wall above the studio. At the top is a small Québec flag, then the text:

> *Ici demeura*
> PAUL-EMILE BORDUAS
> *Peintre québécois*
> *de 1955 jusqu'à sa mort*
> *le 22 février 1960*

By all accounts, Borduas felt lonely and isolated in Paris. Gagnon (who gives the address, incorrectly, as 18 rue Rousselet) writes that "contrary to his expectations, he was more lonely in Paris than he had ever been before" (1976, 25). In Gagnon's later and more detailed volume (1988), he expands on the point:

> *The Paris stay, of which Borduas had had such great expectations, proved to be extremely difficult for him. He found few opportunities to show his work and received little of the hoped-for recognition....We should not forget, [however], the friends he made in Paris, particularly Marcelle Ferron and Michel Camus—Canadian expatriates like himself—who remained loyal to him throughout this period and were a great comfort to him in his loneliness. (1988, 395)*

Gagnon does not, however, mention Borduas' neighbour from two floors up, Madame Antoinette Vincens. She talked often to Maureen and me about Borduas (perhaps because we were also Canadians). She told us that she would see the light on in his studio late at night, and that she would come down and talk with him, for long hours through until morning. Twenty-five years after his death, Borduas remained for her a strong and living presence.

But Maureen and I were not the first Canadians to whom Madame Vincens had confided her love for Borduas. In 1963, the apartment that Terry and Katie lived in in 1976, and in which Maureen and I lived in 1985, had been occupied by another young Canadian exploring Paris: Adrienne Clarkson, author, broadcaster, and eventually Governor General of Canada. Adrienne and I first met in Paris in the 1980s, when she was the official representative of the Government of Ontario, and I was participating in a bilingual conference on poetic translation, partially funded by her office. When we met, she told me that she had read my book *McAlmon's Chinese Opera*, and that she had been particularly struck by the quasi-sonnet of street names (which I quote on page 74), because it included the name rue Rousselet. There followed an almost Euripidean recognition scene:

—*That's because I lived there.*
—*I lived there too.*
—*1975.*
—*1963.*
—*Number nineteen.*
—*Number nineteen!*
—*Ground floor.*
—*Second floor.*
—*Madame Warnier.*
—*Madame Vincens.*

In 1994, Adrienne Clarkson recorded her memories of that period in a CBC television program—part documentary, part dramatization—called *Borduas and Me: a personal fable*. There are a couple of brief shots of the exterior of rue Rousselet, filmed on the actual street.

But the interior shots, as I understand it, were filmed on a stage set in Canada, and they reproduce the interior of Madame Vincens' apartment so accurately that I feel very strange looking at them. (There are fewer shots of Adrienne's/our apartment, but the script does make a point of referring to, though not showing, the bathtub in the kitchen!) The casting also intrigues me. As Adrienne, Sandra Oh seems more naive than I can ever imagine Adrienne being. As Madame Vincens, the distinguished Canadian actress Frances Hyland seems to me almost perfect (allowing for the fact that Madame Vincens has to be twenty years younger than when I knew her) but a bit too sweet— without the touch of ironic *edge* that I remember in the original.

In the film, the young Adrienne rents the apartment from Madame Vincens, who insists (as she always did) that one of the conditions is regular conversations. During these talks, Adrienne discovers to her delighted surprise her landlady's connection to the famous painter. Madame Vincens recalls that "He never seemed to need light," which goes some way towards explaining the ground floor studio. In the film, Madame Vincens still owns one painting by Borduas, which she allows Adrienne to hang in her apartment; and when Adrienne eventually returns to Canada, Madame Vincens gives her the painting as a parting gift. The film then rather uneasily recalls that, a few years later, when Clarkson was in severe financial difficulties, she sold the painting. When she returns to Paris, she guiltily confesses this sale. In a gesture of forgiveness, Madame Vincens refers her to another couple (meticulously anonymous) who have a large and stunning private collection of Borduas, which they protest they will *never* sell. Ending on this note, the film presents this final meeting as a gesture of expiation. But what it conveys most strongly is the deep personal connection between Borduas and Madame Vincens—and the way in which subsequent Canadian renters of that apartment, from Adrienne to Maureen and me, have inherited at least a memory of that connection.

Clarkson returned to Madame Vincens in her autobiography, *Heart Matters* (2006), which devotes some ten pages to a heartfelt portrait and tribute of the woman "after whom I would try to model myself, and who deeply affected my life" (101). In these pages, Clarkson gives a detailed account of Madame Vincens' vivid and tragic life, and of her associations with both Rilke and Borduas. Like me, she continued to visit Madame Vincens whenever she went to Paris, years after our tenancy. "When I think of conversation," she writes, "held by civilized people about topics of eternal importance, I think of those evenings in the room filled with bergenia plants, with a tiny coal fire going and our accented voices taking turns in telling each other stories" (109).

So, when I think of 19 rue Rousselet, all these levels are present for me. Closest of course are my memories of Maureen, and of the year and a half we shared there. But I also remember Borduas, and Rilke, and Cocteau; Jongkind and Beethoven; 1976 and 1985; Terry and Katie and all the friends we knew there; Madame Warnier and Madame Vincens. I know that the glory of Paris is that almost any street, any building, could produce a similarly rich story. But this is my street, my building, my address.

At the same time, no Parisian street is ever *only* your own. Rue Rousselet belongs to many other people—among them, the poet Jacques Réda. I have already quoted, in Chapter 5, from Réda's great book *The Ruins of Paris*. In 2002, browsing through a Paris bookstore, I picked up a 1999 Gallimard volume that republished several of Réda's early books under the collected title *Amen, Récitatif, La tourne*. Glancing through the table of contents, I was stopped dead in my tracks by two poem titles referring to rue Rousselet, both of them originally from *Amen*, published by Gallimard in 1968 (five years after Adrienne, seven years before I ever set foot on rue Rousselet). So, to conclude and supplement my own impressions, here are two poems, written by Jacques Réda in 1968, translated by me in 2002:

Rue Rousselet

De la rue avec son vieux mur on dit qu'elle s'enfuit.
C'est vrai sur quelques pas après l'angle, puis tout s'apaise,
Et le vieux mur devient son propre reflet dans une eau
Très ancienne; et si l'on marchait, changerait-on de vie
Ou d'âme avant d'atteindre l'angle opposé qui navigue
En un temps différent, dans la lente clarté fragile
Des feuilles d'un jardin clos sur les souvenirs?
La clé,

Nous l'avons vue un jour briller entre des livres, doigts,
Nuages oubliés; tous les rayons du soir la cherchent
Parmi la symétrie énigmatique des balcons
Où le ciel vacillant se penche pour attendre une ombre;
—Oblique à travers la douceur fugace de la rue,
Elle s'enfuit déjà par tout l'oblique de nos coeurs. (49)

About this street with its old wall you might say
That it's running away from itself: and that would be true
For a few steps after the corner, then everything settles down,
And the old wall becomes its own reflection
In a very ancient pool; and if you walked here, would it
Change your life, your soul, before you reached
The opposite corner, which sails off in a different time,
In the slow fragile clarity of a secret garden
Closed within its memories?
The key,
We've seen it shine one day between books, fingers,
Forgotten clouds; the evening light looks for it
In the enigmatic balance of balconies
Where the dithering sky bends down
To wait for a shadow. At a slant from the transient
Sweetness of the street, already
It escapes down every detour of our hearts.

L'Automne Rue Rousselet

Déjà le plus sûr est tenu par la simple promesse
Du coin de la rue en automne, et la nuit vient.
La dernière boutique éteint ses lampes; je me tiens
Sous le mur assombri, dans la chaleur d'une détresse.
Des femmes sans passé hésitent, disparaissent
Avec ce geste indéfini dans leurs cheveux.
Je ne sais plus ce que j'attends ici; ce que je veux
M'est remis: ce n'est rien qu'un murmure qui se disperse,
Une lueur qui s'affaiblit au fond des yeux. (57)

Everything I'm sure of is already guaranteed
By the simple promise
Of the corner of the autumn street, at nightfall.
The last shop turns out its lights; I cling
To the side of the darkened wall, in the heat
Of my own distress. Women without a history
Hesitate and disappear
With that vague gesture of their hair.
I don't know any more
What it is that I'm waiting for here; what I want
Has already been returned to me: it's nothing
But a scattering whisper, a fading glimmer
At the back of my eyes.

←-- 14 THE FROG'S KISS --→

Lola Lemire Tostevin and the Mirage of Paris

LOLA LEMIRE TOSTEVIN'S first two novels—*Frog Moon* (1994) and *The Jasmine Man* (2001)—both include dramatically decisive scenes set in Paris. Neither novel takes place exclusively in Paris: apart from one chapter, all of *Frog Moon* is set in Canada, and the greater part of *The Jasmine Man* unfolds in Tunisia. But in both cases, it is the Paris scene that proves decisive: in *Frog Moon* as the climax of the action, and in *The Jasmine Man* as its initiation. Both scenes feature confrontations between the protagonist and a vividly portrayed Other—the otherness being based on gender, race, nationality, and social and political positioning. In both cases the protagonist, defensive at first, is forced into a re-evaluation of her basic assumptions. And in both cases the scene has an undertone of unreality, which cautions the reader against jumping to any simple conclusions. In neither case can we assume an unproblematic identification between the views of the character and the views of the author. Paris is a city of both reality and illusions; it is the home both of romance and of irony.

In this chapter, I will concentrate on *Frog Moon*, giving a detailed analysis of its Parisian chapter, and then will offer some much briefer remarks on *The Jasmine Man*, not so much an analysis but rather an introduction to the questions the novel poses. In both cases, however, I will return to one of this book's continuing preoccupations: the measure of Paris, its streets, and the significance of their names.

--> *FROG MOON* presents the coming of age of a young woman of Franco-Ontarian heritage, whose name is Laure in French and Laura in English.[1] The novel alternates between descriptions of her child-hood and convent schooling (primarily a French-speaking context), and her present situation in Toronto (married to an anglophone husband and with primarily English-speaking children). With great sensitivity, the novel explores the conflicts and contradictions within Laure's situation, as she endeavours to define herself as a woman, as a mother, as a "Canadian," and as a writer. The emphasis on the conflict between her rural Franco-Ontarian background and her urban, anglophone marriage means that neither one nor the other can provide the setting for a resolution of the novel's dichotomies. Rather, the resolution must take place in a setting that transcends and synthesizes both communities: French-speaking, and yet urban-cosmopolitan; neither Toronto nor Montreal: Paris.

So the climax of the novel occurs in the only chapter that is set outside of Canada: "Le Baiser de Juan-Les-Pins," which takes place during Laure's extended visit to Paris. Furthermore, this chapter is set off from the rest of the novel not only by its location but by its more clearly marked demarcation between author and protagonist. This chapter is, in many ways, the most "fictional" section of *Frog Moon*: here, more than anywhere else in the book, there is a consciously ironic distance between author, narrator, and protagonist. In earlier chapters, Laure's perceptions and opinions seem to be more or less directly endorsed by the narrative; in this chapter, the limitations and defects of Laure's perceptions are (it seems to me) clearly implied and critiqued by the tone of the narration. Yet, paradoxically, this is also the chapter in which Laure comes into her own as a writer.

It is also the only chapter in the book whose title is unambig-uously in French. (All the other chapter titles are English, except "Babel Noël," which is arguably in French because of the accent mark, though both words are also used in English.) And thus it immediately sets up a problem of translation, since *baiser* contains an ambiguity that is difficult to reflect in a single English word. Its meaning shifts with context: in a polite context, "baiser" simply means "kiss," and can be used quite innocently and properly; but in an impolite context, the same word can mean "fuck," and would register as a very improper usage. The problem here is its occurrence in a *title*, for which there is as yet no context. The reader cannot yet know whether the reference is to a simple kiss, or to an act of (possibly violent) sexual intercourse. This ambiguity is preserved both in the action of the chapter as it develops (is the taxi driver's "long and astonishingly tender kiss" to be read simply as a kiss, or as a form of rape?), and in the Picasso painting to which the title ostensibly refers. Picasso's visual puns, in which the same graphic shape can be read as either a mouth or a vagina, a nose or a penis, maintain exactly the same ambiguity as exists within the word "baiser" itself.[2]

Questions of translation and bilingualism are at the heart of the novel. On the verge of going to Paris, and acutely self-conscious of the implied cultural stereotypes, Laure (Tostevin?) writes:

> Going to Paris to write seems such a worn-out cliché, belonging to another age, but it also makes the possibility more feasible somehow. Time to throw caution to the wind, Christine says, time to lay down my guard. Visit museums, art shows, immerse myself in everything French, maybe try my hand at writing in my mother tongue, unconstrained by rules, family, expectations. Not that Paris offers superior models, it's just different.... (193)

That is, the question for Laure is not only one of becoming a writer: it is a question of which language she may become a writer in. Rather than follow the clichés of those who "[went] to Paris to write...[in] another age"—that is, the expatriate Americans of the 1920s, who largely maintained a decisive distance from French culture—she will "immerse [herself] in everything French," becoming a dedicated cultural tourist of "museums, art shows," in order to be able to write in her "mother tongue." Yet the very fact that this book is being presented to us *in English* suggests that this choice was not the final outcome. The questions remain.

This climactic chapter of *Frog Moon* will offer an answer, which may also be seen in a curious detail of the text's publication history. The first words of the chapter are "*Il pleut....*" In the published novel they are given in French; in an earlier publication, as an excerpt in the anthology *Likely Stories* (1992), they appear in English: "It is raining." At the end of the chapter, when the novel's narrative self-reflexively loops back on itself and arrives at the point of its own genesis, they are again given in English: "I began to write. *Le baiser de Juan-les-Pins. It was raining....*" The ambiguous "baiser" remains in French; but the "Il pleut" of the first line gives way to the "It was raining" of the last. Thus the novel, with its explicit transition from French to English, marks the moment when Laure finally realizes herself, not just as a writer, but as *a writer in English*. Yet what has produced this self-realization is a series of events that have taken place in French, in Paris.

Tostevin's image of Paris is presented, right from the start, as one that is mediated through cultural references. Laure comes to the city with a fully developed set of preconceptions, which in many ways inhibit her from seeing what is really there.[3] I would argue that Tostevin is aware of these limitations on Laure's part, and that the presentation of them is the ironic point of this chapter. "The various greys of the roofs and sky," the chapter begins, "are the usual greys one reads about in books on Paris, the cobblestones a perfect setting for a Renoir film...." That is, Laure does not come to Paris with an innocent eye. She has read "books on Paris" and indeed assumes that this pre-conditioning through reading is something "one" quite naturally does. She has also seen the films, and is enough of a cinéaste to distinguish the *auteur* characteristics of a film by Jean Renoir, "where almost every shot begins with someone exiting or entering the frame, leaving several frames in between empty." Most of Renoir's great films about Paris were made in the 1930s; the question of how reliable a guide they might be to the reality of the city fifty years later is not raised—at least, not explicitly. So Tostevin acknowledges that the experience of Paris is always a mediated one and that layers of cultural reference inhere in even the simplest perception of roof, sky, or cobblestone.

This intense acculturation of the image of Paris presents obvious difficulties to Laure's stated intentions as a writer. "I've returned to Paris wanting to write," she says, "but too much time is spent gazing out windows or reading about France in France, and not enough time writing what should be written." It's a familiar dilemma, from John Glassco's inability to proceed beyond Chapter 3 of his memoirs, to Geoff Dyer's protagonist in *Paris Trance*, Luke, who abandons his project of writing about life in Paris almost as soon as he begins to live the life of Paris. In Tostevin's presentation, the mediated image of Paris (itself further doubled by the act of "reading about France in France") is still too strong (initially) to allow Laure to find her own voice as a writer. For her, there are still too many echoes; "Paris" is a quotation. Her solution will not be to ignore or set aside the acculturation of the Paris experience; rather, it will be to work *through* it and to realize its potential to nurture rather than inhibit individual creativity.

The mediated nature of the experience of Paris is also apparent in another trope that I have already extensively discussed: the fascination with the naming of Parisian streets. Laure records that her friend Christine's studio

> is on the rue Villiers de l'Isle-Adam, a name I came across last night in [Julian Barnes's novel] Flaubert's Parrot. Only the French would designate a short street after an obscure writer. My own studio is on rue Edouard Vaillant near Levallois. Who were these men?

The first hints of Tostevin's ironic distancing of her own intelligence from Laure's apparently willing ignorance come in Laure's rhetorical dismissal of this question and in her decidedly condescending description of Villiers de l'Isle-Adam not only as an "obscure" writer, but also as one of whom Laure is aware only through the double mediation of his appearance in a trendy English novel. "Who were these men?" Laure asks the question and loftily leaves it unanswered. But Tostevin surely implies that the (unspoken) answer would be relevant.

So: according to the Harvard *New History of French Literature*:

Auguste de Villiers de l'Isle-Adams (1838–1889) was one of the prin-
cipal contributors to the French symbolist movement during the
second half of the 19th century. An admirer of Charles Baudelaire and
a close friend of Stéphane Mallarmé, Villiers' work includes poems,
plays, short stories, and two novels. Most of these works link the
themes of voice reproduction and transmission with haunting, motifs
of possession, the return of the dead, and disembodied spirits. (802)[4]

As for Edouard Vaillant (1840–1915), he was a leading socialist poli-
tician. Early in his career, he participated in the 1870 Commune, after
which he spent some years in exile. Later, he was an active parliamen-
tarian, a close friend of the socialist leader Jean Jaurès, and (according
to the *Encyclopaedia Britannica*) "an ardent advocate of an eight-hour
day and of comprehensive social security." He was also, not coinciden-
tally, Municipal Counsellor for the Père Lachaise district of Paris.

So these two names/street names resonate with many of the
themes of *Frog Moon*: a concern with "voice reproduction," especially
with the voices of the past; the relation between voice and embodi-
ment and/or ghostliness; the political and class divisions within Paris,
which Laure will unsuccessfully attempt to ignore; even the partic-
ular location of the Père Lachaise cemetery. All of these themes are
implicit in the names of the streets that Laure so casually dismisses,
but that Tostevin so carefully records.

Indeed, Vaillant's connection to Père Lachaise is taken up in the
immediately succeeding paragraphs, which describe both images
of the cemetery in the artworks of Laure's friend, Christine, and an
actual visit to the site. Christine's works are diptychs, and duality
is their main characteristic—so much so, that they are almost too
obviously symbolic of all the dualities (past/present; male/female;
English/French) that pervade Tostevin's book. These diptychs are
"the size of French windows," a phrase that again invokes problems
of translation (only in English are French windows called French),
and also recalls the "windows" through which Laure spends too
much time gazing while "reading about France in France." On one

side of Christine's diptychs are black-and-white photographs: "Some are details of a classic Roman Venus taken from different angles, others are shots of streets lined with tombs"—an archetypal duality between love and death. On the other side are sheets of either stainless steel or lead, which again produce a duality, either reflecting or absorbing light. A further duality is formed between the representative (the photographs) and the non-representative, minimalist abstraction (the metal sheets). But while the abstract sides may seem to "say" or "mean" nothing but their own material existence, the fact that they are placed in conjunction with the photographs encourages the viewer to read a quasi-linguistic "meaning" in their context. Most obviously, the lead becomes associated with the tombs. Christine, indeed, is eager to provide her images with the linguistic supplement of commentary:[5] "*she explains* how her diptychs play out the relation between image and object, between past and present. Her photographs of the tombs...are records of the mortal remains, *she says*. The dead evoked by monuments marked by their name" (emphasis added). That is, in her own evocation of the names of the dead, Christine is precisely echoing the themes of Villiers de l'Isle-Adam, on whose street (a monument marked by his name) she lives.

Christine's explanation takes place while she and Laure are strolling through the "hush of the cemetery" of Père Lachaise, in the municipal district of Edouard Vaillant, on whose street (a monument marked by his name) Laure lives. Mediations multiply: there are the actual tombs between which the two women walk; there are Christine's photographs of the tombs, set within the various contexts of her diptychs; there are Christine's explanations of her own photographs; and there is Laure's written re-presentation of the tombs, of the photographs, and of the explanations.

Laure and Christine are here indulging in the quintessential Parisian entertainment of graveyard tourism[6]: an almost fetishistic attraction to the remains of the famous dead, "evoked by monuments marked by their name." Laure's account of her visit to Père Lachaise reflects, once more, a mediated experience of Paris that is stereotypically cultural. The graves she mentions (Colette, Bernhardt, Proust, Apollinaire) commemorate three writers and one actress, while the two she looks for but does not find (Beauvoir and Sartre) are probably evoked as much for their fiction as for their philosophy. Curiously, Laure makes no mention of Stein and Toklas, nor of any of the musicians or painters buried in Père Lachaise (Piaf, Pissarro, etc). But equally, no mention is made of politicians like Faure or Talleyrand; scientists like Arago; engineers like de Lesseps; makers (and/or unmakers) of the city like Haussmann; nor apparently do Laure and Christine visit the memorials to the massacre victims of the Paris Commune or of the Nazi concentration camps. The fairly narrow range of graves that interest them is, I would argue, a further indication of a certain limitation on Laure's sensibility, one which the chapter will increasingly expose and put under pressure.

Leaving Christine, Laure indefatigably sets out for a packed afternoon of cultural tourism in Paris, hitting the high points of the Marais district. In one afternoon, she manages to take in the place des Vosges, the Carnavalet, and the Musée Picasso. And here Tostevin exposes a note of elitism in Laure's responses, a tendency to set herself up as an observer whose cultural tastes and judgements are implicitly superior to those of the mass of tourists. Thus, passing through the place des Vosges and noting Victor Hugo's residence, Laure is "reminded of the extravagant musical about to open in Toronto. Les Miz. The irony of having his words adapted to accordions and kettledrums in spite of his steadfast hatred of music." Whatever one thinks of Les Mis (and I personally am rather impressed with it as an adaptation of Hugo's novel), Laure's tone here is decidedly condescending.

The same note of culturally superior snobbishness persists in Laure's account of her visit to the Picasso Museum in the refurbished Hôtel Salé. Here she notes that "most viewers spend more time inspecting the photographs and biographical details than they do looking at the paintings." In other words, "most viewers" can appreciate Picasso's art only in the reductive terms of biographical reference, not in the "high art" aesthetic terms through which (implicitly) the culturally superior Laure approaches it. But Laure's attempt to distinguish herself from the mass reaction of cultural tourists is complicated by two factors.

In the first place, the "biographical details" that fascinate the common mass of tourists include a photograph of "Picasso at seven with his sister Lola." Here the author—Lola Lemire Tostevin—seems for a moment to peek out from behind the screen of her character Laure, and to acknowledge, in the coincidence of name, her own fascination with Picasso's sister, one of his early inspirations. But this indulgence in vicarious fame is immediately countered by a second factor, Laure's intellectual effort to establish a decided distance from vulgar Picasso-worship by her trenchant feminist criticism of his later work:

> ...the erotic drawings of Picasso's old age. Are these the evidence of an old man's obsession, or the aesthetic affirmation of a vibrant life? I search early paintings of women for an answer, especially those that follow the first bloom of infatuation, but in their fashionable abstract configurations the women no longer speak for themselves. As if each one had been discharged from who she was and condemned to the puerility of the artist's dreams.

This is a vigorous and not at all unreasonable critique of Picasso's distressing tendency to equate his paintbrush with his penis. It seems to represent Laure as a sincere and independent thinker. But a few pages later, Laure will entirely renege on all the assumptions and criteria of this judgement—which action, retrospectively, brings into question the authenticity of her original reaction, and leads one to wonder whether it is not merely a superficial critique, a knee-jerk feminist response, just as "fashionable" as the depictions she condemns.

Laure's busy cultural day continues with an evening visit to the theatre, to see a stage adaptation of Kafka's "Metamorphosis," directed by Roman Polanski. Laure again adopts the role of the sensitive aesthetic critic, giving us a mini-review of the production, particularly praising Polanski's stage device of suggesting the metamorphosis through projected shadows rather than makeup or costumes. "There are at least a dozen curtain calls," she concludes, "and Polanski receives a standing ovation. This is what I came to Paris for." This last comment (surely a little too smug and self-satisfied) again suggests that Laure sees "Paris" through a screen of cultural preconceptions. Or, in the terms that she herself has ironically praised, she sees it as shadows and mediated reflections rather than as physical reality. Again, Polanski provides not real bodies, but "fashionable abstract configurations."

The notion of metamorphosis, meanwhile, resonates back through the whole book. Laure's first encounter with Kafka's story had been when she was given a copy of it, along with Ovid's *Metamorphoses*, by her influential teacher, Madame Wickersham.[7] At that time, Tostevin comments that Ovid's "central theme is the incessant reshaping of different forms of life," and concludes that "I was not to understand until much later the significance of those two books, to my life and to my writing" (180). This "reshaping" of life applies not only to the problematics of translation, the metamorphosis of one language into another, but also to all the complex negotiations of cultural adaptation and assimilation required of a francophone child marrying into an anglophone community. Laure's childhood nickname is Kaki, the Cree word for frog: "By the time you were three months old," her mother tells her, "you answered to the name of a frog" (39). Here, the linguistic transformation is mediated through a third language, Cree, but the Cree form does not entirely obscure the pejorative English use of "frog" as an insulting slang name for "French." Furthermore, frogs are strongly associated with metamorphosis: not only in the strict biological sense of their development from tadpoles, but also in the context of all the fairy tales in which a frog, once kissed, transforms into a handsome prince. What lurks inside these juxtapositions is the racist possibility of suggesting that, in the process of cultural assimilation, the French Canadian frog can be metamorphosed into the English Canadian prince.

There is no kiss for Kafka's Gregor Samsa. But if one returns here to the ambiguity of the French "baiser," there are further suggestions, not only of sexuality but of a possibly violent sexuality. Polanski's early career as a film director (*Knife in the Water, Repulsion*) had associated him with such themes well before their tragic literalization in the murder of his wife, Sharon Tate, by Charles Manson. And although Laure makes no mention of it, the reader may also remember that the reason that Polanski is directing plays in a Parisian theatre (indeed, the reason why Polanski lives in Paris) is that he was a legal fugitive from the United States, having avoided charges of having sex with a minor. So a certain aura of sexual violence is associated with his name. Laure's comments avoid it, staying on the neutral level of the theatre reviewer, but Tostevin's narrative will soon strongly reinvoke it—in, precisely, the context of kissing a frog.

Laure and Christine end their long day with "a late dinner at a Moroccan restaurant in the Marais." The atmosphere is momentarily disrupted by the arrogant comment of a young Frenchman who declares that "he intensely dislikes Canadians, 'Ils sont commes les boches.'" The racist comment is initially laughed off, but it sets up uneasy overtones that will be picked up in the taxi driver's comments on Laure's accent. Laure presents this young Frenchman as "dressed as what is best described as a walking piece of art"—by which she presumably means that he is very (or overly) elegantly dressed. This "walking piece of art" is too beautiful: but Laure is about to confront someone who challenges her to respond to him as a "walking piece of art" that is too ugly.

The slightly uneasy tone is compounded by one of Laure's more supercilious remarks. When asked which book she would take with her to a desert island, "one book to teach you about the world and yourself," she replies "'My own'...not admitting to the fact that I haven't written one yet." It's a smart-ass reply, confirming her sense of her own superiority, already manifested in her disparaging comments about the tourists in the Picasso Museum. There is, it would seem, nothing outside her own self-consciousness that could "teach [her] about the world and [herself]." It is at moments like these that I most strongly sense Tostevin setting up an ironic distance between herself and her protagonist, subtly diminishing the reader's sympathy for her, and setting the scene for the reckoning that must come.

It arrives in the form (the deformed form) of the taxi driver. He is described as "very short....Not exactly a midget, but his proportions are all wrong." His head is "too large for his body," and has a long mane of white hair. His "bushy eyebrows...slant and meet on the bridge of his mis-shapen nose." This last detail explicitly recalls another form of metamorphosis, the folk tales of the *loup-garou* that

Laure was told in her convent school: "She's heard of children who exposed themselves and grew long silken hair on their bodies, and slanting eyebrows that met on the bridge of the nose" (31). Perhaps because of this childhood association, Laure reacts to the taxi driver with instinctive physical disgust. She refers to him consistently, in her narration, as "the monkey," though at one point she also says that he "looks like a rat." Or, like a frog. These metaphors serve to dehumanize him, to exempt her from having to think of him as a human being. She recalls how, living in Paris, she had to "learn how to glaze my focus and walk past beggars or ogling men. As if they didn't exist."[8] By thinking of him as a rat or a monkey, she tries to reduce the taxi driver to the same non-existence. "I dismiss him with a sneer," she attempts to conclude.

But Laure's physical disgust is compounded by the same traits of snobbishness, of class and cultural superiority, which I have noted in her throughout the chapter. "This odious little man bores me," she thinks. "Why should I explain myself to a taxi driver?" And when he starts to challenge her on the topic of Picasso, she says to herself, "Why am I speaking to this monkey about art?" It might be possible to explain or defend Laure's reactions here on the grounds of her understandable unease at the vulnerable position she finds herself in—alone in a taxi late at night on deserted streets with a man who seems to be menacing her—were it not for the fact that her attitudes here match so closely with the assumptions of class and cultural superiority she has shown throughout the day, in perfectly "safe" and unthreatening situations. It is as if her willed ignorance of the socialist Edouard Vaillant is being thrust into her face, as the return of the repressed, in the shape of an immigrant worker, the bottom of the French social scale.

Laure's view of the taxi driver is further distorted by the fact that she sees his face mainly in the mirror, as a reversed reflection. At one point she even refers to him, in a further dehumanization, as "the mirror." Of course, he sees her the same way. The climax of their encounter comes when he climbs into the back seat, breaking down the conventional barrier between taxi driver and passenger, and "orders [her] to face him"—directly, without the mirror's reversal.

Their first skirmish concerns accent. She guesses that he is Spanish; he replies that he is Portuguese, but has lived in France for many years. In turn, he recognizes that she is not French, but when she tells him that she is Canadian, he replies, "Ah! I wouldn't have guessed it. Swedish, Swiss perhaps, but not Canadian. You don't speak French with a Canadian accent." This exchange strikes directly to the heart of all Laure's uncertainties and vulnerabilities about her own national and linguistic identity. The taxi driver refuses to recognize her as either Canadian or French-Canadian; her accent is neither the *joual* of Québec nor the proper Parisian French that the nuns had attempted to teach her. By identifying her as Swiss, or even more bizarrely as Swedish, he is denying her any national or linguistic base for her identity. He is placing her, as it were, on the periphery—just as the taxi itself is heading for the boulevard Périphérique.

Laure attempts to counter this challenge by saying, "I speak French in many languages." At one level, this is another smart-ass reply; it's a self-consciously paradoxical epigram that deliberately blurs the distinctions between accents, dialects, and languages. But on a deeper level, it relates to the continuing ambivalences of Tostevin's own linguistic position. In "Criticism as Self-Reflection," the introduction to her volume of essays *Subject to Criticism*, Tostevin writes of "a dilemma that had paralysed me for years":

> *I felt disabled by my own mother tongue. The French I spoke at home was not the French I spoke at the convent where I went to school, or the French in which I wrote my school lessons, all of which were different still from the French spoken to me when I lived in France. The French I spoke at home was not even a written language.* The various French dialects I've spoken over the years have been so varied they have often felt like different languages. *To some, the French I write is pretentious and not "French Canadian"; to others, the French I speak is flawed and not "good enough." Under such circumstances it was easier for me to write in English, although it was never entirely a matter of choice: English eventually chose me.* (17; emphasis added)

Here, Tostevin's directly autobiographical account makes the same elision of "dialects" and "languages" that she attributes to Laure in the novel. For Tostevin, this "paralysis" contributes, at least in part, to her eventual decision to write in English. Similarly, Laure's comment here prefigures her decision, at the end of the chapter, to become a writer *in English*. Her claim to speak French not just in many *accents*, but in many *languages*, could be extended to mean that writing in English may still be, for her, a way of speaking in French.

The question of peripheral accents recurs when Laure remarks that she has a friend who is an artist and a Catalan. To herself, she thinks that "In France, Spain isn't so different from Portugal, and surely he [the taxi driver] wouldn't hurt someone who has a friend who's both a foreigner and a Catalan." It's an astonishingly obtuse and insensitive thought, full of lazy national stereotyping—rather like saying that, to an outsider, there's no real difference between Canadians and Americans. It ignores not only the very real differences between Spain and Portugal but also the differences within Spain, between Castillian and Catalan. For someone who is so sensitive to linguistic distinctions between French and English, and between Québec and Ontario French, Laure is being singularly stupid at this point and thoroughly deserves his sarcastic rebuke: "Ah yes, the French love artists, especially if they're Catalan. Unfortunately, they don't feel the same about foreign taxi drivers." Even here, though, Laure's narration defensively attributes this reply not to a person but to a thing: "the mirror says."

The taxi driver's reply here points to a variety of social divisions— between native Frenchmen and immigrant workers, or between culturally validated professions such as "artists" and mere "taxi drivers"—which would have been of great concern to a politician like Edouard Vaillant (to whose street the taxi is heading) but which have been largely ignored by Laure (who lives on that street). But the other reference here is to the Catalan artist most beloved by the French: Picasso. Of course, since Laure has previously deprecated the biographical approach to Picasso, the idea of approaching his work in the political context of Catalan nationalism is alien to her.

But now the taxi driver turns the conversation precisely to Picasso, and to questions of beauty and abstraction in his work. He challenges her to "define for me the value of an abstract body," and Laure replies:

I suppose it resides in its form and is independent of the subject of the painting. It has nothing to do with meaning or with the body painted, but with lines, colours, and surfaces. The subject can't be compared to other subjects but exists through its form.

The taxi driver ironically applauds this statement—"Bravo, madame. You are the first passenger to give me such an eloquent answer"—but his voice is nevertheless "filled with scorn." As well it should be. For what Laure has given here is merest cliché: a standard, conventional explanation of "abstract" art—Art History 101. Moreover, it's the kind of pure formalism, divorced from context, which (as Leo Steinberg famously complained) enabled art historians to talk about Picasso's *Les Demoiselles d'Avignon* for fifty years without ever mentioning that it was a painting of five naked women in a brothel. But even more to the point, what Laure says here is a total denial and abandonment of her own earlier position. Just that afternoon, in the Picasso Museum, she had scorned those other tourists who appreciated "fashionable abstract configurations," and had taken pride in her own more critical, feminist insight. For Laure that afternoon, Picasso's art (and the failures of Picasso's art) had *everything* "to do with meaning or with the body painted." She refused to accept that the subject exists only through form, but insisted on looking for, and lamenting the absence of, "the women [who] no longer speak for themselves."

So Laure's reply is really a gesture of bad faith: "Why am I speaking to this monkey about art?" She is still condescending to him, speaking as if someone who is a foreigner, who is physically deformed, and who is a mere taxi driver, could not possibly be expected to have any finer appreciation of art. She withholds from him her real opinion and instead feeds him a conventional set of superficial platitudes about abstract art. That is, she still refuses to take him seriously as an interlocutor, or indeed as a human being.

But further, her taking refuge in this formalist explanation is an attempt to deflect the conversation in "safe" directions, to keep the discussion itself at an "abstract" level, and to avoid at all costs any engagement with real bodies. Earlier, she had seen the obnoxious young Frenchman in the restaurant as a "walking piece of art"; now, the taxi driver insists that she confront the implications of this metaphor more literally. His climbing into the back seat is a transgression of all sorts of boundaries: the class divisions between worker and employer; the sexual divisions between deference and assault; but also, in a way, the artistic divisions between image and reality. Up until this point, she has seen him like a painting, "framed" in the mirror. Now he is like a painting come down off the wall, seizing the detached museum viewer by the arm, demanding to know the difference between aesthetic response and real-life response, and forcibly deconstructing the paradox of an "abstract body."

> Tell me, if I were a Picasso invention would you find me interesting? Would you spend hours before me figuring out why my nose is flat, my nostrils so dilated? How would you interpret a chin that juts too much to one side and legs that are so short and bandy?

Laure has no answer to these questions. Indeed, the whole history of her long day of Parisian cultural tourism has trapped her into a position where she can have no possible answer to these questions. All that is left for her is one moment of absolute honesty. When the taxi driver asks her again whether, despite all her aesthetic appreciation of metamorphosed bodies in Picasso and Polanski, she finds his actual body disgusting, she answers, despite the extreme vulnerability of her position and the imminent threat of rape, with a simple "Yes." And the taxi driver (monkey, rat, frog) rewards her with a kiss.

It's still a highly ambivalent kiss, balancing between the two meanings of "baiser." It has all the elements of erotic foreplay—"The flat of his hand glides down my chest, stops at my breast. The cotton of my blouse and the lace of my brassiere grate gently back and forth against my nipple"—yet for all the suggestions of sexual intercourse or rape, it remains no more than a kiss—"a long and astonishingly tender kiss." What astonishes and disconcerts Laure is her own sexual response:

> As his mouth searches, reaches a nipple, I'm startled by the convulsive turbulence invading me. A warm sensation shoots to the pit of my stomach, explodes inside my groin. I'm horrified. This reaction is banned, taboo, transgresses everything I know to be right. Yet the sensation has assumed the force of an unknown, unnamed law that possesses me so completely that it divests me of who I am. Who I thought I was.

In other words, she has an orgasm and is ashamed of it. Feminism teaches that what she "should" experience is (as she says only a paragraph earlier) "repugnance and fear." Yet the physical sensations overcome the intellectual prescriptions.[9] And the effect of this surprising reaction is to disrupt all her presuppositions about "Who I thought I was."[10] In a chapter so concerned with cultural and linguistic identity, the questions have been resolved in favour of physical sensation, sexual (be)coming.

The taxi driver lets her go, the rape remaining both real and virtual. The conventional screen of politeness is restored—"Very well, madame"—and he meticulously gives her the correct change. The end of the incident is narrated with startling abruptness. In the space between the end of one paragraph and the start of the next, Laure is cinematically jump-cut from inside the taxi to inside her bathroom, all the intervening action (getting out of the taxi, opening her door, coming into her apartment) having been elided—the exact opposite of the leisurely editing technique attributed to Renoir in the first paragraph.

The effect is to reinforce the undertone of unreality beneath the whole episode. Laure "stand[s] before the mirror as if to corroborate what has happened." Did this incident really take place, or was it a dream? A nightmare, or an erotic fantasy? Could such a bizarre, deformed body really exist? Or are we in the realm of fairytale, specifically, the fairytale evoked throughout the novel, the fairytale of metamorphosis, the frog beseeching a kiss from the princess? Except that here, of course, it is not the frog that is transformed but the princess: the metamorphosis will take place within Laure herself.

Returned to her "self," Laure takes refuge (as always) in culturally mediated forms. The "corroboration" she seeks is in a mirror image, framed and controlled, like a painting on a wall. And then she consults her purchased guide to the Picasso Museum, which had been the crux of her aesthetic/corporeal argument with her "monkey," and she arrives at *Le Baiser*:

> ...an image dated 1925 lunges at me. In an explosion of garish colours, two intertwining bodies kiss, their limbs and organs so topsy-turvy it's impossible to tell which ones belong to the man and which to the woman. Each detail—a mouth which could also be an eye or female genitals, a phallic nose, a corrugated cardboard foot—is part of a puzzle whose pieces have been scattered in order to bind the two figures in a passionate but violent embrace. The commentary beside the image states, "Art is never chaste."[11]

The irony here is that Laure is accepting as an authority on art the same "Picasso" whom she has previously criticized. Picasso's possibly sexist notion that art is not bound to conventional notions of sexual morality is held up as the justification not only of Laure's inadvertent *jouissance* but also of the linguistic promiscuity of her decision to write *in English*. So:

> I pick up my pen and on the first page of the French scribbler I bought more than a month ago, I begin to write. Le baiser de Juan-Les-Pins. It was raining....

And here, finally, the ironic gap between author, narrator, and protagonist is closed. For it is both Laure (intradiegetically) and Lola Lemire Tostevin (extradiegetically) who write these words, who give a title to the chapter (not Picasso's title), and who transform the initial "*Il pleut*" into "*It was raining*." Laure has been shocked out of her expectations—even, indeed, out of her own sense of identity. Her highly conventional, acculturated image of Paris has been forcibly confronted with another image: the taxi driver, whose physical metamorphosis has broken down the divisions between artistic image and corporeal presence, between cultural tourism and political reality, or (most simply of all) between the back and front seats of a taxi. But it is precisely this flux that enables Laure/Tostevin to begin writing. If "art is never chaste," then perhaps a spot of linguistic promiscuity may also be accepted; the language for Laure's Parisian self-discovery will indeed be English. "I speak French in many languages," she told the taxi driver. Now, on the page in front of us, she begins to speak French in English.

--> THE OPENING SCENE of *The Jasmine Man*—the initial encounter between Amy and Habib in a Parisian park—reads like a replay, in a lower key, of the climactic scene of *Frog Moon*. Many elements are similar. Again, there is a protagonist, a Canadian woman temporarily resident in Paris, who is confronted by a character who is other than her in terms of gender, nationality, race, and social and political positioning. Again the encounter is marked by a physical infringement of boundaries: Habib is "sitting too close to me on a park bench" (19). Again the discussion involves questions of language, accent, and pronunciation. Like the taxi driver, Habib uses meticulously polite forms of speech, but in such a way as to suggest an edge of irony or antagonism. Again the protagonist is marked by a certain political naivety or ignorance: "I couldn't imagine the police going out of their way to arrest someone simply because he might be Algerian" (23). (Just ask Gail Scott.) Again she finds herself on the defensive and is annoyed at herself for being so: "Why was I justifying where I lived? What business was it of his?" (29). And again the result is a decisive change in the protagonist's life.

It is, however, a low-key replay. Habib sitting too close on a park bench in a populated square at midday is scarcely the same thing as the taxi driver climbing into the back seat on a deserted street at midnight. The antagonism is less overt, while the physical attraction is more open. This scene is, after all, not an end but a beginning: the beginning of a romance.

That is, *The Jasmine Man* operates within the frames and conventions of romance, but it is of course a highly ironic and distanced version of romance (just as *Frog Moon* is, ultimately, an ironic and distanced version of the autobiographical coming-of-age novel). Rather than offer an extended reading of the ways Tostevin works with and against romance conventions throughout the book, I will concentrate here on a single detail of this opening scene: the name of the park in which it takes place. Robert Schumann Square.

I have already talked at length about writers' fascination for Parisian street names, and about the many ways in which they can be used. One obvious tactic is to exploit the historical and cultural associations of the real people after whom the streets are named; and in the previous section of this chapter, I have suggested that Tostevin does just this in *Frog Moon* with her evocations of Villiers de l'Isle-Adam and Edouard Vaillant. So what associations are suggested by the name Robert Schumann?

The most obvious response is to invoke Schumann as the archetypal Romantic artist, writing all that swooning music; pursuing an obsessive love interest against the opposition of the bride's father and turning his marriage to Clara into a great nineteenth-century love story; suffering depression, attempting suicide, dying in agony. A fitting character, it might appear, to preside over a romance.

Even at this level, however, one can detect a strong possibility of irony. Isn't Schumann just a bit too much?—as an image of romance, he's way over the top. His life story exaggerates Romanticism to the point of parody. Furthermore, one can consult more realistic (or cynical) contemporary biographers, who say that all his depression and glamorous illnesses were actually symptoms of tertiary syphilis. Schumann's name undercuts romance fully as much as it promotes it.

But there is a further, even more intriguing, consideration attached to the name "Robert Schumann Square." Does such a place even exist? There is no "Robert Schumann Square" on any map of Paris that I have consulted, nor is the name listed in an exhaustive directory of Paris streets available on the Internet. (There is an avenue Robert Schumann, in the 7th arrondissement.) I have to conclude that Tostevin has done something that I described in Part Two as extremely rare: rather than using an existing Parisian street name, she has invented a fictional one.

Tostevin herself has been very careful neither to confirm nor to deny this speculation. In correspondence with me, she wrote:

"Whether Robert Schumann Square really does exist or not, maybe, just maybe, it existed at the time when Amy thought such a place did exist but perhaps it no longer does....I'm not sure that Robert Schumann Square is a non-place, but, as in a mirage, rather a refraction, a change of direction as a result of a place travelling along a different wave front through time."[12] In this comment, Tostevin links the possible non-existence of the street name with the later imagery, pervasive in the sections of the novel set in Tunisia, and especially in the desert, of mirages: the convincing perception of things that do not actually exist.

But Paris, as I said in the opening paragraph of this chapter, is a city of both reality and illusions. There does exist a map, a directory of names, according to which Robert Schumann Square—the site of ideal romance, the evocation of nineteenth-century Romanticism—*does not exist*. Thus the whole "romantic" affair of the novel takes place in a place (or a Place—Square?) which has no place. It is an imaginary site. The entire story is cancelled out from the beginning—or at least it is placed under a Derridean mark of erasure. The name that is not a name (le nom qui est un non) names and unnames the whole narrative. So everything that follows has to be read as not existing, in a non-time and a non-place, defined and excluded by the map of Paris.

←-- 15 A TRAVEL OF
INDETERMINATE STOPS -->

Gerry Shikatani's Aqueduct

THE BARON HAUSSMANN was never much noted for his sense of humour. But once, in 1857, at the height of his power, he managed a witty response to a guest at the Emperor's table who suggested that the Baron should be made a Duke. Not enough, replied Haussmann: "I should be made an aqueduke."[1]

The literal creation of aqueducts was, of course, a great part of Haussmann's achievement and legacy: his reform of the Parisian water supply was as profound, if less spectacular, as his transformation of the city streets. For Canadian poet Gerry Shikatani,[2] the creation of aqueducts is more metaphoric: "Aqueducts collect speech, there is this direction outwards" (316). *Aqueduct* is the title of his major book of poetry, published in 1996, and is also the title of Book III, "Aqueduct 1984–87," within it. "Aqueduct" in turn includes a poem (to which I shall return) entitled "The Baron Haussmann" (284–85). There is, alas, no confirmed indication that Shikatani knew the "aqueduke" story.

Aqueduct consists of three sections ("Books"), made up of poems pertaining to three separate trips to Europe: in 1979, in 1982, and over the more extended period of 1984-87. The three "Books" have subtle but decisive differences in tone and in authorial stance, and Shikatani was widely urged to publish them as, indeed, three separate books. But, courageously, he held out for the publication of the complete manuscript as a single volume, even though its size (400 pages in the eventual edition) seemed to make the cost prohibitive. The appearance of *Aqueduct* in 1996 was made possible only by an unprecedented collaboration between three small presses—The Mercury Press, Underwhich Editions, and Wolsak and Wynn Publishers—who pooled resources (grant money, promotion budgets, distribution, etc.) in order to realize the book as Gerry had envisioned it. The publishers of these presses deserve enormous credit; they should all be made aquedukes.

At this point, before I go any further with this chapter, I should enter several provisos and disclaimers. First, there are a couple of aspects of *Aqueduct* that might make it seem as if I had a conflict of interest in offering a critical appraisal of it. The 1996 edition carries on its back cover two glowing blurbs, pre-commissioned by the three co-publishers; one is by Lola Lemire Tostevin and the other is by Stephen Scobie. Further, one of the poems in the book, "The Pont Neuf" (268), bears the dedication "for Stephen and Maureen Scobie." I intend to discuss this poem in detail, including the dedication. So the reader will have to accept that my critical stance in this chapter is not entirely disinterested.

Secondly, my treatment of *Aqueduct* is going to be very selective. Not surprising, perhaps, in a short chapter on a 400-page book—but, in concentrating on the Paris poems, I will be omitting huge sections of Shikatani's writing on England, Italy, Spain, and even non-Parisian France. This narrow focus will inevitably distort the book as a whole.

Finally, I should note that a good deal of my information about *Aqueduct*, especially the circumstances of its composition, comes to me directly from Gerry Shikatani, in the form of an interview I conducted with him in spring 2002.[3] I have tried to exercise scepticism towards "authorial intention," but some of my readings do indeed depend upon Shikatani's statements in this interview.

⇢ THE THREE "BOOKS" of *Aqueduct* were written in different circumstances and from different authorial stances. Book I is entitled "21, Rue des Rosiers (1979)," and is mostly set in Paris (with a few side trips to Spain and the Midi). But the poems were not actually written in Paris at the time. Shikatani recalls:

> *That whole section was written after I got back from France. I took no notes. The thing about '79 was that it was my first trip to Europe, and I decided to write almost nothing while I was there, because I didn't want to shape my vision of what I was seeing. So that section is really something I did back in Toronto. But I was doing it from a recollection of Rue des Rosiers in the Marais. (I)*

So the point of view of writing *in* Paris is retrospectively reconstructed—and indeed, a degree of fictionalization extends, in Book I, both to the character of the narrator and to the Parisian setting itself.

Book II is entitled "A Traveller's Journal (1982)." Whereas the title of Book I had focused on a place, an address, a single static setting within which action would unfold, this title focuses on a character, a journal writer, and on movement between various different settings, travel. According to Shikatani, this section started out within the conventions promised by its title, with the poems being written day by day, as the events happened, in the locations described. "I decided to write a journal of this trip, in poems" (*I*). But personal problems intervened, and

> *I stopped writing these journal poems. So what happened was that when I came back to Toronto, for much of the Book, for probably half of that journal, I sat down, and each day I had to say "this is such and such a day": I had to recall what I did on that day, and write poems out of that. (I)*

So the journal format of Book II is retrospectively faked (in an odd echo of John Glassco). But the events described, and the character of the narrator, are far less fictitious than in Book I.

Only in Book III, "Aqueduct (1984–87)," do we arrive at poems actually written *in situ*:

I found it hard to write in Paris the first two trips, but by the third time I was there....I really love Paris, I was so fascinated by the idea, I really wanted to see what it was like to actually live there, and to see if I could write in Paris. (I)

We can trace a progression here, which may be described in terms of narrative. Book I, deliberately written at a distance and after the fact, constructs a narrative, with a quasi-fictional narrator and a highly manipulated setting. Book II adopts the narrative line of a journal (albeit reconstructed), and that narrative line is determined by *travel*: quite literally, it follows the sequence of a journey. These are tourist's poems—a very intelligent and sensitive tourist, but a tourist nonetheless. In Book III, the tourist becomes a resident: hence the timespan, four years as opposed to a few months. And the *narrative* element basically disappears. Each poem stands alone, as a moment of pure perception (almost, but not quite, pre-articulate perception). The presence and personality of a narrator, so evident in Book I and still perceptible in Book II, increasingly dissolve into a perceiving and recording consciousness, no longer dependent on any narrative context. "So that was important," Shikatani concludes, "just to see what would happen if I was there, in Paris, to write" (*I*).

In his interview with me, Shikatani proceeded directly from that statement about writing *in* Paris to another thought, which (in this interview at least) he doesn't fully succeed in articulating[4]:

And the other thing was that...there was a real conscious thing that was happening in terms of my language, my line length, so I had to look at that as well. (I)

Line length (even in prose poems) is, for a poet coming out of the Black Mountain tradition, ultimately a question of breath. But the intake of breath is also the medium of smell and, indirectly, of taste. For Gerry Shikatani (gourmet, restaurant critic, professional writer on all aspects of cooking and eating), food is not so much a metaphor as it is a condition of his writing, a form of discourse. Throughout *Aqueduct*, food and meals are described with a sensual intimacy equalled only by John Glassco. Compare this passage from *Memoirs of Montparnasse*:

> All day long I was hungry. I lowered my eyes when passing the windows of pastry shops, unable to endure the beauty of their displays—the éclairs, millefeuilles, gâteaux mocha, pavés suisses, barquettes de fraises, madeleines, cake anglais, and those lovely ones whose name I never knew, shaped like the hull of a sailboat, half the deck plated with chocolate, the other half with mocha, and full of a rich deposit tasting of nuts and nougat. (131)

with this from *Aqueduct*:

> I can remember then, the precision of that meal, when the proprietor had ushered me to the corner, the corner table, and I ate by candle-light, the wax dripping off-line, onto the cotton cloth. Eggs, hot, yet still liquid and yellow in their sweet warm cream, the tureen to fingers was hot, I would taste and inhale the odours into me. And the crisp, almost smoke salt skin of a duck confit in its soft giving sauce, a tableau of puréed carrots fanned with ridges, and those sweet white potatoes, still vegetable crisp, speaking of their presence in the earth. (248)

The sensuality of food may at times function as a metaphor for sexuality (or as a displacement of frustrated sexuality), but it also exists for its own sake. If it is a form of discourse, then it is certainly what Roland Barthes would call "a lover's discourse." Indeed, the Barthes connection is made explicit in the first Parisian poem of Book II, "Paris, Early July":

> breath exchange food,
> food exchange breath!
> (O-la!)

Roland Barthes, truly yes yes wings a-beat
hard on this page, landing signal,
carrier of,
this day. this is the day: pass, step,
walk around parked car.
car, Camus, a car accident he was killed
by, gingerly
step on street, drivers
seldom give way less time for thought,
souvenir, Parisien philosophy, literature
and myth of course
(67)

Both Barthes and Camus were killed by car accidents. But "car" in French also means "because," a sign of causality: thus "carrier...parked car...car accident." Accident is not wholly unmotivated. (There is also the food pun on "gingerly." And "myth of course" of course refers to Barthes' *Mythologies*.)

This whole connection between food, breath, and writing is given definitive expression in "Notes on Writing and Meals" (230), which I here quote in full:

> *The everyday type of writing and everyday meals continue the line longer, break each rule cooked breathing of breath, taste the perfume, breathe to carry it further into the nostrils and at the stove or table sniff, or the loss—sustenance that happened you see, on the boulevard St. Germain or avenue Bosquet—or never part of the planetree leaves that fall with each autumn. Breathe do I the plain breathing is as plane leaves fall, that autumn in these lungs and every day, every day we are at pots and pans and scrubbing away. Such talking away such meals say Chez Germaine talk and order push the line, with now lower lip ready muscatorily defined with that anticipatory, that habit of ready, to try to speak to a community, every day.*

"Writing and meals" become metonymies for each other, linked through breath: the intake of food ("taste the perfume"), the length of the line. Both are "everyday" activities, usually conducted at tables—often indeed, in Paris, at café tables. They are "everyday" both in the sense of "ordinary" and in the sense of "continual," and this mundaneness of activity "continue[s] the line longer"—in this case, into the rhythms of a prose poem. Both activities merge, in turn, into the realities of the city around them: "plain" breathing echoes the ubiquitous "plane" trees of Parisian streets. A street name—"boulevard St. Germain"—mutates and feminizes into a restaurant name—"Chez Germaine."[5] Such verbal echoes "talk and order push the line," so that the activities of talking, writing, cooking, and eating all "try to speak to a community."[6] This community is, ultimately, the context within which Shikatani's poems take place—and, sometimes, mistake place.

⇢ THE ACTION OF Book I of *Aqueduct* "takes place" in a very specific setting—"21, Rue des Rosiers," the title of the Book—yet it also mistakes that place, fictionalizes it. I began my interview with Shikatani by asking him: "Was that an address you lived at, or was it a café, or what was it?" "It was nothing at all," he replied. "It was totally out of my imagination" (*I*).

What that imagination does is to take several quite distinct aspects of Right Bank Paris and bring them all together at this quasi-fictional address. There is in fact an actual 21 rue des Rosiers, but it shares little with Shikatani's fictional location.[7] He makes very little, for instance, of the fact that the rue des Rosiers is the heart of the Jewish quarter of Paris—indeed, this aspect is specifically set aside in references to bars with "cured ham" (31) or brasseries with "salt pork ribs and bacon" (39). Perhaps more important is a sense of the street as being both intensely traditional—the living site of Jewish inheritance—and in transition. The whole area of the Marais was, at the time Shikatani was writing, in the midst of a major urban transformation, emerging from centuries of neglect into accelerated gentrification.

In the seventeenth century, the Marais had been the centre of fashionable and aristocratic Paris, but towards the end of the reign of Louis XIV there had been a massive shift west, towards the areas of the Faubourg Saint-Honoré and the Faubourg Saint-Germain (Hazan, 86). The area then fell into a long period of decay:

*Having escaped the piercing interventions of Haussmann—only
just; the Baron planned to extend the rue Étienne-Marcel all the way
to the boulevard Beaumarchais—the Marais remained in neglect
until the middle of the 20th century. In the years 1945–50, it was
still a poor quarter, where the courtyards of the great mansions were
piled up with delivery vans, steel-roofed shacks, stacks of wooden
crates, and carts with iron-rimmed wheels. The de Gaulle-Malraux-
Pompidou years corrected this archaism. The real-estate agents
weren't slow to see the end of buildings so historic, so run-down, and
inhabited by people so little able to defend themselves. In twenty
years the Marais became unrecognisable, and the old mansions—
surfaces scrubbed clean, security guards enclosed in plastic, parking
assured—were again in the hands of a privileged bourgeoisie, in
a shift the opposite of that which, two centuries earlier, saw it
emigrate, in mass, to the west. (Hazan, 87–88, my translation)*

This transformation must have been, in 1979, almost complete but
still ongoing, a function of the living memory of the quarter. The grand
classic mansions of Rohan and Carnavalet, or the superb arcades of the
place des Vosges, co-existed with run-down buildings and cheap
garrets—the ideal setting for the archetypal "starving artist" figure
that Shikatani's poem uses and manipulates. It was still, at that time, a
marginal district, on the edge of its own developing history.

Shikatani refers to several other settings, but he is vague enough
about them that a reader not familiar with Parisian geography could
easily suppose that they are all part of the same neighbourhood
(which they are not). For example, the "square" where artists paint
"their ridiculous landscapes" (21) is clearly the (hideous) place du
Tertre, all the way up in Montmartre; but the phrasing makes it sound
as if it was just down the street. One reference to the prostitute places
her, plausibly, on the rue Saint-Denis, at least a kilometre to the west
(37), but other passages (9, 19) make it sound, quite implausibly, as
if she was working the rue des Rosiers itself. The key incident of the
blind man's death (35) is specified as taking place at Le Drouot on the
corner of the boulevard des Italiens, nowhere near rue des Rosiers,
but again it is assimilated into the composite setting of the poem.

Such elements—painting in Montmartre, street prostitution on Saint-Denis, a famous restaurant on the Grands Boulevards—are all (in Shikatani's words) "translated/transplanted" (I) into the Marais, where they create and inhabit a composite, imagined address on the rue des Rosiers.

This address *has to be* fictional, because so too, to a great extent, is the protagonist. Shikatani explains:

> *The whole work, the whole thing I was playing with, was...doing the cliché "artist going to Europe," and so I wanted to bring in all that romantic imagining of the artist, the suffering artist....I just really wanted to play the whole thing, with a certain kind of consciousness about it. So that's why I converted all these things, and the Marais seemed like a perfect kind of venue for that....It went against the way I would normally, especially in that period, have been writing, which was at that time very minimalist, and very fragmented....So "Rue des Rosiers" was my sort of take on doing a real narrative. (I)*

As a narrative, "21, Rue des Rosiers" is still, it seems to me, minimalist and fragmented. The "story" emerges only by hints and indirections, and can never be fully specified. But enough is there to suggest the directions it might take.

The very fact that the protagonist of Book I is a painter, not a poet, already indicates the fictional distance Shikatani is setting up from the narrative voice. (In the following paragraphs, I will use "the painter" to refer to the fictional narrator of Book I.) If one is to "play" with romantic notions of the suffering artist, a painter is closer to the common cliché than a writer. In some lines, Shikatani stretches the irony to the edge of parody: "the sketchbook burns / my fearful hands" (10). And the artist's garret at 21 rue des Rosiers comes equipped, of course, with "brown cockroach-stains by the sink" (7).

The painter makes the familiar sexist equation (repeated so many dreary times in later Picasso) between paintbrush and penis: "the round firm paintbrush" held by the hand "in / the trouser pocket" (8).[8] Some kind of sexuality is indeed identified as the source of artistic vision: "this was the way I painted," he writes (9), referring not only to the paintbrush in his trouser pocket but also to watching the prostitute on the street below him:

> and each night
> I would watch her,
> standing at my window
> follow this whore
> home with my eyes,
> turning each step
> the lamps out
> until only remained
> the echoes of her heels,
> this was the way I painted.
> (9)

As I have said, this passage is fictionalized in terms of location (there are no streetwalkers on the rue des Rosiers), but this displacement works to push the image into wish-fulfilment fantasy and erotic obsession. The painter seems to have a fetish for leather heels: the reference here recurs in every description of the prostitute (19, 20, 36, 38).[9] There is also the idea of voyeurism and even more of surveillance: by page 19, the painter has noted the number of her room, with its "closing door." As a watcher, he keeps his distance; it is the power he maintains over her; it is also "the way I painted."

When this distance begins to break down, it is, ironically, because of another, different instance of voyeuristic detachment. Pages 32–33 introduce a new character: a blind man with a cane, selling lottery tickets. The painter presents him as an object of curious, inverted *envy*: "the blind (white cane / I covet)" (32). The artist of sight and vision covets, in some sense, the obliteration of that vision, a totally negative visual world:

> travel of indeterminate
> stops, cane,
> I covet a sign possible,
> possibly mine.
> (33)[10]

But then the blind man is killed, in a traffic accident (like Camus, like Barthes), "killed instantly, / the cane was intact, the lottery tickets / ignored on the pavement" (35-36).

At first, the painter claims that he was "the only witness" to the accident; and the point appears to be that he refuses to accept the social responsibility of *being a witness*. That is, the death was caused by a failure of vision (the blind man could not see the vehicle that killed him), and this failure extends into the painter's refusal to acknowledge what he, the artist of sight, has seen:

> *I was the only witness*
> *at the zinc bar*
> *and turned back*
>
> .....
>
> *no other witnesses and*
> *what could I say?*
>
> .....
>
> *the waiter insistent by and*
> *above me,* "Oui, monsieur?"
> "Un express,"
> *I routinely said.*
> (35-36)

It is a familiar trope of urban alienation, given definitive expression in Baudelaire's "Les Yeux des Pauvres"[11]: the watcher inside the privileged place (café, restaurant) who sees, but refuses to acknowledge or take responsibility for, the reality of what goes on outside the windows, on the street. The painter's "routine" request for a coffee dismisses the blind man's death and forecloses on the empathy, or envy, which the previous pages had suggested.

But on further examination, it is clear that the painter is *not* "the only witness": the poem twice mentions "the feather in the hat / she seated there" and "feather in the hat, the leather / of her heels" (35-36). That is, the prostitute, the object of the painter's heel fetish and voyeuristic obsession, is also present: *she too sees*. And presumably, like the painter, says nothing. Previously the object of the gaze, she now becomes complicit in the guilt of his gaze. She too becomes a subject, responsible, and failing to respond.

So the distance they both maintain from the blind man's death results, ironically, in the breaking down of his voyeuristic distance from her. In the next poem, he at last approaches her directly, rather than watching her from a distance. His approach is still extremely ambivalent:

> *rue St. Denis half*
> *hidden a shyness half*
> *hidden a cruel*
> *desire half*
> *hidden (image*
> *want and not want).*
> (37)

On the one hand, there is still this hesitancy, which works itself through the repetitions of a "desire half / hidden," so that he is scarcely able to articulate what he wants/does not want:

> *"do you, do you?" stop.*
> *a nervous flick.*
> *"suck[?"]*
> *.....*
> *"do you?*
> *how much?" (her heels)*
> (38)

As if their complicity in refusing witness to the blind man's death has finally allowed him to ask for this sexual favour ("suck"), and to connect it to his fetish ("heels"). On the other hand, this faux-naïf bashfulness (how could anyone really doubt that a Saint-Denis street-walker would offer a blow job?) is accompanied by repeated hints of violence. There are several references to a "tangle of rope...around her bare feet" (37), and to "the slick stockings / 'click' tightened by her garters / tightened to his neck" (37). These images come together in a deeply equivocal passage:

he walks the street [sic: *"he"*]
again, hope hidden
the tangle of rope
around her bare feet
the man he does not
want to be
but paints with
his single desire
(37–38)

Nothing is explicit here. Do the suggestions of strangulation in the tightening of her garters around his neck extend reciprocally to the rope around her feet? Has he in fact killed her? Has he in some sense become her, since it is now *he* who "walks the street"? What he wants and what he does not want are tangled together. He does not want to be a man who buys sex from prostitutes, yet this is the "single desire" that produces his painting.

Such ambiguities are perhaps as much as Gerry Shikatani was, in 1979, prepared to offer in terms of conventional narrative resolution. "For they say the pain / is an Achilles' heel," he concludes (41). The woman's heel (point of obsession, fetish) has become vulnerable: it lets in death (Achilles), it lets in pain, and of course it lets in paint. The implied pun between pain and paint (as well as the echo of "heel" in "Achilles") are perhaps the ultimate stage of Shikatani's parodic presentation of the cliché of the romantic artist. Book I's "play" with that image pushes it into some very dark areas, and locates them all on the street of rose bushes: the beautiful flowers, and their thorns.

⇢ AFTER THE NARRATIVE of Book I, the Parisian poems in Books II and III move deeper into the city, into the experience of *living* there, rather than merely visiting. That is, the poems concentrate less on narrative sequence than on moments of perception: spatial rather than temporal, the accumulation of a specific site/sight rather than an event in a continuing line. Often, Shikatani's poems will deny even the fully formulated expressions of retrospection, but will plunge (by means of a fluid and sometimes incomplete syntax) into the moment of perception itself, before that perception has become fully articulate. As always, the central experience is simply "the long poem of walking" on Parisian streets:

> To feel such streets, place and this
> the right slant,
> angle askew
> an answer that departs
> .....
> [the] way the mouth pours out
> the streets of Paris pull
> in.
> (204)

The streets of Paris insist upon being named, and the names form the groundplan of the poetic imagination, as in the poem named (precisely) "The Plan":

> In its every thing, is one at once located, how place insists its name. I do locate this city everywhere with its implicit time-quartered map. I am walking from Notre Dame towards the Pont de la Tournelle and then the Bastille, past the bordering concrete walls of the Seine; or seated for seemingly endless minutes with a coffee at L'Atrium on the boulevard St. Germain.... (298)

"Place insists its name": the experience of the city (urban, topographical) requires its linguistic identification, that moment when "a bridge across the river" will not do: it has to be "Pont de la Tournelle." That textual pleasure recalls, again, Roland Barthes, (in a poem suggestively called "Contexte"):

> The mix of pleasure, The Pleasure of the Text set in the mode of held glasses of muscadet at the bar, taken by patrons, set in the words of pleasure in the reading, right [write?] the way ideas set and the space in the voices arranged, and the smell of cigarettes. The way— the painted tiles of 1900 Les Halles, tin metal bar called Le Plat du Jour and the frosted rose lamps produce all that my body can bear of pleasure.... (243)

Here, text, body, pleasure all concentrate in a remembered (nostalgic?) image of the old market, "1900 Les Halles." So "the words of pleasure in the reading" (or in the righting/writing) are "set in" the "context" of a place both real and imagined (Les Halles, but Les Halles "1900," not 1984). The poem does not, in any narrative or retrospective sense, "describe" a place, a setting, or even a context. It *produces* that context in the immediate, word-to-word movement of its experience.

This sense of arrested movement, not time but space, not narrative but immediacy, relates these poems to painting. Thus, some of the best poems in Book III respond to paintings in Parisian museums, such as "The Measured Movements: The Jeu du Paume" (269–74)[12] and "The Post-Impressionists" (304–05). The book provides brilliantly concise, if elliptical, evocations of painted scenes: "the place of lunches and / delighted word" (270) (Renoir); "the hillside of red poppies" (271) (Monet); "the metaphor, the lean /gesture: balanced / on a naked foot or / slippered" (272) (Degas); "that smoke of distant fires, / season's dusk of sweet chestnuts from charcoal / on the stone terrace landing" (304) (Pissarro); "Admiration between two sisters / who have aged in distant worlds" (305) (Vuillard). In each case, it is as if time has been stopped—first in the painting itself, the act of fixing a visual image, and second, in the poem, where the elliptical syntax interrupts any sense of strict discursive sequence. These poems are not "stories" about what the paintings are "about": they evoke, directly and without art-historical distance, the moments of standing before them, in Paris, in the dimly remembered Jeu du Paume.

--> ONE PARISIAN who had no interest at all in stopping time was of course Haussmann; and in *Aqueduct*, as in so much Parisian writing, the Baron cannot be ignored. The poem title "The Baron Haussmann" (284–85) is, however, more metonymic than literal. The poem says nothing, directly, about Haussmann himself—his history, his personality—rather, it concentrates on his most visible legacy, the Grands Boulevards, including the one that now bears his name.[13] In my interview with Shikatani, I tried to elicit where he stood in relation to the kinds of controversy I described in Chapter 2. "How do you ultimately feel about Haussmann?" I asked him, and then, rather reductively, "Do you like what he did to the city?" "Yes," he replied, "it represents the power...." (*I*). But then he broke off, and his answer shifted direction. He began to talk about the sense of space and energy in the Grands Boulevards, and to relate this sense, as he also does in the poem, to his childhood memories of Spadina Avenue in Toronto.

"Power," however, remains an essential word. Haussmann certainly represented power, not only in political terms, but in the brute physical transformation of the city. The word most often used (for example, by Eric Hazan) for the process by which he cleared out old ramshackle neighbourhoods and pushed through what the poem calls his "straight and harmonious" boulevards is "penetration." And I don't think that the sexual connotation is irrelevant.

One of the major accusations against Haussmann is that he depopulated neighbourhoods: that the vibrant street-life of a working-class (and therefore potentially revolutionary) area was replaced by the empty spaces of wide boulevards, suitable only for bourgeois carriages, or for cannon-fire and cavalry charges. Does Shikatani allude to this uneasiness when he talks of "the sunny emptiness of days in repose, when *the people have gone*" (emphasis added)? Or is he only referring to the traditional emptiness of non-tourist Paris in July and August?

And how does Spadina enter into this argument? The poem nostalgically idealizes "that avenue I knew, its own wide walks upon which I'd played hockey and ball." Yet Spadina was also the site (in the late 1960s) of a major Haussmanian project for urban redesign—the Spadina Expressway—and of a singularly successful resistance to such "improvement"—it was cancelled in 1971. (See Dennis Lee's exultant "The Day We Stopped Spadina.") For Shikatani to evoke Spadina *in support of* the Baron Haussmann is, to say the least, paradoxical.

Yet at the same time, Haussmann's Grands Boulevards are an area of Paris that Shikatani genuinely enjoys (more so, I admit, than I do). Here is the full statement from our interview:

> SS: *How do you ultimately feel about Haussmann? Do you like what he did to the city?*
> GS: *Yes, it represents the power....I came upon it as that one section of the city, the Grands Boulevards, the whole energy of it....I'm*

talking about the government, the shopping, and also, what I
still like about it, is that it starts to open up....I mean, you get
past the Grands Magasins, you start going west, and it's a part of
Paris I really like going to. I like going to the cafés there, I like the
light around there, I like going to Saint Augustin....It relates to
my growing up in downtown Toronto. I know this wherever I go.
Growing up in Toronto, at College and Spadina, it was right in
the middle of downtown, and I've always liked going down to the
business area, Bay Street, at dusk, and in the evening, because
I like that sense of the modern structures, and the contrast, the
opening up of it....In some sense, there is for me that same feeling
on the Grands Boulevards, going shopping, being part of that
massive crowd, seeing the way the trees are formed as you go
along the Boulevards.... (I)

These trees are evoked in the poem's opening:

The Grands Boulevards, straight and harmonious, filled with the
sunny emptiness of days in repose, when the people have gone.
The trees, true down these avenues presence silent comfort a
practiced ease and thus, invitation to think while cutting this hour
with walk not talk.

So, for Shikatani, some of the most public and grandly designed
urban spaces in Paris become also private, intimately personal: they
become, again, the space of the flâneur. The streets provide a "silent
comfort," an "invitation to think," a time to "walk not talk": the essen-
tial conditions of flânerie. The Grands Boulevards "do lead so on into
the quiet interiors of pronounced elocution of the muscle private, the
heart" (284).

The scale, however, remains personal. What he sees on these
streets is not the grand drama of imperial display, but rather chil-
dren playing hopscotch or pinball, or men "cleaning their motorbike
engines," or a woman whose skirt is blown up by an urban gust
of wind. Everything is concentrated down into a single, bitter-
sweet moment: a chocolate truffle, bought at a market on the rue

Treilhard,[14] which offers "a single bite, not all, a wetness does not describe the concentration." So the whole grand spectacle of Haussmann's transformation of the city "disappeared sweetly, with a gust, before gentle voyeur could hold onto such light." Paris, and especially Parisian *light*, endures, far beyond even the most massive projects of urban redesign, concentrated into the taste of a sweet bought at a market on a minor street.

--> THIS POEM had better be quoted in full:

The Pont Neuf
for Stephen and Maureen Scobie

The point is
that, a new one way, to jump next
to, the from here and
that which, an interesting proposition
that which I can taste as fort as
something sautéed just to the point
of it, so suddenly, and a love for this,
all this place, big as a cow,
that is the point is
a departure is that new that's what
I'm sighing a sign
it's new the always
the Pont is new.

b. (crystal)

Wrapped and un-
wrapped, shining heart
with Christo
un rivering gift wear
the wrapture sol-soleil-
so sequined ! dressed
to-the-9s.
(268)

As I acknowledged earlier, the dedication here sets me apart from ideal standards of critical objectivity. I do think that this is a very good poem, but then, how could I not? Maureen and I met Gerry Shikatani in Paris in 1985; after Maureen's death in 2001, Gerry sent me one of the most beautiful and heartfelt tributes I received about her. Gerry always had good recommendations for out-of-the-way restaurants in various cities (such as an Indian restaurant in London called "The Last Days of the Raj: a Workers' Co-operative"), but one of the few places to which *we* took *him* was on the Pont Neuf. It's the Taverne Henri IV, right at the (one-way) entrance to the place Dauphine. In those days (1985), it was owned and run by a man called Monsieur Cointepas. (I think his first name was Henri, but I always thought of him, with deep respect, as "Monsieur.") He served very rough country fare— coarse bread with cheeses, pâtés, cold meats—and a small, personally selected choice of fine but inexpensive wines. In recent years, alas, Monsieur Cointepas has become ill and has had to pass on ownership. In its new incarnation, the Taverne Henri IV is still a good place to go, but (here is my own version of "Paris perdu" nostalgia showing) it's not the same as it once was. Not the same as when Maureen and Gerry and I went there in the spring of 1985.

The poem is built upon multiple word-plays, and I hope it will not be tedious if I spend some time pointing them out. Literally, pointing: "The point is" (first line of the poem), the point is that the Pont crosses a point. The Pont Neuf crosses the western point of the Île de la Cité: the point, that is, where the divided river, split by its two islands, rejoins itself and becomes again the single Seine. Between the Pont Neuf and the point of the island lies only the narrowing park of the Vert Galant.[15]

The point is a bridge, *un pont*, and a "new one," though the irony is that the "New Bridge" (completed in 1607) is in fact the oldest surviving bridge in Paris, the *least* "new." Here the name retains an historical reference drastically disconnected from its contemporary relevance. The bridge is also "to the point," that is, relevant, significant, well phrased. But in French, "au point" also describes a perfectly cooked meat, not too rare, not too well done, but just "au point," to the point, at the point of perfection. It is also a "point...of departure," that is, something new. New and old mix together: "I'm sighing" (conventional gesture of nostalgia for the old) "a sign" (the obvious pun) for "its new...the always...the Pont is new." And it is (new, always) the Pont Neuf, a site that evokes "a love for this, / all this place."[16]

The love "for" this place further echoes the multiple possibilities of the italicized "*fort*." If the word is read in French, then it is an adjective meaning "strong" (as a taste may be), but it is also a homophone for the English "for." If it is read in English, the final "t" is pronounced, and it becomes a point of fortification. If it is read in German, again the "t" is pronounced, and it means "away"—which is how it functions in the phrase *fort/da*, used by Freud to explicate the Pleasure Principle.

Then comes Christo. In 1985 (just too late for Maureen and me to see it), Christo and his collaborator/partner Jean-Claude executed on the Pont Neuf one of their "wrapping" projects, in which a major public building or installation (such as the Reichstag in Berlin) is enclosed within a material surround (in the case of the Pont Neuf, nylon polyamide). The effects are always intensely paradoxical. "Gift-wrapped," the familiar and taken-for-granted site is suddenly offered to the public as a gift, as something to be discovered in and as a present. It is both concealed (the texture of the particular stones is covered) and exhibited (the classic outlines of the bridge are accentuated in its wrapped form). And the wrapping is very beautiful in itself: the pleats, the texture of the material. The wrapping isolates the bridge from its context of urban utility, yet also permits that utility to continue (traffic continued to move across the Pont Neuf throughout the period of the installation).

Thus, the second half of Shikatani's poem begins with the pun between "crystal" (emblem of clarity and transparency) and "Christo" (emblem of wrapping and concealment). The wrapped bridge "wears" its "gift [ware]," and is exalted into "[w]rapture." The "sol" (ground) of the bridge-span meets the "soleil" of the sun. So, in celebration, the whole bridge is "dressed // to-the-9s," that is, in French, to the nine / neuf.[17] (The "new" bridge is always, also, "bridge nine.")

What Shikatani's poem amounts to, then, is the evocation of a particular Parisian place by means of a dense intertextual weave of allusions (both private, "for Stephen and Maureen Scobie," and public, "Christo"), and of wordplay (pont/point, wrap/rapture, new/nine). The syntax is fluid, at times indeterminate ("to jump next / to, the form here and / that which") in ways which may recall Gertrude Stein. So there is no *narrative*; one might almost say that there is no *description*. There is only the linguistic moment of consciousness, a "travel of indeterminate stops," one of which happens to be, wonderfully, the Pont Neuf.

PART SIX --> *Personal Postscripts*

←-- 16 THE FIRST TIME

I SAW PARIS (1970) -->

FIRST IMPRESSIONS of a city are often decisive. How many stories
have I heard, over the years, of people who declare that they don't
like Paris at all; and how often has this dislike been due to something
that happened on their first visit: a surly waiter, an awful hotel, being
cheated by a taxi driver, or finding the Louvre closed on the one day
they had allotted to see the *Mona Lisa*. My own first few hours in Paris
were a catalogue of disasters and minor frustrations. In retrospect,
I shudder to think how close I must have come to just such a lifelong
aversion.

It was the early summer of 1970, and Maureen and I were making
our first extended trip together to Europe. I had never been to Paris
before; indeed, throughout my Scottish childhood, my only trips
abroad had been one student excursion to Germany, and a couple of
visits to the profoundly foreign city of London. Maureen had spent
several months in Paris, as an au pair, in the early 60s, before we
were married, so I was relying on her expertise.

We arrived by train, from London, in the mid-afternoon: it must have been at the Gare du Nord, though the few fleeting visual impressions I retain would better fit the layout of the Gare de l'Est. We were without any advance hotel reservations (a mistake which I have never allowed myself to make again). But Maureen had confidence in her memories of hotel-booking agencies located in train stations; and, sure enough, we found such an office tucked into a corner of whatever station it was, where Maureen, negotiating her rusty French, secured a room for us in an inexpensive hotel near Châtelet. We had one hour to get there and pick up our reservation.

So we emerged from the station, into the full pandemonium of *une grève*—a French word that I learned, definitively and permanently, that afternoon.[1] Paris was in the grip of a full, twenty-four-hour bus and Métro strike. No public transportation of any kind. And the line-up for taxis bore little if any resemblance to an organized queue (indeed, it took several years after this experience to persuade me that French civilization had any grasp whatsoever of the concept "queue"): rather, it was an undignified rammy, in which the strongest and most assertive pushed their way ruthlessly forward towards anything that looked like a vacant cab.

Aghast, we retreated into the station, to the booking agency, and asked them to phone the hotel to explain that it might just take us a little longer than an hour to get there. Out of the question, monsieur et madame: you have one hour, or you will lose the room. Get there.

How we did it, I really don't know. Memory draws a blessed blank over the next half hour or so. I assume that we became as rude and ruthless as all those around us, and that we pushed our way to the front of the non-queue. It is possible that Maureen recovered unremembered reserves of colloquial French (as I did, several years later, when a Montparnasse hotel denied any knowledge of a room reservation for my mother). Or maybe we looked so pathetic that some taxi driver took pity on us (though this conjecture seems highly unlikely). But somehow we got a cab and made it to the hotel in time.

The hotel was certainly inexpensive. In fact, our room was something like the classic Parisian garret for starving artists, right up under the roof, with odd slants to the ceiling and a small window looking out over rooftops. I have no memory of the name of the hotel, or even its exact location. Later Parisian hotels I remember very well: the Clément, near the old Marché Saint-Germain (before it was boutiquefied); the Michelet-Odéon, alongside the noble pillars of the Odéon theatre; the Saint-Pierre, across a narrow street from a branch of the Sorbonne and the birthplace of Sarah Bernhardt. But of this first hotel I have only vague and imprecise memories. I know that it was on a very narrow side street off the west side of the place du Châtelet, in behind the flower and livestock markets of the quai Mégisserie. Looking at a map, I think it may have been on the rue Jean-Lantier, or possibly the rue Saint-Germain-l'Auxerrois. What I do remember is that the corner of the street was patrolled—there is no other word for it—by a solitary prostitute: a rather large woman, in her forties or fifties, appealing to that small but very defined section of the Parisian clientele that wants to be mothered, if not smothered.

Having unpacked, and taken the measure of our garret room, we set out from the hotel, ready at last to walk around the real Paris. Maureen was eager to show me the sights of the Left Bank: Notre-Dame, the Latin Quarter, the Cluny Museum....But as we approached the Pont au Change, to cross the Seine, we found our way barred by a line of heavily armed policemen. Apparently there was a student demonstration at the Sorbonne, and the authorities—barely two years after May 68—were taking no chances.[2] The whole area was sealed off. And not just by police, but by the special riot squads, the CRS (Compagnies Républicaines de Sécurité), whom the justice minister, Poniatowski, euphemistically described as "the forces of law and order." Riot police are intimidating at the best of times, but the CRS always looked particularly menacing, waiting in their sinister grey buses with wire-meshed windows. Paris that evening presented a forbidding spectacle.

Baffled and disappointed, we retreated from our proposed walk and decided that the best thing to do was to get something to eat. We didn't want to go very far—the Métro strike was still on, and the traffic, chaotic enough because of the strike, was now further congested by not being able to cross the river—so we just settled on the closest place we could see, a restaurant in the place du Châtelet called Le Dreher.[3] And here I ordered a simple dish of sole meunière.

It was a revelation. Simply the best restaurant meal I had ever had, up to that point in my life. In retrospect, I scarcely think that Le Dreher can have represented the peak of Parisian gourmet cuisine; it was probably a very ordinary restaurant. But that's the point: that even an "ordinary" Parisian restaurant can produce such a meal and can take the production of it *seriously*. It's one of the things that I have always most liked about Paris, and which I began to learn that evening: not just the imagination, but the care, attention, and respect devoted to *pleasure*. Pleasure, not as something incidental or vaguely disrespectable, but as a serious pursuit, a worthy aim of civilization. That sole at Le Dreher was the real beginning of my love affair with Paris.

We lingered over the meal. When we went out again, later, the bridge was still sealed off, but the atmosphere seemed to have relaxed; the demonstration had passed peacefully. For now we were content just to lean on the parapet at the end of the quai Mégisserie, gaze across the river to the squat twin towers of the Conciergerie, or look farther west, downstream, to where the slender point of the Eiffel Tower reached into the evening sky.

And all of the day's frustrations melted away—the strike, the taxi queue, the hotel, the riot police, the barriers—none of it mattered any more. Standing by the Seine that evening with Maureen, I knew that I was at home in the city of my dreams.

←-- 17 CATASTROPHE AND SHAME --→

Paris Journal (2002)

IN MAY 2002, Paris was gripped by a sense of catastrophe and shame.[1] The two words were everywhere: "catastrophe" in the newspaper headlines and editorials, "honte" in the graffiti and private conversations. From academics to waiters in cafés, from street demonstrations to magazine placards, "shame" was the keynote word.

The occasion was the fact that, in the first round of the presidential elections on April 21, Jean-Marie Le Pen, leader of the far-right National Front, had come in second to (ex-Gaullist) President Jacques Chirac, and ahead of (Socialist) Prime Minister Lionel Jospin, thus ensuring that the final ballot, due on Sunday, May 5, would be a straight run-off between Chirac and Le Pen, with Jospin eliminated.

This result seems to have been a gigantic accident of the French electoral system. Everyone (probably including Le Pen and his supporters) had simply assumed that the second, run-off ballot would be a straight choice between Chirac and Jospin, and the evident inevitability of this assumption had enabled people either to vote for other, fringe, candidates, or else to abstain from voting altogether.

After all, in French politics, no one ever quite goes away (unless, like Mitterrand, they manage to die in style, on the wings of a prohibited songbird[2]). In the weeks that I was in Paris, a major European Community task force on social problems was being headed up by Valéry Giscard D'Estaing, who was President of France so long ago that Tony Blair must still have been in diapers. The Chirac/Jospin choice was so old, and thus so inevitable, that no one really believed that anything they did in the first round of voting would make any difference at all.

How wrong they were.

Suddenly France was faced with the serious possibility that a political monster, Jean-Marie Le Pen, ex-torturer and murderer from the Algerian campaign, the man who had dismissed the Holocaust as a "detail" of history, the most egregious Fascist politician in contemporary Europe, had a legitimate candidacy for the Presidency of the French Republic. Only two words seemed appropriate.

Catastrophe.

Shame.

Graffiti, spray-painted through stencils, on the rue de l'École de Médecine:

21 Avril:
Je pleure

21 Avril:
J'ai honte

21 Avril:
Je crie

21 Avril:
J'ai mal au coeur

[I weep; I'm ashamed; I cry out; I'm sick at heart, I'm nauseous]

Nor can I ignore my personal sense of catastrophe. Je pleure. This was the first time that I had been in Paris since Maureen died in 2001. And she was always with me, as I walked the streets of the city, as I passed through so many places she had known before me, places she had taught me to love. Place Furstemberg (where, on one chilly winter day in 1976, we had heard a recording drifting down from an open window: "Winter Lady," by Leonard Cohen). Cluny. Rue de Sèvres. Saint-Germain. Above all, the tip of Île de la Cité, park of the Vert Galant, where thirty years ago I took the photograph of her that I still carry, tattered and frayed, in my wallet; the photograph that appears on her memorial card. I went there. I sat on the spot where that photograph was taken. I took the original print out of my wallet and sat there looking at it. Trying to guess which was stronger: her presence or her absence. The way she still gave meaning to my life, or the way in which her death deprived me of all meaning.

I walked up from there to one of our favourite places: the Taverne Henri IV. Monsieur Cointepas still behind the bar, slower in his movements now, wearing for the past few years that slightly unfortunate moustache. Suspenders hiked across his shoulders. The grey-haired, nameless waiter doing all the work. Glasses of wine; plates of cheese and eclectic variations on ham. Monsieur Cointepas' voice (on the few occasions he chooses to speak) deep and forceful. Who (I wonder) did he vote for?

Thirty years I've been coming to this bar. Times with Gerry Shikatani: remember, in his poem, "a love for this, / all this place." So many times with Maureen, more times than I can count. Her presence with me in every choice I make. Ham or cheese? And all of Monsieur Cointepas' meticulously chosen wines: Brouilly, Fleurie, Sancerre?

Île de la Cité, April 29.

In thirty years the trees
have grown backwards: pruned

in the severe French manner, fists
trimmed to their knuckles. In

the photo I carry always with me
they're taller. Even the trees

along the Seine are not reliable
markers of time, or

measures of loss.

April 30, in the Luxembourg Gardens.

I sit here watching children riding docile donkeys down that wide alley of the Luxembourg, which leads from the central, ceremonial pond towards the distant entrance that comes in from the rue de Fleurus (and that must have been used so often, daily almost, by Gertrude and Alice). The children mount the donkeys with so much trusting expectation of an endless journey. Yes: as long as they're still on the way out, backs to the Senate, it's not over; it's less than half; they will have this, and this much again, all the way back.

But as soon as they turn, there is a limit. As they ride back, towards that eternal view of the Panthéon dome looming between the chestnut trees, everything diminishes.

You must dismount. The ride is over.

The statues in the Luxembourg all now have spikes inserted at the top of their heads, a sort of surrogate crown. The reason seems to be so that birds can't sit on them, or (more pragmatically) shit on them. It seems a pity, though—I always liked pigeons settled on the heads of queens or goddesses. It brought them down to earth, those regal or mythological personages.

Meanwhile, at Saint-Germain-des-Prés, Picasso's bust of Dora Maar is back in place. It's a lovely image, donated by Picasso as a memorial to Guillaume Apollinaire (a slightly odd choice, since Apollinaire was long dead before Pablo met Dora). It stands under the chestnut trees in the garden of the ancient church, just across from my favourite café, Le Bonaparte, at the end of the (very short) rue Guillaume Apollinaire. For the past few years it's been missing, so I'm delighted to see it back: cleaned, gleaming almost, though already a bird has visited it. Maybe it needs one of the Luxembourg's spikes.

Talk about uniting all one's dearest obsessions. Today, April 30, both in Paris, I saw a movie by Jean-Luc Godard and a concert by Bob Dylan. Both of them are to me not only artists who first asserted themselves in the revolutionary years of the 1960s, which they also, centrally, defined, but, more importantly, artists who *survived* that early reputation and became the most advanced and important workers in their media for decades afterwards.

The Godard movie I saw in Paris today (at Le Forum Lucernaire, on the rue Notre-Dame-des-Champs, the same street on which Joyce and Hemingway lived) was his idiosyncratic 1987 version of *King Lear* (denied any formal French distribution until now, on account of copyright problems), which I have actually seen many times on video in Canada, but which continues to impress me with its virtuoso quotations not only from Shakespeare but also, stunningly, from Virginia

Woolf—how the death of Percival in *The Waves* comes to echo the death of Cordelia. (One Parisian review, commenting on its saturation of quotations, refers to it as *Le Roi Lire*.) Editing Shakespeare's text produces, as the final line, "She lives!"—Cordelia, or maybe even Virginia Woolf. At the end of the screening, I spoke briefly with a woman in the audience. It was her first viewing of the film; it was my 10th or 12th; we were both equally devastated.

Then in the evening I went to a Dylan concert at La Zénith, on the north edge of the city. Walking in the door, I ran straight into Jean-Louis Dreau, an old friend whom I had not seen for many years. I once gave him a guided tour, in my halting French, of Dylan's home town, Hibbing, Minnesota. During the concert, Dylan sang "Visions of Johanna": the first time I had heard it performed live since Vancouver in 1966. Afterwards, I got a ride back into town, with Jean-Louis' friend, Jean-Paul, driving as maniacally as only a true Parisian can.

May 1, *Fête du Travail.*

I bought my sprig of *muguet du bois* (lily of the valley) early in the morning, from a table at the Métro stop at Odéon. This purchase, somewhat amateurishly pinned to my jacket, fended off most other sellers, except for a very insistent one at Trocadéro, who couldn't see why I shouldn't celebrate twice.

At the gold shivering statue of Jeanne d'Arc, battered by the media, ten thousand of Le Pen's followers gather to pay tribute to an idealized image of French national glory. Across the river, parked outside the Musée d'Orsay (closed for the holiday), buses of riot police wait patiently. A couple of miles east, at République, a million people gather to march to Bastille, and to vote, NO!!

Surrounding the base of the triumphal column of Bastille, they use the most regrettable invention of the twentieth century, spray-paint cans, to inscribe the memorial of 1789 with an inescapably monolingual twenty-first-century message: "FUCK LE PEN."

I keep a cautious distance. Having read all the demonstration routes in *Libération*, I know where not to go. On a wall on rue Visconti, I take note of the emphatic message:

MIEUX VAUT UN ESCROC
QU'UN FACHO! VOTEZ!

[Better a crook than a fascist! Vote!]

All those fine French Socialists, holding their noses and voting for
Chirac.

Down among the trees below Trocadéro, la Tour Eiffel is barely visible
through the blossoms of lilac branches. Clouds scud across the sky
behind the tower; fresh wind, on an unseasonably cold morning,
scatters the blossoms across the paths. They lie there so thickly, it's
like walking to a wedding on a bed of flowers. One couple on a bench
seems almost intent on consummating such a wedding; she sits on his
lap and devours him. Studiously, I watch the other inhabitants of the
park. One solitary man smoking his pipe. Another solitary man (me)
writing in his notebook.

Still life: at the market of the avenue
du Président Wilson.

Whole baskets of luminous
deep red strawberries:
amongst them white
thick stubby (contrast
of colour) asparagus.

At the Métro stop Saint-François-Xavier:

A doorway entrance, with
two lions, or
that is how I
remember them: today

one lion is so
overgrown with ivy
it is impossible

to say whether two
totally abstract green
shapes now guard

the doorway, or is it two
inhibited fauves: wild overgrown
Parisian beasts.

-->

On the rue Joseph Bara
(little drummer boy) a children's
playground. Drum,
drum to whatever
war you have waiting.

-->

Tonight in the restaurant
(Latin Quarter) a party
of five priests
come in, sit down, and order
unproblematically
bread and wine. Untheologically,
so do I. And so
does the man beside me
who is wearing
a plain black T-shirt
with one
white word:
"Décadence."

May 2.

Outside the Arsénal, on rue de Sully: a column of cavalry; horses in
colour-matched pairs (grey to grey); riders in long black raincoats,
gleaming black helmets, red plumes. All the horses at slow walk, beating
out a rhythm with their hoofbeats. Reaching the corner of the boulevard
Henri IV, they turn right, paying no attention at all to the traffic lights.

In the evening I went to a film at the Cinémathèque Française—which may seem a simple statement, but for me it is redolent with memory. Memory, specifically, of the winter of 1975–76, when I would go to the Cinémathèque regularly, two or three times a week: really, my post-graduate education in film. Back in those days, the Cinémathèque was still being run on a fairly haphazard basis. There was never any guarantee that the film being shown was the same as the film advertised. You might go there expecting a French classic (Vigo, Renoir), and end up seeing a Japanese samurai film with Bulgarian subtitles. Or, if you were lucky, an entirely illegal print of Hitchcock's *Vertigo* (unavailable at that time for complicated copyright reasons) disguised under the title "Cold Sweat." It didn't matter. You took whatever they gave you and absorbed it into an eclectic vision of world cinema, more strange and more comprehensive than anything I have known since.

And you sat there, under the high ceiling, under the soaring arch that frames the screen, terribly conscious of those ferocious young intellectuals who had sat in these front-row seats in the 1950s: Rohmer, Chabrol, Rivette, Truffaut, Godard...[3]

Tonight was Robert Bresson's *Lancelot du Lac*, a film of austere and relentless grimness: a vision of Arthurian "romance" in which nothing is romantic, chivalric combat is blood-drenched fiasco, and all the "visual pleasure" of cinematic spectacle is systematically denied by camera positions that are always too close, always too downward-looking, to afford the traditional distancing of action cinema.

And yes, the film was exactly the one that was advertised. And a notice outside the hall assured us that the state of the print was "bon." Thirty years ago, neither of these facts could have been taken for granted.

So then I took the Métro home: from Trocadéro, coming up out of the underground at Passy, crossing the Bir-Hakeim bridge (which features in two great films: Godard's *Alphaville* and Bernardo Bertolucci's *Last Tango in Paris*), with the illuminated Eiffel Tower on my left, reflected in dark waters of the Seine. Change at Motte-Picquet-Grenelle, to the line through Duroc (where I would have got off in 1975) to Odéon. Back then, I would have known every change, where to stand on the platform, which end of the train would be closest to the exit I needed to take.

But I also remember the nights when the mad dash from a late showing at the Cinémathèque to the Trocadéro Métro wouldn't work: the "Last Métro" (title of a film by Truffaut) would already have departed, the station would be closed. Then there would be the long walk home, which I may have resented in 1975 but which lives mythologically in my memory. Down past the silent fountains of Trocadéro. Across the Pont d'Iéna. Under the iron skeleton of the Tour Eiffel. Up the midnight deserted expanse of the Champ de Mars. Cut left at École Militaire, along to the looming dome of Les Invalides, Napoleon's megalomaniac tomb. Past the clunky church of Saint François-Xavier, past the rue Babylone with its spectacular Pagoda. Left on Oudinot, under the bureaucratic walls of the Ministry for Overseas Territories, then right on rue Rousselet—which was, in 1975 and again in 1985, home.

This walk across a midnight Paris. Confident geography, habitation of history. I can follow it still in my mind, no need to look at a guide. It is still the street map of my memory, the inscription of desire.

May 3.
In my hotel bathroom, I have to say, I notice a water stain on the floor, almost exactly the shape and outline of a map of France. Even the mildew is patriotic.

And an addition now to the graffiti on rue de l'École de Médecine.

21 Avril: J'ai honte

Added in spray paint, simply:
Moi aussi!

And more complexly:
T'étais déjà pas fier?!

[You already had nothing to be proud of?!]

Dinner tonight at a new restaurant on the rue des Grands-Augustins, which is called [sic] "Ze Kitchen Galérie." Every review I've read of it begins with the words: "Despite its awful name...." Right on both counts.

But somewhere in the course of this evening, my mood turned morose. I'd spent too much time in my all-too-familiar tense of the past conditional: "Maureen would have loved..." this restaurant, for example, this sweet-potato soup, this ginger ice cream.

On the one hand, I am detached from everything; I don't care; because for me the worst has already happened. I don't much care what happens to me for the rest of my life, because nothing, including my own death, can be as bad as what I've been through in the past year. And there's a certain comfort in that feeling. If I went home to Victoria and found that my house had burned down, I would be sad, angry, devastated by the things I'd lost, but I'd know that the *most* beautiful thing had already been lost, so, fundamentally, *it doesn't matter*. Not that I'm stepping rashly into the mad flow of Parisian traffic, or going to rabid National Front demonstrations and shouting "Fuck Le Pen!"—I take care of myself—but at some level, it just doesn't matter.

On the other hand, the flip side is that the *best* thing has already happened to me too. No matter what I do—how much I enjoy Paris, how many Dylan shows I go to, how many gourmet meals I eat—none of it will ever be as good as it once was, as it once was with Maureen. Again, I'm not going to stop trying to enjoy myself. I'd still rather be at a Dylan concert than listen to a Neil Diamond cd; I'd still rather eat at Ze Kitchen Galérie than at McDonald's. But there is a final level of contentment that I will never attain again, simply because I can never share it with Maureen, either directly (her being there beside me) or indirectly (me telling her about it when I get home).

So I left the restaurant feeling pretty down. I strolled along the Seine, came up the rue des Saints-Pères, browsed in a couple of book-shops, and settled in on the terrace of the Bonaparte to drink cognac and write some postcards.

I've been coming to the Bonaparte for over thirty years. Over those years, waiters have come and gone with predictable irregularity (all of them men, by the way: this year is the first time ever that I've seen a woman serving at the Bonaparte). In all that time, the most consistent has been one: a small, neat, Asian man. He's been here for so long that he seems to me a fixture of the place, as immutable and unchanging as Picasso's statue of Dora Maar in the churchyard opposite. Tonight, unusually, the café is very quiet, and I take the chance to engage him in conversation. His name is Thao Louang Rath; he comes from Laos; he has been working at the Bonaparte for twenty-one years. (So I was, by a few years, here before him!) Another two or three years, he guesses, and he will have enough money to retire. He wants to go back to Laos—I do not ask him about the political implications of such a move. He wants to live in the country, away from the noise and bustle of big cities. He doesn't like Paris; he doesn't like this centre of Paris, Saint-Germain-des-Prés, which for me he has come to epitomize.

For some reason, I am immensely cheered by this conversation, and the evening's depression, at least briefly, lifts.

May 4.

Breakfast at Le Danton, place de l'Odéon. Two cops on bicycles have decided to give a ticket to a woman also riding a bike. For the life of me, I can't make out what her offence has been. It wasn't riding one-way the wrong way down one of the many restricted streets. Given the general craziness of traffic at this seven-way intersection, it's hard to see what anyone could possibly have done wrong. The process seems interminable: it takes at least fifteen minutes to fill out all the forms. Sometimes the cops seem to be doing nothing at all, as if waiting for some superior authority to arrive. The woman looks vaguely embarrassed but says a cheerful hello to several acquaintances who walk past while all this is going on. Only towards the end does she seem (from where I am sitting, drinking a coffee and eating a croissant) to be disputing the cops' version of events, waving her hands (though not with much conviction) towards the site of the alleged offence. Of the two bicycle cops, I notice, only one is wearing a helmet.

Today I hear rumours that Le Pen is secretly polling around 40 per cent, but the results have been suppressed. He might even win.

"Catastrophe" is no longer a strong enough word. Anything close to such a result would be the end of French civilization.

A café at the corner of the boulevard Saint-Germain and the rue Solférino (whose name reminds several writers, from Walter Benjamin to Adam Gopnik, of the fiery element sulphur, rather than the Bonapartist battle): a café, that is, conveniently close to the Musée d'Orsay. It provides one tiny corner, no more than three tables, designated by the sign "Zone Non Fumeur." (Not even noticing such a concession, I sit somewhere else.) At the middle table of this "zone," a man sits down and starts smoking a pipe. His wife joins him, lights a cigarette, and goes to another table to fetch an ashtray. The waiter does nothing. Sulphur.

Going to a museum like Orsay is now, for me, mostly a case of visiting old friends. Pissarro's red roofs. Cézanne's stolid peasant woman in that ultimate blue dress. A young girl sleeping in Vuillard's bed. I love them all and embrace them all the more for their "intimations of mortality," knowing that Maureen will never see them again, and how many times will I?

So it is really a shock (a stunning, delightful revelation) to come across, in a special exhibit at Orsay, something totally new. In fact, it's like discovering a completely new painter, and a great one at that, from a period I thought I knew well. Here is an artist who began his work in the 1890s, painting imitations of Impressionism. But so much more than imitations—these are not student exercises—already he knows what he is doing. These canvases could stand alongside any examples of late Impressionism. And so it goes on, as, in the first decade of the century, he runs quickly through all the major "isms" of an orthodox art-history account. Deep brooding landscapes on the edge of Expressionism; a sudden explosion of Fauve colour; inspired pastiches of Cubism that totally miss the central Cubist ideology but catch Braque's colours with uncanny virtuosity. I love and covet almost every painting in this show. There's a *Red Cloud* from 1907, which in my opinion wipes the floor with every canvas of that year except Picasso's *Demoiselles d'Avignon*. Why it is not reproduced on a large scale in every history of twentieth-century painting is now beyond my comprehension. It is one of the three or four greatest paintings of the first decade of the twentieth century.

By about 1912, this painter is at last becoming familiar to me. I have seen his work before, especially in the New York Guggenheim. He is entering conventional art history. But all this early work, anything before 1910, I had never seen before. As I said, it is like discovering a whole new painter, a great painter, in a period I thought I'd known inside out. And here he is on the walls of Orsay, delighting me, astounding me. The greatest landscape painter of the decade. And his name is Piet Mondrian.

Because it is cold
because it is raining

the terrace canopy
of the Café Bonaparte
is lowered

so we can feel as we drink
last midnight cognacs
the artificial heat
of electric bars

but we can't see under
that lowered shade
to the floodlit tower
of Saint-Germain

which is why we came
here in the first place
to see that tower
and to drink that cognac

because it is cold and
because it is raining.

May 5.

Today they are voting. Not many signs of it as I cross the city in its Sunday quiet; the voting stations do not advertise themselves very prominently. But you can see, at the Mairies, a steady trickle. I have my camera with me today, the only day of this trip that I'm allowing myself the mediation of the viewfinder and the lens. I photograph the graffiti on the rue de l'École de Médecine. On the rue Oudinot, I find a poster proclaiming that "Chirac, c'est la France" plastered above a traffic detour sign, a set of bright red arrows pointing decisively right.

I photograph a placard for the magazine *Courrier*. It shows an archetypal Frenchman, holding a bottle of wine in one hand, with a loaf of bread tucked under his arm. But the wine bottle has a swastika on its base, and the baguette's upward slant ends in the stiff extended hand of the Nazi salute. The headline reads "France, l'Europe te regarde (le monde aussi)." Is this the key to the repeated use of the word "honte"? Does the "shame" of April 21 reside in the way that France is seen by its partners in Europe, in the world? Not the internal shame—we allowed this to happen—but the external shame—other people saw us allowing this to happen?

Then, on a corrugated iron fence around a construction site, a somewhat more comprehensive statement (spray-paint cans being, again, the medium of choice for today's philosophers):

LE PROGES?

UN LUMINEUX

DESASTRE

[Progress? A shining disaster!]

I'm walking round my old neighbourhood, rue Rousselet. Number 19. Noting which windows are open, which remain shuttered. Who is still alive, who has been succeeded. The tailor's shop where I bought one of my favourite ties has disappeared.

Influenced by Mavis Gallant, I go inside the Chapel of Saint Vincent de Paul, on the rue de Sèvres, which I had blithely passed, God knows how many times before. I climb the winding stair to the saint's relic.

It's tiny: a body scarcely five feet tall. I am moved, not to piety but to doggerel:

> Was Saint Vincent de Paul
> really that small?

Bourgeois Sunday lunch at the Hôtel Lutetia. I've always been deeply suspicious of this place. A sign outside takes pride in recording that, at the end of the Second World War, it was a major clearing-house for the return of deportees; it doesn't mention that, during the War, it was the favoured Parisian hang-out of the Gestapo.

The clientele is mostly elderly, and a surprising number of them have trouble figuring out the push/pull on the heavy entrance doors. At the next table, a group of three women, all in their thirties, all competitively dressed and coiffed, sit with one grey-haired man, who takes absolutely no part in their conversation.

Later that night, I go up rue Mouffetard, behind the Panthéon, the street in which every second door is a Greek barbecue or a Swiss fondue. I choose Swiss. But standing outside an Irish pub, I watch through the window French national TV reporting the vote in favour of Chirac. 82 per cent. The entire street erupts in cheers.

Full-page, front-page headlines in the left-wing newspaper *Libération*:

> *on April 22, day after the first round of voting:*

> ***NON!***

> *on May 1, advocating a vote for its hated opponent Chirac:*

> ***OUI!***

> *on May 6, reporting the result, showing the back of Le Pen's head:*

> ***OUF!***

Le Pen, predictably, blamed his defeat on the "Stalinist and totalitarian" tactics of the French media. Coming from Le Pen, the word "totalitarian" is a laugh. But in this case he wasn't entirely wrong. I have never in my life seen such a concentrated, hysterical campaign as all the French media waged against Le Pen this last week. Reporting the final result, *Libération* proclaimed it as "82% pour la République": not 82 incredible per cent for one candidate, but 82 per cent for the state, for the ideal of the Republic, for, in effect, France itself.

By the next week, indeed a few days later, *Paris-Mode* had come out with an issue headlined "La Victoire de la République," featuring a photograph of Jacques and Madame Chirac, in the Presidential Garden, home for another five years. He has one arm paternally around her shoulders. She is wearing a very dull, conservatively cut, brown suit. Her smile is equally dull, conservative, and brown. In the background however, in front of a bed of yellow tulips, a white poodle joyously bounds towards them.

May 6.

A difficult day for me. It would have been our thirty-fifth wedding anniversary. It is *still* our thirty-fifth wedding anniversary. Is it too romantic that I spend the evening at a Wagner opera?

Morning coffee at Port-Royal. Table of three next to me, one man and two women, all in their thirties. All three smoking incessantly. Several times their conversation breaks into song, sketching out tunes from popular shows, but once, in the middle of a lively discussion of yesterday's elections, they all join in a mock-pastiche version of "La Marseillaise."

I did my laundry. I mailed thirty-three postcards.

I met Jean-Louis Dreau for lunch at the Brasserie Balzar. When we came out, the whole street was blocked off by police. Bomb scare at the Sorbonne. Jean-Louis shrugged. It happens every time that Chirac is elected, he said.

Notice on the railings of the (rather small)
garden on the south side of the church of
Saint-Germain-des-Prés.

En cas de tempête, ce jardin
sera fermé.

[In case of tempest, this garden
will be closed.]

When does a mere rainfall
become a tempest?
Hopeless, homeless citizen,
when do they close the door?

May 7.

9:45, late breakfast. The sun is shining almost straight down rue
Saint-Sulpice, east to west, past all the scaffolding that enshrouds the
north tower of the church, shining through the flickering leaves of the
plane trees in front of the pretentious shopfront of Christian Dior, and
producing its own Impressionist pattern of dappled light that falls on
the terrace tables of the Café de la Mairie du VIème Arrondissement,
where I sit, as always, divided between memories of Djuna Barnes and
the practical assessment of this morning's croissant et grand crème.

The 63 bus slides by. I know its route so well. Forget about the tour
buses. If you know the normal routes, you can see all of Paris, at ground-
level, cheap. 63, 87, 39, 70, 82, 38: if (as is rumoured) they ever change
the system of numbering Parisian bus routes, I will be totally lost!

Time for a big, blow-the-budget meal. Which, in practical terms,
means lunch. At the really top flight of Parisian restaurants, you can
still get lunch at prices that are merely very expensive, as opposed to
dinners, which are beyond reason. It's also just possible to sneak into
a place without reservation, whereas dinner will be booked for weeks
ahead. So, today for me, lunch for one at Le Grand Véfour, Palais-
Royal, a mere 70 Euros (plus wine). Every table bears a brass plaque

with the name of some famous person associated with the site. Colette is a couple of tables to my left. I am sufficiently delighted to be sitting at a table assigned to Camille Desmoulins, Revolutionary politician and friend of Robespierre, whose fiery speech, here in the Palais-Royal, was one of the major sparks of the French Revolution. But what would he have made of lunch today? The swarm of formally dressed waiters, almost outnumbering the customers, obsequiously remembering a couple of regulars from Australia? Or the *amuse-bouche*, a cream-of-pea soup reduced to the merest froth? The chicken thighs surrounded by little circles of pâté. A superbly flavoured roast pork. A cheese plate disappointing only in its brie. An architectural extravaganza of chocolate. Half-bottle of Château Lafon-Rodet 1988.

All of this menu written down in my notebook, to be recalled, as always, in the past conditional.

Notice on the door of the Church of Saint-Julien-le-Pauvre (one of Djuna Barnes's Nightwood churches).

*Seule la prière permet
de communiquer
avec Dieu
Içi le portable est
inutile*

*[Only prayer allows you
to communicate
with God
Here your cellphone
doesn't work]*

May 8.
I have undergone an inordinate number of holidays (banks closed, reduced bus service, no special rates at cinemas). A week ago was Fête du Travail, Mayday, workers' holiday. Tomorrow is Ascension. And today, I'm not even sure what it is, something religious: Corpus

Christi? Again the uncanny silence on the busy intersections of Odéon. The city taking a quiet breath.

Lunch again at Henri IV, and afterwards, sitting for a while in the tree-shaded luxury of the place Dauphine. On a working day, there would be games of *boules* on the dirt under the trees: civil servants from the Palais de Justice, serious games contested by daily experts. Today there is only one game going, and only one serious player, a young shirt-sleeved Frenchman fooling around with three amateurs, all of them English, two of them women. The Frenchman, basically indulgent (a connoisseur of this, one of the finer points of French civilization, condescending to the unfortunate barbarians), cannot resist the occasional show-off shot, knocking out opponent's balls at full toss, with a casual flick of the wrist.

Meanwhile two Scotch terriers, loose of leashes, chase each other across the square. One sniffs the other's tail, then enthusiastically mounts. "No! No! No!" Impeccably clad in Parisian black, but speaking English, the mountee's owner comes running across the square to drag her away. The game of boules continues, uninterrupted, but the Frenchman seems to have lost his touch. His shots are going spectacularly awry. The two dogs' owners settle down again at the Bar du Caveau du Palais, their securely leashed charges still eying each other a little wistfully.

At the Fontaine Saint-Michel, a Scottish bagpiper is playing his heart out, accompanied by an African bongo drummer.

This evening my sense of justice is feeling aggrieved. I was having a pre-prandial kir at the Café de la Mairie du VIème, and listening to two young American women at the next table. They had just arrived in Paris that afternoon, and they hadn't the faintest idea where they were. They had a clumsy, large-scale tourist map, and they couldn't find Saint-Sulpice on it. They didn't know north from south. So I took pity on them, pointed out exactly where we were, where they could find Notre-Dame, places they might eat, etc. And what was my reward for this altruism? To be landed, in the restaurant I myself chose, with a next-table group of the crassest tourists possible. They wanted the salad, but not with the (delicious) foie gras topping. No, they didn't want any wine; they'd like Coca-Cola Lite, with lemon.

It was La Marlotte, on the rue du Cherche-Midi, and something had gone drastically wrong with it. It used to be one of our favourite restaurants; Maureen and I came here on visits that were seldom, but choice. It was dark and intimate, and the clientele was profoundly bourgeois French. Now it's somehow light and airy and there isn't a word of French to be heard.

Just this loud dialogue at the next table.

—They pushed the daughter out.

—Naw, they didn't.

—They pushed the daughter out.

—No, they pushed her husband out.

—It wasn't anything to do with her.

—No, it was just business.

—Can she still get me on a flight home?

May 9.

Ascension Day. If Christ had been rising straight up out of Paris today, He wouldn't have remained visible very long. A low thin mist hung over the city all day, never fully clearing, yet not particularly cold.

In the morning I took a 21 bus down to the Parc Montsouris, an area of the city that I don't know very well. The park itself is very pleasant, inhabited early in the morning mostly by joggers. On the north edge of the park, there is a series of narrow streets that run off uphill; the streets are very close together, some of them looping round as crescents, some of them *impasses*. Street surfaces are still cobbled; the house fronts are covered in ivy or else shaded by well-established trees. Birdsong is clearly audible. It's an intensely private, quiet neighbourhood.

One of these streets is called the rue Georges Braque. "Peintre cubiste," the street sign defines him, accurately if a little restrictively. Braque was "cubist" only in the great years between 1908 and 1914, when he defined himself and Picasso as two climbers roped together on a mountain. Yet the sign is also true: Braque's later work, from the 1920s on, remains true to the principles of Cubism and is, in my opinion, infinitely superior to the work of the later, unfocused, self-indulgent Picasso. Braque lived on this street from 1927 until his death in 1963. I'd never seen it before, but it is a delightful location, a place of beauty.

I wander to the top of it, which is sufficiently elevated that you can look back down its narrow perspective to a framed view of the joggers circling Parc Montsouris. A woman comes out of number 14, the front of which is totally overgrown with ivy. (Braque lived at number 6.) She locks the front gate, then reaches her hand back through the railings and drops the key into a box hidden under the ivy. She doesn't see me standing there watching; without a backward glance she strides off down the street.

Yet somehow I am sure that, if I put my hand through the railings and picked up her key, a dozen pairs of eyes would be watching.

Afternoon coffee at Le Danton. At a table by the window onto the carrefour de l'Odéon, there's an elderly man, smoking a small cigar and contemplating one of the great problems of the modern age: how to get the shrink wrap off a new CD. He has a whole stack of them, and he's picking away with his fingers. A subversive idea occurs to me: "Burn it off," I think, and damn me if that isn't exactly what he does!—flicks his lighter and holds it briefly to a corner of the CD. The wrapping comes off quite easily.

Late-night dinner in the retro splendour of Vagénende, boulevard Saint-Germain, an 1890s proliferation of mirrors. Over the past few days, I have become quite adept at eavesdropping on the conversations at adjoining tables; but it's still a difficult art, when the surrounding noise is so loud, and when you're not even sure what language is being spoken.

This couple next to me is speaking mostly a kind of muffled English, but at times they move into French. At one point she says something about a Québécois accent, but it doesn't sound that way to me.

She's wearing a hat pulled down to her eyebrows and a woollen roll-neck sweater up under her chin: she must be *very* hot. He's older than her, and for most of the meal he seems to be feeding her some world-weary and sophisticated line about living the liberated life. "If you're sexually frustrated," he tells her, "you must find out *why*, and decide what to do about it."

"Well," she replies, "I know that on some level."

"What *level*?" he snaps. "There are no levels, only being conscious or unconscious." Later he tells her, "Do as I do," then immediately adds, "but not tonight."

So, I wonder, is this a seduction already accomplished, or still to come? At one point he refers to "our hotel" and seems very concerned that *she* knows the way back. He repeats this twice.

Then they get all giggly together, and she takes a photo of him clowning around with the wine bottle, which is disappointingly called Château Brown. They are taking a very long time to finish their meal. They had eaten their main course when I came in, and already I've overtaken them.

Suddenly, the free spirit pulls out a cell phone and calls his lawyer, to whom he speaks in very clear, unaccented English. "Do I have to come in for interrogation? [Pause.] So, the tactic seems to be: make it difficult for Alexander, and then he will try to buy me out to get rid of the problem." He hangs up, and says to the girl, "The fight is on, big time."

"Vamonos," she replies, adding another language to the mix, and they disappear into the night. After a while I follow them out onto the boulevard, turn right, and head to the Bonaparte.

May 11.

There are many farewells to Paris, and none of them is ever final. Each time I leave I assure myself that I will return, hanging on in my wallet to some small token: a Métro ticket, a carte orange. On my last full day in Paris, I went for a second time to see the show of early Mondrian paintings, uncertain whether I would ever have the chance to see them again. And the astonished discovery of the first visit settled into a deeper satisfaction.

The political life of France seemed to be returning towards normal. With the parliamentary elections coming up in June, predictable positions were being staked out. Chirac was trying to consolidate his newly achieved high ground as saviour of the Republic. The Socialists were looking for a leader. Le Pen was huffing and puffing on the margins. The spray-painted signs on the walls of the rue l'École de Médecine will long outlive their occasion. J'ai honte. J'ai mal au coeur.

I went back to the Taverne Henri IV and shook hands with Monsieur Cointepas, hoping to see him next year. I went back to the Vert Galant, to the tip of the Île de la Cité, and once again I took out Maureen's photograph. As she sat there, thirty years ago, so beautiful. I spoke to her in my heart, and I promised again to return.

NOTES

INTRODUCTION

1. I have generally followed the French practice of not capitalizing words such as "rue" and "boulevard" in street names. However, in quotations, I will follow the English style of capitalizing such words if this is the usage in the original text.

2. The classical usage of the phrase "the judgement of Paris" refers, of course, not to the city but to the Trojan Prince—though it has been retrospectively applied to the city in such books as Ross King's *The Judgment of Paris*, which is a history, not of the Trojan War, but of Impressionist painting. For the possible associations between the city and the mythological Paris, see Chapter 10.

3. And modern politics died, one might venture to suggest, on the streets of Paris in May 1968. What follows is postmodern politics: "the end of history," or the world defined by CNN. The exemplary case study would be the films of Jean-Luc Godard.

4. Walter Benjamin (1892–1940) was a historian, a sociologist, a literary critic, a cultural theorist: one of the most wide-ranging and influential minds of his time. In the last decades of his life, he accumulated material towards a vast project, a book that was never completed, on nineteenth-century Paris, using as his central image the "arcades": indoor, covered

shopping streets, which flourished in Paris in the early part of the century. Benjamin died in 1940, attempting to escape the Nazi occupation of France. His huge assembly of notes was finally edited and published in Germany in 1982: *Das Passagen-Werk*, edited by Rolf Tiedemann. It appeared in English translation in 1999.

5. For practical purposes, I am taking 2007 as the cut-off date for resources used in this study.

6. That is, English Canadian. French Canadian writers have a whole different cultural dynamic to deal with in writing about Paris. I have attempted to deal with the Québécois experience of Paris in my transla-tion (together with Marie Vautier) of the poetry anthology *Paris Québec* (Montreal: Éditions Trait d'Union, 1999; Victoria, BC: Ekstasis Editions, 2003).

PART ONE

1--→ CONSPIRACY THEORIES

1. HLM is the abbreviation for *habitation à loyer modéré*: low-rent housing. The term is notoriously associated with hundreds of highrise towers erected in the suburbs of Paris, especially in the early 1960s. The defin-itive representation of this disastrous urban phenomenon is given in Jean-Luc Godard's 1967 film *Deux ou trois choses que je sais d'elle*—"her" being both the major character (played by Marina Vlady) and the whole Parisian region (Parisienne).

2. I have also used this pun in the translation I did, with Marie Vautier, of the anthology *Paris Québec*. There, it translates the title of a poem by Bernard Pozier. But Pozier himself was already punning on the phrase, since his title is "Les paris perdus," literally, "lost bets."

3. For a good example, see the photograph of the way the façade of the Hôtel de Sully was covered over by shop signs in the early years of the twen-tieth century: *Paris Then and Now*, 112–13.

4. Cf. Alastair Gordon: "In Paris a building is never just a building. New public architecture gets served up as a gourmand's feast of allegory and national politics" (in *Paris: Travelers' Tales Guides*, 1997, 81).

5. Woods quotes this phrase as an existing maxim, without giving a specific source. I am irresistibly reminded of Phyllis Webb's great Parisian poem, "Breaking": "A war is architecture for aggression" (46).

1. Jean-Luc Godard's 1965 film *Alphaville* presents Paris (though filmed entirely in the present) as a future dystopia controlled by an all-powerful computer.

2. A somewhat better version of this story is given by Michel Carmona: "Apparently Octavie let slip at dinner parties that she had no luck with her real estate purchases because whenever her husband advised her to invest in a particular block, it was always pulled down a few months later" (351). At the same time, Carmona defends Haussmann against any charges of outright corruption, citing (rather convincingly), Alphonse Alland: "Such a man, haughty and proud as he was, could never have agreed to the humiliation of a dishonest deal that would have made him bow his head before an accomplice, whoever he might be" (352). But Haussmann did die in comparative poverty: after his downfall, no tucked-away slush funds or hidden bank accounts were available to him.

3. Both books are cited by Eric Hazan as examples of "l'historiographie actuelle" (139). Hazan himself is having none of it. He complains that both Valance and Carmona "minimise to the point of the absurd" the extent of Haussmann's "préoccupations anti-émeutières": that is, concerns against riots, street demonstrations, barricades, revolution. See further discussion in the main text, below.

4. That is, Voltaire. See the quote at the beginning of this chapter. One of Haussmann's constructions was indeed named the boulevard Voltaire.

5. Equally, there is the counter-myth of the barricade itself as a privileged site. This myth extends from Victor Hugo's *Les Misérables* to its Broadway realization in the striking stage sets for *Les Mis*. Nor was it entirely missing from the iconography of May 1968.

6. Eric Hazan quotes an effective and striking passage from Dolf Oehler [my translation]: "To whom, among all those who today traverse the place Saint-Michel, do the figures on the fountain (surrounded by outlets for beer and Coca-Cola) have anything to say? Who would be able to interpret for tourists this allegory in its historical setting? Who could recognize that the Archangel, with his spear pointed at the back of Satan, must at the time have represented the triumph of the good over the evil people of June 1848? But during the period of the insurrections, on the threshold of a real revolution, this statue had an utterly unequivocal meaning. Everyone knew that this Saint-Michel symbolized the Second Empire obliterating the demon of revolution, and that the rue Saint-Jacques and

the Latin Quarter were supposed to recognize their own image in that of the hellish beast cast down to the ground."

7. Here as elsewhere, Cobb uses the term "Alphaville" to refer to the soulless suburbs, highrises, and HLMs around Paris. But he never attributes the word to its source: Jean-Luc Godard's 1965 film *Alphaville*, a futuristic dystopia filmed entirely in contemporary Paris. See also note 1, Chapter 1, for Godard's even more mordant revisiting of the theme in 1967.

8. If the place Dauphine is indeed, as André Breton claimed, the vagina of Paris, then it should be noted that the narrow passage between it and the Pont Neuf is now a one-way street. You can drive in, but you can't drive out; you can penetrate the womb, but you can't be born. See also Chapter 5, note 23.

9. Fair enough: but the next time after reading this passage that I was in Paris, I tried it out. I stood directly under the front façade, looking straight up, and tried to pretend that there was no open space behind me, that I could not get any farther back, could not get any more distanced view. And yes, I did get the sense Sasaki speaks of, of a tactile, physical weight pressing down on me. Yet at the same time, I also registered a very striking *visual* sensation: of the elongated perspective, of the layer upon layer of decoration pressing down on me yet also rising up from each other. Perhaps I am just a creature of the twentieth century, but it was still sight rather than touch that dominated my response.

10. "In 1765 the Parliament of Paris issued a decree that inaugurated...one of the most remarkable cultural revolutions of modern France: it banned all future burials in churchyards and called for the removal of the two hundred or more parish graveyards within Paris out beyond the city's formal limits, where huge new municipal cemeteries would in due course be created" (Burton, 130). A hundred years later, a proposal for a further logical extension of this idea—a mass graveyard even farther out of the city, accessible only by train—made a major contribution to the downfall of Haussmann (Burton, 134; LaFarge, Chapter 22).

11. At the same time, I recognize the attraction of Jane Jacobs's fine phrase, "the fundamentally deconstructive space of the local" (69).

12. Jones also notes that the trope persists, and that the innovations of the nineteenth century become in their turn fetishized: "Paris, the city of nineteenth-century modernity, was in danger of being set in aspic, with modernity transformed into nostalgia" (470).

1. Personally, I don't mind the top, above-ground level of the Forum des Halles; it has some quite pleasant places to stroll or sit in. But the underground shopping levels are indistinguishable from second-rate malls anywhere in Europe or North America. Louis Chevalier writes that the "so-called [sic] Forum des Halles...doubly offends me; by the removal of the original les Halles and by its replacement with this" (260). The buildings that were removed were not, of course, "original." Thirty years later, the whole complex is being rebuilt and redesigned.

2. As cited and translated in Evenson, 132. Evenson also (158) quotes André Hallays, from the same 1909 article that I cited on the first page of this section: "Yes, the sense of proportion today is abolished; but why should it not disappear in a city where, for more than twenty years, palace and church have been dominated by a useless hunk of metal three hundred meters high?"

3. I am delighted to note that I am shared in this ambition by no less than Socialist Prime Minister Lionel Jospin: see note 1, Chapter 10, Burton, *Blood in the City.* In his main text, Burton writes (and I applaud every word): "Sacré-Coeur is the least loved of the major Paris monuments. The left detests it because of the politics of its origins, liberal Catholics are embarrassed by its mixture of nationalism and religious masochism, and its neo-Byzantine massiveness benumbs the feelings and intellect even as it overwhelms the eye of the politically and religiously neutral" (174). Burton gives an extended commentary on the cult of the Sacred Heart and its link to the most extreme right-wing politics and writing of the period.

4. *A Fairly Good Time* (Laurentian Library edition, 1983); *Overhead in a Balloon* (Random House edition, 1985); *In Transit* (Penguin edition, 1988). The end-papers of William Weintraub's memoir *Getting Started* reproduce the front cover of an early edition of *The Other Paris*, which also shows the Eiffel Tower, but I have seen this image only in reproduction.

5. One of the very few exceptions is, oddly enough, Julien Green: "On one of my bedroom doors the sun has laid a fiery window. It is one of the windows in the Montparnasse Tower. I can see the original from my room, coloured ruby-red by the setting sun. I stand looking out for a moment, then turn, and there it is again, a little farther round on another door, a blazing pink and so clear that I can count the four panes. I have never seen such a beautiful refraction phenomenon except in the mountains" (123). I myself have some fond memories of the Tour

Montparnasse. From the street on which Maureen and I lived in both 1975 and 1985, rue Rousselet, the tower was exactly framed by buildings at the rue de Sèvres end of the street, and it formed a landmark by which to guide ourselves home. On the other hand, I have always resented its intrusion on the skyline over the trees of the Luxembourg Gardens.

6. It is to be hoped that the Pyramid will survive the crazier speculations attached to it in Dan Brown's irresponsible potboiler, *The Da Vinci Code*.

7. But it is worth noting that her "Introduction" to *Paris Notebooks*, written a mere five years later, reverses one of her main conclusions. The essay says that the Museum is "disorganized, inefficient, with a depressed and dwindled staff putting together shows of steadily diminishing quality" (172). The introduction concedes that the Museum is "now run with taste and imagination" (4).

8. See Chapter 17 for my own, rather disrespectful, response to this holy relic. The body was installed on the site in April 1830 and almost immediately gave rise to visions of the Virgin by Catherine Labouré, which in turn were commemorated by "miraculous medals," which continue to exert their force until this day (see Burton, Chapter 6).

PART TWO

"I IS AN OTHER"

1. In the past few decades, autobiography has been the subject of a great deal of theoretical speculation and redefinition. I make no pretence here to survey this large and fascinating field; what follows is a personal and fairly pragmatic summary. Neither am I preserving any very strict distinction between "autobiography" (which tends to be a retrospective summary of a whole life) and "memoir" (which tends to focus on a specific portion of a life, often defined by a delimited time and place— "Paris in the 20s").

2. See J. Gerald Kennedy's comment on Hemingway: "Inevitably, the Paris of *A Moveable Feast* is an imaginary city, a mythical scene evoked to explain the magical transformation of an obscure, Midwestern journalist into a brilliant modern author" (128). Here, Kennedy extends the process of fictionalization from the position of author/narrator/protagonist to the setting itself, the city of Paris, which becomes fully as imaginary, or as textual, as the constructed positions of the autobiographical voice.

3. In, that is, all later editions of the book. The first edition (New York: The Literary Guild, 1933) maintains the fiction: its title page reads simply *The Autobiography of Alice B. Toklas*.

4. Similarly, the book's most devastating dismissal of James Joyce is attributed not to Stein herself, but to Picasso, in a sideswipe that also takes care of Georges Braque, whom Stein always drastically undervalued (260).

5. For more discussion of this point, see Chapter 10.

6. See, for example, the concoction of the Dayang Muda's memoirs by Kay Boyle (161), and Glassco's own invention of the entirely non-existent memoirs of Madame Daudet (171).

7. If nothing else, Glassco had ensured the eventual revelation of his secret by leaving all the manuscripts to Library and Archives Canada. Some passages were written on the back of pages advertising horse shows in the 1960s. Much of the manuscript was also written in ball-point pen, a technology not existing in 1932. It is clear that Glassco enjoyed the deception for as long as it lasted; it is also clear that he did not intend it to last into posterity.

8. For Glassco's 1960s correspondence with Kay Boyle, see Michael Gnarowski's Introduction to the Second Edition of *Memoirs of Montparnasse*, xviii-xxii. Glassco may also have come across Matthew Josephson's *Life Among the Surrealists* (1962). A good extract from this book is included in Adam Gopnik's anthology *Americans in Paris*.

9. Kay Boyle (1902–1992), born in Minnesota, first came to France in 1923 with her husband, a French student named Richard Brault. Stifled by provincial life, she drifted towards Paris, where she worked for Sylvia Beach, and attached herself to the American expatriate group. She became devoted to the tubercular writer Ernest Walsh, and cared for him until his death in 1926. She was one of the founding editors of the literary magazine *This Quarter*. She then married Laurence Vail, and eventually returned to America. She was a successful and prolific author, publishing fourteen novels and numerous short stories. She also became a radical social activist, following her experiences in the 1950s as a victim of McCarthyism, and in the 1960s at universities in California. In the 1960s, she renewed an old friendship with John Glassco; their intense correspondence is discussed by Michael Gnarowski in the Introduction to the 2nd edition of *Memoirs of Montparnasse*.

10. "In one curious gesture," writes Kelly Pitman, "Boyle both appropriates McAlmon's writerly space and inscribes her own self-effacement. Her revised *Being Geniuses Together* is at once an act of homage and an act of terrorism" (seminar paper, University of Victoria).

11. For more discussion of the political implications of "nomads" from "the south," see Chapter 9.

PART THREE

4 → MISSING THE DIRECT WAY

1. The Balzac epigraph is as quoted by Priscilla Parkhurst Ferguson, *Paris as Revolution*, 90. The Gail Scott epigraph is from *My Paris*, 19.

2. Desnos, who was Jewish and active in the Resistance, was arrested and deported a mere few days before the Liberation of Paris. He died in a concentration camp at Terezin. In *Being Geniuses Together*, Kay Boyle gives an eloquent account of his funeral: "You were not permitted to fulfill the promise as 'one of the hopes of French literature,' but there was one more eternal moment written in the history of that literature when the great and the humble of Paris kneeled in the streets outside St. Germain des Prés (kneeling in homage even on the terrace of the Deux Magots) the day of your funeral, of the burying of the handful of bones that were left, in 1945, of all you were" (301). Desnos is commemorated now in the Deportation Memorial at the eastern end of the Île de la Cité, one of the most moving (and one of the least visited) sites in Paris. On the walls are carved the concluding lines of his great poem "Je vous ai tant rêvé." This poem, in adapted form, provides the opening to Part III of my Governor-General's-Award-winning book, *McAlmon's Chinese Opera*, and I have also attempted a full translation of it, which is included in my Selected Poems, *The Spaces In Between* (115–16). The appreciation of Desnos is one of many gifts I personally owe to John Glassco. To a shopkeeper on the rue de Seine, I owe the realization that both "S"s are pronounced: "Deznose," not "Deyno."

3. The best account of Kiki is by herself: *Kiki's Memoirs*, in the 1996 edition edited by Billy Klüver and Julie Martin, which includes her original text, translated by Samuel Putnam; a typically supercilious introduction by Ernest Hemingway; a selection of the many famous photographs of Kiki taken by her lover Man Ray; and a few reproductions of her own charming and naive paintings. The detailed description of Kiki was, apparently, an impromptu effort on Glassco's part. William Toye asked him for a more vivid portrayal, and he responded overnight. See Gnarowski's "Introduction," note 21, xxv.

4. It is a measure of the mock-sophistication with which Glassco presents himself that he should here so casually claim expertise in the drinking habits of Parisian prostitutes. Similarly, when "Narwhal" (Man

Ray) makes some interesting comments about de Sade, the response of Glassco's precocious young persona is not that he should read de Sade, but that he should *re*-read de Sade! (29).

5. The rue de la Glacière is actually a couple of hundred metres in the *opposite* direction from the one Glassco describes himself taking. Coming out of 147 rue Broca (now rue Léon-Maurice-Nordmann), one turns *right* to get to the rue de la Glacière; but one turns *left* to get to Glassco's described route via the Santé Prison and the Lion de Belfort. Does such an error really matter? Only if you are taking pride in the accuracy and expertise of your references to Parisian topography. But the wrongness of the detail helps to emphasize the degree to which Glassco here is constructing a fictional image rather than merely reporting on memory.

5 → THE STREET MAP OF PARIS

1. Michael Gnarowski annotates: "A heroic monument at the Place Denfert-Rochereau commemorating the heroism of the citizens of Belfort during the siege of that city in the Franco-Prussian war of 1870–71" (Glassco, 203). The very impressive lion was sculpted by Frederic Auguste Bartholdy, the creator of the Statue of Liberty. For more details on the place name Denfert-Rochereau, see below.

2. There is one, rather problematic, instance of a fictional name in Lola Lemire Tostevin's *The Jasmine Man*. See Chapter 14.

3. Gopnik is entitled to his opinion, but I personally would argue that, having crossed the Pont des Arts, he turns the wrong way. He should instead have turned east, towards the Pont Neuf, the Île de la Cité, and Notre-Dame.

4. The rue Gît-le-Coeur is a particularly narrow and, at one time, disreputable street, on the Left Bank just west of St.-Michel. In the mid-twentieth century, it featured a cheap lodging widely known as the Beat Hotel, due to the residence there of Gregory Corso, Allen Ginsberg, William S. Burroughs, and others. (See Barry Miles, *The Beat Hotel*, 2000.) Nowadays, the street is somewhat more upscale, with a couple of luxury hotels at prices the Beats could never have dreamed of.

5. To be nit-picking, however, one might point out that the rue du Pot-de-Fer does not intersect with the rue St.-Jacques!

6. In his *Mémoires*—quoted (without page attribution) by Eric Hazan, 25–26. For further discussion of Haussmann see Chapter 2.

7. In transcribing this passage, I have silently omitted Scott's habit of printing some (though not all) place names in bold face.

8. Véro and Dodat were both pork butchers, of humble origins. But Benoît Véro married a rich woman and prospered greatly. He and Dodat built the arcade in 1823–26, and took great pride in its opulence, especially the marble floor. Alas, the prosperity did not last. By 1845, Véro's sons were bankrupt, and one of them brought the story full circle by ending up working as a butcher's assistant. See Carmona, 130–31. As Scott testifies, the *passage* still exists, and is one of the loveliest of the remaining arcades.

9. I am using the word "index" in the sense developed by Pierce and Saussure, as a sign that directly points (like a street sign) to its referent.

10. The title is a line from Baudelaire's poem "Le Cygne," probably the single most frequently quoted line in discussions of mid-nineteenth-century Paris, and in the "Paris perdu" rhetoric discussed in Part One. "The form of a city changes faster, alas, than the human heart." Roubaud's book was published in an English translation by Keith and Rosmarie Waldrop (Dalkey Archive Press, 2006).

11. "And all that,—By Orient Express?—No, by Métro, with a simple Orange Card 2 zones." The "orange card" is the weekly or monthly ticket that allows unlimited travel on the Paris bus and Métro systems.

12. On Réda, see also "19, rue Rousselet," Chapter 13.

13. The area is not much better now. The "military depot or prison camp" is now the Jussieu campus of the Université de Paris V, a grim, concrete slab.

14. The context of this quote is not particularly flattering to Hemingway. He has been talking about not having enough money and about how he and his wife, Hadley, did not have enough to eat. Then Sylvia Beach delivers to him a cheque for six hundred francs from a German magazine. Beach tells him, very sensibly, "get home now and have lunch" (72)—that is, share the good fortune, the money, and the food with Hadley. But Hemingway does no such thing. Instead, he treats himself to a meal alone at the Brasserie Lipp (during which he again recalls the story of Hadley losing his manuscripts). Even then, though he notes that "walking up the rue Bonaparte [was] the shortest way home" (76), he does not go home, but goes to the Closerie des Lilas to drink coffee and "work." Hadley is not mentioned again in this chapter.

15. See Higonnet, 163–64: a system of street numbering was introduced in 1779, but it was irregular and confusing. Systematic and compulsory numbering was introduced under Napoleon in 1805.

16. Dorothea Tanning, American painter and wife of Max Ernst, recalls: "The rue Guillaume Apollinaire was a subject of much jesting among literary buffs and artists who would point out to you its doll-like length occupied by two massive gray buildings *sans* numbers, *sans* entrances, these being located around the corners on its two busy right-angle streets. You could *walk* on the rue Guillaume Apollinaire but you could not *live* there. Max said Apollinaire would have laughed and loved his phantom street....[A] few years later the city fathers got busy when no one was looking and had a couple of doors punched in the side of their building...and numbers conspicuously added to dress them up" (*Americans in Paris*, 607-08). The street now has an excellent cinema, the St.-Germain-des-Prés, with deep associations to the Nouvelle Vague. For a rather different memory of the Café Bonaparte, see Stan Persky, *The Short Version*, 237-40.

17. Not strictly true, as I noted above.

18. At this point, I am concerned with the "poetry" inherent in the *names* of Métro stations. But there is also, more literally, the question of poems written by and about riders on the Métro. For a contemporary example, see Marc Lapprand, "Jacques Jouet, Metro Poet," *SubStance* 96 (Vol. 30, no. 3), 2002, 17-26.

19. Richard D.E. Burton reports that "antisemitic fantasists of the Belle Époque believed [the Métro] to be part of a Jewish plot literally to undermine Paris" (289)!

20. Walter Benjamin actually answers this question—see below.

21. See Chapter 14.

22. Similarly, in one of Colette's earliest novels, *Claudine in Paris*, when Claudine goes out for her first unaccompanied walk on the streets of Paris, she is followed by a "very good-looking gentleman" who "passed me, pinching my behind with a detached expression" (29). This incident occurs, of course, on the rue des Saints-Pères.

23. Years later, Breton elaborated a symbolic "map" of Paris as "the body of a recumbent woman whose vagina is located in the Place Dauphine" (Sheringham, 89).

24. Parts of this discussion of the proper name are reproduced, or modified, from some of my earlier works, notably discussions of the "alias" in relation to Bob Dylan. See *Alias Bob Dylan Revisited* (Calgary: Red Deer Press, 2003), 42-43.

25. There are some exceptions: for example in totalitarian countries, where living dictators are all too eager to name boulevards and parade grounds after themselves. In Canada at any rate, it seems accepted that Montreal's

transformation of "Dorchester" into "René Levesque" could have taken place only after the latter's death. Indeed, the reaction to Jean Chrétien's hasty proposal to rename Mount Logan after Pierre Elliott Trudeau led to a proposal for a five-year moratorium before any renaming in honour of the dead. (Another possible exception might be found in the renaming of an Edmonton street "Wayne Gretzky Way": but, symbolically, Wayne Gretzky has been dead in Edmonton ever since he was traded to the Los Angeles Kings.) There is one wonderful instance of strategic renaming in Glasgow, where in the early 1980s the city fathers renamed Royal Exchange Place as Nelson Mandela Place, thus forcing the South African Trade Commission, located at that address, to include on all their letterhead and official communications the name of the man who was still, at that time, as far as the South African government was concerned, a jailed terrorist.

26. Scott's entire book, *My Paris*, may be read as an extended tribute to, or dialogue with, Benjamin. On the second page of her novel, she tells us that when she moved into her studio, she found that the previous occupant had left behind a copy of the French translation of *The Arcades Project*, and for the entire course of the novel, she reads from it, quotes it, cites it as an authority. It is rare to go for more than two pages in *My Paris* without running across a reference to Benjamin.

27. "Haunts," here, as in the quote from Ferguson above, may be no more than a figure of speech. But the relationship between the proper name (identity) and the ghost (especially in Derrida) is an endlessly fascinating one. Again one might refer to André Breton's *Nadja*, which on its very first page comments that the word "haunt" "makes me, still alive, play a ghostly part, evidently referring to what I must have ceased to be in order to be *who* I am" (11).

28. Both Cobb and Benjamin mention Solférino, which is situated in a particularly staid district of the 7th arrondissement. Is it because Solférino, as the name of a Napoleonic battle, contrasts so much with the mundane realities of government bureaucracy; or is it because the name suggests a sulferous whiff of the underground as Hellfire? "It is owing to these stations," Benjamin writes, "that the names of places where Napoleon I gained a victory are transformed into gods of the underworld" (847).

29. As quoted (and translated) by David Frisby, in Tester, 81. The quotation comes from Hessel's *Spazieren in Berlin*, Vienna/Leipzig, 1929, a book that was reviewed by Walter Benjamin. One of the earliest stages of *The*

Arcades Project was a proposal for an essay to be written collaboratively by Benjamin and Hessel.

30. Benjamin refers specifically to "the excellent publication by Taride, with its twenty-two maps of all the Parisian *arrondissements*" (85). I don't have a Taride publication, but I assume that Benjamin is talking about a small book similar to two that I do have: *Paris par Arrondissement* (Éditions L'Indispensable) and *Plan de Paris: rues, métro, autobus* (Éditions Leconte). The point is that all these "maps" of Paris are in fact *books*, the maps being preceded by an exhaustive index of street names, and bus routes. So in its very form—as a small softcover which one can slip into a pocket or a purse—the map of Paris *is* a book.

31. De Certeau's perception of the World Trade Center as a privileged site of power was to be confirmed, all too tragically, by the events of September 11, 2001, twenty years after he wrote this passage. See also Chapter 3 for a similar account (via Maupassant and Barthes) of the Tour Eiffel as "a viewpoint and nothing more."

32. See, for instance, the endless mappings and re-mappings of "Yugoslavia," which for over a hundred years have not only *reflected* violence, but have actively *produced* it. Many of these maps were of course drawn up in Paris, in the negotiations leading up to the Treaty of Versailles. The definitive account is given by Margaret MacMillan in *Paris 1919: Six Months that Changed the World* (New York: Random House, 2002).

33. No "accurate" maps perhaps: but certainly there had been maps, of some sort, for centuries. Colin Jones notes that the first printed maps of Paris appeared in the 1530s, and that "over a hundred" appeared in the eighteenth century—though he makes no claim for their accuracy. "Maps, guidebooks and almanacs were increasingly made available in pocket-book size...for the inquisitive pedestrian" (178)—that is, for the flâneur.

34. "Cognitive mapping describes the assimilation of sensory impressions about the places we inhabit or traverse not as raw impressions but as a 'code' of meaningful signs which collectively produce a mental map. This cartography enables us to function by producing a sense of distance and relation and by schematizing our experiential world in terms of valued or significant sites" (Kennedy, 13–14).

35. Note that Marie here retraces part of the route taken by Jake and Bill in *The Sun Also Rises* (cited above): the Île Saint-Louis, the wooden footbridge, the prospect of Notre-Dame. She might thus see, at the end of Île de la Cité, the grilled window to the Deportation Memorial, with

its inscription from Robert Desnos. The Memorial was opened in 1962; Gallant's story was published in 1966.

6→ THE FLÂNEUR

1.   Even so, my spell check does not recognizes it, and suggests instead "flamer," "flanker," "flayer," and "fanner"—all of which offer promising shades of meaning.

2.   See *The invisible flâneuse?: Gender, public space, and visual culture in nineteenth-century Paris*, ed. Aruna D'Souza and Tom McDonough (Manchester: Manchester University Press, 2006).

3.   Most accounts of the nineteenth-century flâneur stress that he moves through the crowds unseen: a watcher who is himself invisible. The Internet has coined a word for precisely this quality: lurker.

4.   But, on the other hand, see Benjamin Franklin's observations, from as early as 1767: "the Streets by constant Sweeping are fit to walk in tho' there is no pav'd foot Path. Accordingly many well dress'd People are constantly seen walking in them" (*Americans in Paris*, 4). By 1833, however, Ralph Waldo Emerson found Paris to be "a loud modern New York of a place" (*Americans in Paris*, 54)!

5.   One of the arguments against the possibility of twentieth-century flânerie is that the automobile again rendered Parisian streets unwalkable. And, indeed, it is true that no one would want to stroll at a lobster's pace across any of the major boulevards. Yet I personally feel that what has been rendered impossible by the choking traffic of contemporary Paris is not so much walking for pleasure as driving for pleasure (not to mention parking). On the side streets, the pedestrian can still negotiate Paris traffic without anything near the discomfort Levenstein describes for the early nineteenth century. And traffic circulation does not entirely rule Parisian streets. Whole streets can still be closed down for regular markets, or for festivals like the midsummer-night Fête de la Musique (when one can indeed stroll down the boulevards and experience the pure anarchic pleasure of standing in the centre of the intersection of the boulevard Saint-Germain and the boulevard Saint-Michel). Or there is the quintessential Parisian experience of a street being entirely blocked by a delivery truck, whose driver is carrying a package to a fifth floor *sans ascenseur*, blithely ignoring the honking horns of the cars backed up behind him. The pedestrian casually slipping past this blockage, or wandering through the street market on the rue de Buci, is still, to my mind, a flâneur.

6. The fact that White's book is an extremely disappointing and superficial sketch should not obscure the significance of its title.

7. Ferguson notes that Balzac also uses the verb *jouir* in relation to the flâneur, with the same erotic connotation (90).

8. There is a fine ironic comment on this point in, of all places, Alfred Hitchcock's film *Vertigo*. The film's protagonist, Scotty, defines what he does, quintessentially alone, as "wandering." Later, as his equivocal relationship with the woman he knows as Madeleine develops, there occurs between them the following exchange, which to me reads almost as a conscious commentary on the solitariness of the flâneur:

> *Madeleine: I just thought that I'd wander.*
> *Scotty: That's what I was going to do.*
> *Madeleine: Oh yes, I forgot. It's your occupation, isn't it?*
> *Scotty: Don't you think it's kind of a waste of time for us...*
> *Madeleine: ...to wander separately? Only one is a wanderer. Two together are always going somewhere.*
> *Scotty: No-o-o. I don't think that's necessarily true.*
> *Madeleine: You left your door open.*
> *Scotty: Be right back.*

9. The argument that "women shop" is the criterion most often advanced for excluding women from the possibility of being a flâneur. "She is unfit for *flânerie*," writes Ferguson, "because she desires the objects spread before her and acts upon that desire" (Tester, 27). And again, "The flâneur desires the city as a whole, not any part of it. No woman can disconnect herself from the city and its seductive spectacle. For she must either desire the objects spread before her or herself be the object of desire.... Women figure the observed, they cannot possibly reverse roles to join the observers" (*Paris as Revolution*, 84–85). While these surprisingly sexist distinctions between male and female attitudes towards desire (and shopping) may be valid in terms of nineteenth-century social assumptions, it still seems to me a weak argument. To go out deliberately seeking and purchasing a specific object is certainly not flânerie: but what about window shopping, or browsing? Ferguson may not see window shopping as flânerie, but Baudelaire certainly did: Christopher Prendergast quotes a line from one of his notebooks: "La flânerie devant les boutiques, cette jouissance" (36). As the arcade evolves into the department store and the shopping mall, more and more sophisticated techniques are used to

induce the passer-by to purchase, but it is still possible for a flâneur, male or female, to maintain a state of detachment; to look but not to buy; to be, in Solnit's words, "more than an audience but less than a participant."

10. Note that, for Baudelaire, dandyism is far more a mental attitude than a matter of dress and fashion: "Contrary to what a lot of thoughtless people seem to believe, dandyism is not even an excessive delight in clothes and material elegance. For the perfect dandy, these things are no more than the symbol of the aristocratic superiority of his mind" (420). This point seems to me important in relation to John Glassco. Glassco could not *afford* the fine clothes of a Beau Brummel-type dandy (though he always aspired to them). Nevertheless, I am sure that he always thought of himself as a dandy in Baudelairean terms. See "Brummell at Calais," Glassco's fine tribute to "A foolish useless man who had done nothing" (*Selected Poems*, 56–57).

11. This image of an older, purer Paris might also be seen as another form of "Paris perdu" rhetoric.

12. It should be noted, though, that Chambers, unlike Ferguson, sees this role as existing mainly in the pre-1848 period. Later, he argues, "The shift that Baudelaire was to introduce into this understanding of the flâneur involved turning him from an inspector (of the working class) into a critical reader (of the class configuration itself), and it required him to overcome his bourgeois sense of solitude and invisibility in order to accept both the reader's connectedness to the city-text and a sense of community with the peripheral figures this new, parasitic, mediatory status associated him with" (219). This view, which offers an alternative history of the flâneur's development, is argued in somewhat dense detail in "Flâneur Reading (On Being Belated)," a chapter in Chambers's charmingly titled book *Loiterature*.

7 → DEVIOUS ROUTES

1. All quotations from Sheila Watson's Paris diary are taken from the text published as part of Fred Flahiff's biography, *always someone to kill the doves: a Life of Sheila Watson* (Edmonton: NeWest Press, 2005). Flahiff notes that he has silently corrected many misspellings, in both English and French, especially of French place names. Having seen a copy of the original typescript, I agree that such mistakes were numerous. Flahiff's biography is the major source (along with my own personal knowledge) for facts about Sheila Watson's life.

2. Flahiff always refers to this woman, rather too coyly, as "Wilfred's young friend." Her identity is well known to those who were close to the Watsons, but it has not entered the public discourse. I myself do not know the woman's name.

3. See the diary entry for April 12: "There is marriage and there is a marriage contract—the contract is material and temporal. Marriage itself is an act of faith and consequently an act of perfect love—or inversely and perhaps more truly, an act of perfect love consequently an act of faith. Only a belief such as this would have made and did make the first years of our marriage possible" (149–50).

4. For a full discussion of Wilfred Watson's poetic career, one that attempts to discuss it on its own merits, without reference to Sheila, see Stephen Scobie, "Love in the Burning City: The Poetry of Wilfred Watson." *Essays on Canadian Writing*, 18/19 (Summer/Fall, 1980), 281–303.

5. Watson uses the phrase "Peripatetic speculators" just once (113). It's a sentence fragment whose reference is not clear, wedged ambiguously between references to crabs and to books by Jean Cocteau! But it is an almost ideal definition of the flâneur.

6. This is as far as I am prepared to go down the invidious path of comparing the literary accomplishments of Wilfred and Sheila Watson. In the light of Sheila's achievements in *The Double Hook*, *Deep Hollow Creek*, and *Five Stories*, it is all too easy to dismiss Wilfred's work as minor, and to become annoyed, even furious, at the extent to which she was prepared to subordinate herself to him. But Wilfred continued to produce remarkable work, both in poetry and in theatre. Sheila's devotion to him may have been hurtful to herself, but it was never entirely misguided.

7. In addition to the passages quoted here, see, among many possible examples, a "great circuit" around the Tuileries (101); a long walk from the Opéra to the place des Vosges (108–09); and another slow approach to the place des Vosges (152).

8. That is, to the quai des Grands Augustins and to the rue des Grands Augustins, where Picasso lived in the 30s and 40s, and where he painted *Guernica*.

9. Watson is here just a couple of years early for the occupation of the famous "Beat Hotel" at 9, rue Gît-le-Coeur, by Ginsberg, Corso, Burroughs, et al. The Beat heyday at this address fell between 1957 and 1963. See also Chapter 5, note 4.

10. Some of it overlaps the route covered by Gertrude Stein on her visits to Picasso—see Chapter 11.

11. In addition to the explicit quote from Hopkins, might one not read here at least an echo of Ezra Pound's "In a Station of the Métro": "petals on a wet, black bough"?

12. For Hopkins, "inscape" was the quality of utter individuality and beauty that every thing possessed; "instress" was the active force by which that quality was realized and communicated.

13. There is no sexual edge to this stress on solitude. Watson's journal never gives any hint that she might feel sexually threatened by being a woman alone on the streets of Paris. If Gallant feels at risk, it is more from political than from sexual violence. In Scott, however, sexual danger is always present.

14. "Nasser" indicates a reference to the buildup towards war over the Suez Canal, which broke out some three months later. One week earlier, on the occasion of the July 14 national holiday, Watson had written: "There was no real sense of a fête. The war in Algeria is too much a fact" (158).

15. Cf. her comments on the novel in "What I'm Going To Do," transcribed and edited by Stephen Scobie, *Open Letter*, Third Series, 1 (Winter, 1974–75), 181–83.

8→ MAVIS GALLANT ON THE STREETS OF MAY 68

1. "Events" is the usual term, somewhat euphemistic, applied to the political upheavals in France in May 1968. They began with student protests in the universities and workers' strikes in the factories; the unexpected joining of these two separate movements shook the authority of the French state to its foundations. As students occupied their universities and workers their factories, there were mass demonstrations against the government of President Charles de Gaulle. De Gaulle indeed at one point left France, but only to ensure the loyalty of French army units posted in Germany. After a few dizzy weeks, the government reasserted its authority, and "May 68" faded into memory and mythology.

2. "Don't get near" may simply be an abbreviation, omitting the "I." But it can also be read as a warning, the writer advising herself to keep a safe distance.

3. The formulation here is strikingly similar to John Glassco's "This young man is no longer myself: I hardly recognize him" in the "Prefatory Note" to *Memoirs of Montparnasse*. It would be tempting to read Gallant as alluding not only to Glassco's "Note" but also to the manifest falsity of that "Note." But by and large I have chosen to take Gallant's Notebooks at

face value, and not to worry too much here about the problematics of the autobiographical "I."

4. One of Gallant's continuing preoccupations, as witness her long-mooted book on the Dreyfus Affair, is French anti-Semitism and xenophobia. The support given to Cohn-Bendit by French students was one of the first things that attracted her attention early in 1968; and clearly, for her, the moral high point of the month is reached on May 22, when she hears a demonstration of students chanting *"Nous sommes tous des juifs allemands* [We are all German Jews]": "It is the most important event, I think, since the beginning of this fantastic month of May, because it means a mutation in the French character: a generosity. For the first time, I hear a French voice go outside the boundaries of being French" (*Paris Notebooks*, 33).

5. See Gallant, *Paris Notebooks*, 23–24. De Gaulle's words were "La réforme, oui; la chienlit, non." Gallant reports that "Nobody knows what it means." She finds it in a dictionary as "carnival mask," but a friend reports that it is "a filthy expression." Gallant implies, but does not state directly, that it really is three words, chie en lit, shit in bed. The word is all over the papers; "everyone is shocked and upset." But what Gallant and her friends were not, apparently, aware of is that 1968 was not the first occasion on which de Gaulle had used this word to describe a situation of civil unrest on the streets of Paris. When he re-entered Paris in August 1944, de Gaulle intensely disapproved of the near-anarchy that prevailed immediately after the Liberation, and he moved quickly to impose a sense of order. He displayed, according to Jean Dutour, "a horror of this *chienlit*" (quoted in Burton, 242; see Burton, 239–43 for the full context). Dutour was a Resistance fighter who published his memoirs, which include this citation of the word, in 1965. So it is just possible that de Gaulle, if he had read Dutour's book, may have been reminded of "chienlit" less than three years before May 68. One of the Readers of this manuscript has informed me that the word goes back as far as 1740 and was used by Montherlant to mean a person poorly dressed: dirty, unruly, disorderly.

6. It is interesting to note how many of Gallant's short stories are about refugees: about foreigners in Paris who (mainly for economic reasons) do not have the freedom to "pack up and leave."

7. All the quotations in this passage are from *The Arcades Project*, but Clark does not give specific references—a rather unhelpful gesture, when reviewing a thousand-page book.

8. This "impulse to walk" is echoed on a humorous note, late in the Notebooks, on June 1, when Gallant listens to a news broadcast from the BBC, and learns that "The world's walking record has been broken by a man named John Sinclair. He walked a hundred and seventy-six times around an aerodrome" (90)!

9. For a detailed account, see Adam Gopnik, *Paris to the Moon*, "The Balzar Wars" (228–38) and "A Handful of Cherries" (271–95). Gopnik concludes that the struggle to preserve the character and standards of the Balzar was, ultimately, lost. My own reaction on recent visits has been equivocal: I've had good meals there, and mediocre ones as well. But I still go. For a short time after Gopnik's book appeared, the Balzar suffered from a rush of American tourists; but it now seems to have resumed a stolidly French clientele.

10. See my entry for May 6, 2002, in Chapter 17.

9→ "LOVING WALKING HERE"

1. Passing the famous Montparnasse cafés, the Dôme and the Sélect, Scott comments: "Where Hemingway declaring. Paris belonging to him. Situated only few blocks from leisure lottery studio. Reinforcing sense of having stumbled into some mythological space" (35).

2. Some very fine distinctions hinge on that "or."

3. In this chapter, I am largely assuming a straightforward identification between author, narrator, and protagonist. But for a more problematic discussion of these positions in *My Paris*, see Part Two.

4. As I have already noted, Benjamin is her authority throughout the book. She refers to him constantly, rarely going for more than two or three pages without a citation. But none of these references is critical. *The Arcades Project* is accepted, at face value, as an authoritative text.

5. I cannot quite bring myself to see a Métro-rider as a flâneur. But perhaps a case could be made for a bus-rider, since knowledge of the Parisian bus-system is a truly arcane subject. If the flâneur's true habitat is the Parisian *street*, then it must be noted that the Métro ignores streets (except in the names of its stations), whereas the bus system is entirely dependent on streets, especially one-way streets, which often determine the vagaries of its routes. There are few better "walks" through Paris than the 38, the 39, the 63, or the 82.

6. The choice of "wanderers," rather than "walkers" or "strollers," surely echoes Robin Vote, in Djuna Barnes' *Nightwood*, whose "wandering" (42) is both literal and metaphorical.

7. I myself remember a similar incident. In 1985, I stayed in Paris for six months and went through the proper bureaucratic procedures (including the expedited queues) of applying for a Carte de Séjour. It was issued to me one day before I was due to leave. For the much easier experience of Wilfred and Sheila Watson, see her journal (115) and the reproductions of their actual cards (92–93).

8. Not unconnected, perhaps, to the attacks of eczema she suffers throughout the book.

9. "Raining in Sarajevo" (35, 61, 113); "In Sarajevo people strolling in fog" (42); "Raining in Bosnia" (77, 83); "Snowing in Sarajevo" (137); "Blizzard in Bosnia" (146); "Snowing in Bosnia" (150).

10··▸ JOHN GLASSCO AND THE ETHICS OF PLEASURE

1. "By 1900 Paris had an all-time high number of cafés—27,000, which, together with wineshops and cabarets, gave it more drinking places (11.25 for every thousand residents) than any other major city in the world" (Rearick, 28).

2. Engels himself was not immune to the pleasures of Paris. In *The Arcades Project*, Benjamin copied out at length an ecstatic rhapsody from Engels on the subject of French wine: "And what wine! What variety—from bordeaux to burgundy, from burgundy to full-bodied Saint-Georges, to Lünel and the South's Frontignan, and from there to sparkling champagne! What a choice of whites and reds—from Petit Mâcon or chablis to Chambertin, to Château Larose, to sauterne, to Vin du Roussillon, and Aï Mousseux! Bear in mind that each of these wines produces a different sort of intoxication, and that with a few bottles one can pass through all the intervening stages from a Musard quadrille to 'La Marseillaise,' from the wanton pleasures of the cancan to the fiery ardor of revolutionary fever, thence to return, with a bottle of champagne, to the cheeriest carnival mood in the world! And only France has a Paris, a city in which European civilization attains its fullest flowering, in which all the nerve fibers of European history are intertwined, and from which arise, at regular intervals, those tremors that shake the terrestrial globe; a city whose population unites, like that of no other city on earth, the passion for enjoyment with the passion for historical action, whose inhabitants know how to live like the most refined of Athenian epicures and to die like the most unflinching Spartan—Alcibiades and Leonidas rolled up into one; a city which really is, as Louis Blanc says, the heart and brain

of the world" (704–05). This is not the kind of rhetoric one normally associates with the founding member of international Communism.

3. Would it be fanciful to hear in this phrase a parodic echo of Hemingway's "Movable Feast"? It may also be noted that very similar inflatable erections were deployed in the ceremonies attending France's staging of the soccer World Cup in 1998.

4. Hera is notoriously vindictive, and is of course the wife of Zeus. If we combine these characteristics—power, vindictiveness, wife—we come up with something very close to "Mrs. Quayle [quail]." Thus, the ending of *Memoirs of Montparnasse* could well be read as Hera's revenge on Paris for choosing Aphrodite.

5. Adam Gopnik, discussing the question of fashion (why the Café de Flore remains fashionable while Aux Deux Magots has fallen from favour), quotes an unnamed Parisian friend as saying: "The reason that when you place any two things side by side, one becomes chic and the other does not is that it's in the nature of desire to choose, and to choose *absolutely*. That's the mythological lesson of the great choice among the beauties: They are all beautiful—they are goddesses—and yet a man must choose. And what was the chooser's name? Paris" (85).

6. Aragon gives a hilariously straight-faced description of the transactions in a "handkerchief" shop in the Passage de l'Opéra: "I have often noticed, from my observation post in the Certa, that this is the way the proprietress invariably treats her customers. A single one is allowed in at a time, he remains for ten or fifteen minutes, the door locked from the inside, then he leaves again and the door stays open until the arrival of a new visitor. Coyness, infirmity? People must need to blow their noses very frequently when they are no longer very young" (96). And later, of one of the customers: "he is in something of a hurry to disappear into the shadows where I can just make out the languid movements of a pair of hands. Follow your inclinations boldly, stranger. You have my blessing, and that is a great deal, believe me. He grows taut. He writhes. Oh, he certainly didn't take very long, did he!" (102).

7. An error on Glassco's part. The name should be spelt "Archevêché," and it is not a rue, but either a pont or a quai.

8. Thus we return again to the same cityscape celebrated by Hemingway and Gallant, the view of the Deportation Memorial, with its ultimate tribute to the memory of Robert Desnos. The Memorial was opened in 1962, so it is unlikely that Glassco would have been aware of it when writing the first draft of the *Memoirs* in 1964; however, he did visit Paris

again in 1967, before the publication of the revised version, so at least the possibility exists that he may have been aware of Desnos's subliminal presence in this scene.

9. A final triumph of the compulsion of names: even when Glassco is down and out, he has to inscribe the name of the bridge he sleeps under.

10. The same church whose gargoyles did not speak to Sheila Watson.

PART FOUR

11··→ A WALK WITH GERTRUDE STEIN

1. There are several other uses of the phrase, in texts such as "An Elucidation" and "Stanzas in Meditation." I make no pretence here to an exhaustive listing.

2. Compare Stein's comments on how she reacted to her full comprehension of Cézanne's paintings: "This then was a great relief to me and I began my writing" (*Lectures in America*, 77).

3. For a splendid discussion and defence of Stein's egotism, see Karin Cope, *Passionate Collaborations: Learning to Live with Gertrude Stein* (Victoria, BC: ELS Editions, 2005). Cope also discusses the challenges to Stein's self-confidence evident in the 1930s, especially in *The Autobiography of Alice B. Toklas* and *Everybody's Autobiography*.

4. Or, she might have added, Scottish poetry: Robert Burns, "O my Luve's like a red, red rose" (1794).

5. Though even here, we might ask: What is it that makes a rose smell "sweet"? Are we not culturally preconditioned (partly through the associations of the name) to find the scent of a rose "sweeter" than the scent of a skunk?

6. Frank Muir and Dennis Norden appeared on a BBC radio show called *My Word*. Their weekly challenge was to come up with a comic explanation for the source of a well-known phrase. I heard this story on the radio forty years ago, and I have no precise citation for it. I remember the punchline, but I have reconstructed the build-up. This is not a precise quotation, but I owe it all to Frank Muir.

7. For a short list, see the Wikipedia website on this phrase, which lists references from Hemingway to Margaret Thatcher, from Aretha Franklin to Jeannette Winterson, and a Scottish rock band called Idlewild. Two fairly rudimentary tributes are included in my own *Stone Poems* (1970).

8. Gertrude Jekyll was one of the most important figures in British garden design and theory in the early twentieth century. "Jekyll" is pronounced to rhyme with "she-kill." I will always remember Ian saying to me

(sometime in the 1970s), "Don't you know her, Stephen? She's the gardener lady"—with the particular inflection of "gardener lady" (strong stress on the first syllable) giving it an undying music.

9. At the foot of the rough track leading to his home at Little Sparta, there was an inscription that read, accurately, "The way up and the way down are one and the same."

10. Of all the Stein biographies, there is only one that I am aware of that attempts to reconstruct this route. Linda Wagner-Martin, in *"Favoured Strangers": Gertrude Stein and Her Family*, writes: "[Gertrude] traveled several times a week to the flat in the Bateau Lavoir, called the 'laundry boat' because of its misshapen structure. Sometimes she walked the four miles, going down the rue des Saints Pères, crossing the Seine near the Louvre and continuing down the rue de Richelieu past the Bibliothèque Nationale; at Boulevard Clichy, the cobbled streets ascended toward Montmartre. On other occasions, she took the horse-drawn omnibus across Paris from the Odéon up to the Place Blanche and then continued up hill to the little square that adjoined Picasso's studio" (72). This route closely accords with the one that I worked out for myself, looking at the map. Wagner-Martin cites as her source for this description Barbara Pollack, *The Collectors: Dr. Claribel and Miss Etta Cone* (Indianapolis: Bobbs-Merrill, 1962), 74.

11. The Larousse encyclopaedia defines "Lorette" thus: "Au debut du XIXe s., jeune femme élégante et de moeurs faciles."

12. It has been widely documented that her early book *Three Lives* owes a great debt to the *contes* of Flaubert; and Linda Wagner-Martin makes an interesting case for her self-identification with Georges Sand. Despite her close friendship with Guillaume Apollinaire, there is little evidence that she read a great deal of early twentieth-century French literature. Her knowledge of French was certainly greater than that of many of the American expatriates (such as Djuna Barnes, who spoke little to no French), but in conversation she tended to exercise it more in the countryside than in Paris.

13. Nowadays, like Saint-Sulpice (see below), the Pyramid has been hijacked into the ludicrous fantasies of Dan Brown's *The Da Vinci Code*.

12-→ WRESTLING WITH THE ANGEL

1. Which, incidentally, shares with Wilfred Watson's *Friday's Child* the editorial benediction of T.S. Eliot.

2. Matthew O'Connor, the fictional character in Barnes's novel, is based on an actual person, Daniel Mahoney, who also appears, under the barely disguised name Dan Maloney, in John Glassco's *Memoirs of Montparnasse*. O'Connor's anguished monologes are among the greatest rhetorical *tours de force* in *Nightwood*.

3. I am assuming that Robin and Felix live close to Saint-Sulpice; actually, this is one of the few addresses on which Barnes is not explicit. Of Felix's "rooms," she says only that he chose them because of their association with "a Bourbon [who] had been carried from them to death" (9); she never says where exactly they were.

4. The 1995 scholarly edition of *Nightwood*, edited by Cheryl J. Plumb, annotates this convent as "unidentified" (220)—which is somewhat surprising, since Barnes's description identifies it quite clearly. There is only one convent on the rue Picpus with a cemetery which includes the grave of Lafayette; it is not a secluded location, but offers a guided tour every afternoon.

5. See the editorial note: *Les Misérables* (Penguin, 1982), 427.

6. One week later, in Hamburg, I walked into an exhibition by the Scottish poet Ian Hamilton Finlay, who was fascinated by the issues posed by the French Revolution, and found myself in the middle of his profound and moving tribute to the victims of the Picpus Cemetery.

7. Perhaps the most famous example is Perec's novel *La Disparition* (1969), which entirely omits the letter e. It was translated into English, by Gilbert Adair, as *A Void* (1994). For a recent Canadian example of Oulipian virtuosity, see Christian Bök, *Eunoia* (2001).

8. For someone who knows the Parisian bus system, the numbers act as metonymies for the whole route. The 63 is one of my favourite bus routes in Paris; I ride it often. So the mere number evokes for me a whole urban landscape.

9. I actually met Etel Adnan once, and, not surprisingly, it was at Saint-Sulpice. Each June, the square in front of the church is transformed into a Fête de la Poésie, the whole space crammed with stalls of small publishers specializing in poetry. I had already read *Paris When It's Naked*, so when I saw a stall stocked with other Adnan books, I went up to it and soon realized that the woman behind the table was Etel Adnan herself. We had a very pleasant conversation. She signed a book for me and told me a wonderful story of tracking down the reclusive Djuna Barnes at her Patchin Place apartment in New York.

10. For a very similar incident, see my own poem on the Café de la Mairie du VIème, "For Djuna Barnes" (*The Spaces In Between*, 110).

11. In all my reading of Delacroix, Jacob, and the Angel, there is an intertextual undercurrent, which may be no more than an entirely personal flight of association on my part, of Bob Dylan. I make no claim for any deliberate allusion on Dylan's part; indeed, I would find it unlikely. My own association depends in part on a painting that I once saw but can no longer trace or give a definite reference for: a portrait of the young Delacroix that looked to me uncannily like the Dylan of 1965. Accidental or otherwise, there are plenty of cross-references. Jacob's renaming as Israel is perhaps the greatest single instance in the Old Testament of the alias as destiny, the new name that will found a nation, in the same way as Robert Zimmerman's renaming of himself as Dylan was the foundational gesture of his career. The limp that Jacob carries as a result of his struggle (*Genesis* 32: 31) is not only the "wound in the thigh" of Oedipus or the Grail legend's Fisher King, but also the literal trace of polio in Dylan's father, Abraham Zimmerman. Like his Biblical namesake, Dylan's son Jakob is the grandson of Abraham. In the year of Jakob's birth, Dylan wrote a love song for his mother, Sara (the Biblical Abraham's wife), which begins: "You angel you / You got me under your wing" (324). One year later, in "Tangled Up In Blue," Dylan wrote of a semi-autobiographical protagonist who worked on a fishing boat "outside of Delacroix" (331): the reference is to the fishing port on the Gulf of Mexico, but it can also be read in relation to the painter's name, to that name's literal meaning ("of the Cross"), and to the whole problematic of parenthood implicit in the painting. All of these themes are discussed in detail in my book *Alias Bob Dylan Revisited* (2003). Most of the echoes remain, I admit, accidental: yet they accumulate into a rich intertextual weave that persists, for me, only just "outside of Delacroix."

12. Jacob may in many ways be seen as an instance of the Trickster (another parallel to Dylan). See also the profoundly funny *Beyond the Fringe* sketch on the text "I am a smooth man" (*Genesis* 27: 11).

13. For a full treatment of this topic, see Jean-Paul Kauffmann, *Wrestling with the Angel: The Mystery of Delacroix's Mural* (2003). While I find much of Kauffmann's book overstated, I am indebted to it for a good deal of my fascination with Delacroix's painting.

1. Rue Rousselet is in fact equidistant between the Vaneau and Duroc Métro stations. Which stop you get off at depends on which direction you're coming from. In terms of buses, the corner of rue Rousselet and rue de Sèvres is serviced by the 39, 72, and 87 routes. The 39 and 72 go both ways, but the 87 has a different route heading back out from the centre: it goes down the rue de Babylone, stopping at the wonderful cinema called La Pagode and thus demands a slightly longer walk (via the rue Monsieur) back to rue Rousselet.

2. I'm describing the quarter as it was in 1975. As far as I can tell, going back there most recently in 2008, most but not all of these shops are still there. I think the horsemeat butcher closed some time ago. The tailor, alas, is gone, and so, tragically, is Peltier's. See Part One, "Paris Perdu," for a guard against nostalgia. But the quarter is no longer what once it was. For another account of shopping on this stretch of the rue de Sèvres, some ten years earlier, but in many of the same shops, see Adrienne Clarkson, *Heart Matters*, 99.

3. Christian Ivaldi has gone on to a distinguished career in performance and recording. His discography shows a special interest in collaboration, often including works for two pianos.

4. For some of these details, I am indebted to the biographical sketch by Adrienne Clarkson, 101–09.

5. I quote from two books by Gagnon, both of which are entitled, simply, *Paul-Emile Borduas*. The first was published by the National Gallery of Canada, Ottawa, in 1976. The second, much more substantial volume, is from the Montreal Museum of Fine Arts, in 1988.

PART FIVE

1. Since the chapter I am dealing with presents her primarily in a French context, I will use the name "Laure" throughout. In this chapter, all quotations (unless otherwise noted) are from the chapter "Le Baiser de Juan-Les-Pins" (197–209). Since it is quite a short chapter, and since I will basically be going through it in sequence, I will not give page annotations for every individual citation.

2. The *Musée Picasso Guide* (Paris: Éditions de la Réunion des musées nationaux, 1985), to which Tostevin herself later refers, indicates that the painting in question was previously called both *Sur le Plage* and *Femme Assise* before Picasso settled on the ambiguous title *Le Baiser*. In this

catalogue, it is also clear that the painting is entitled simply *Le Baiser*, and that "Juan-Les-Pins" is the place of composition. The chapter title, "Le Baiser de Juan-Les-Pins," is thus Tostevin's amalgam.

3. For a very full, indeed almost programmatic, account of such influence, see Mavis Gallant's "The Other Paris" (1953; *Selected Stories*, 99–117).

4. While the relevance to Tostevin's novel seems somewhat distant, it may also be worth noting that Villiers de l'Isle-Adam was a passionate advocate of capital punishment, and in 1885 he protested bitterly against a new regulation that did away with the scaffold, and decreed that all executions be carried out at ground level. The steps of the scaffold were, he argued, "the *property* of every condemned man." Villiers attended so many executions that even the executioners themselves "considered him an 'enlightened connoisseur' of their art." For all these citations, see Burton, 115.

5. For an extended discussion of the "supplementary" relation between visual images and verbal commentary, see my book *Earthquakes and Explorations: Language and Painting from Cubism to Concrete Poetry* (University of Toronto Press, 1997).

6. For the definitive guide, see the charmingly entitled *Permanent Parisians: An Illustrated Guide to the Cemeteries of Paris*, by Judi Culbertson and Tom Randall (1986).

7. Whose name, intriguingly, concludes with the suggestion of inauthenticity or misrepresentation: "sham."

8. This is of course a widely observed feature of the alienation of modern city life. The classic early statement of it in relation to Paris is Baudelaire's prose poem "The Eyes of the Poor."

9. Compare this reaction with her own earlier experience, guided by an anatomy text book, of arousal and orgasm: "In the process of naming parts of her body she didn't know she had, she is unable to find words to describe what she's feeling. She is bewildered by sensations to which she readily submits. A trembling on the verge of fulfilling a secret yearning" (135). Note that the emphasis here is as much on verbal articulation as on physical experience; and that, again, this new knowledge comes to her through the mediation of a "third" language—in this case, Latin.

10. Note the verbs here: "who I *thought* I was," "everything I *know* to be right." Intellectual thought, or even knowledge, is no match for physical experience.

11. In the 1985 edition of the tourist guide to the Musée Picasso, the relevant passage reads: "En même temps que Picasso propose une image qui

n'est pas vraiment explicite (ce tableau s'est appelé jadis 'Sur le plage' ou 'Femme assise'), il multiplie les représentations dont la signification est de toute évidence sexuelle: les nez ressemblent au sexe d'un homme, la bouche à celui d'une femme: 'L'art n'est jamais chaste,' disait Picasso" (57).

12. Private e-mail correspondence, July 2001, quoted by permission of Lola Lemire Tostevin.

15--> A TRAVEL OF INDETERMINATE STOPS

1. Quoted in Carmona, 276. Carmona describes this pun as "Offenbachian humour"—an odd choice of adjective, considering the later use of Offenbach's *Contes d'Haussmann* as a punning attack on the Baron. Christopher Prendergast, in his review of Carmona's book, somewhat ungenerously describes "aqueduc" as "a grinding pun."

2. Gerry Shikatani was born in 1950, in Toronto, of Japanese parents. He has worked as a poet, a prose writer, a text-sound artist, a filmmaker, and a writer on food. His other publications include *1988—Selected Poems and Texts, 1973-1988; A Sparrow's Food;* and *Lake and Other Stories.* He has lived in Toronto, Montreal, Paris, and Spain.

3. Quotes from this interview, which remains unpublished, are indicated by the parenthetical citation (*I*). The transcription and editing of the tape are mine.

4. Transcribing the tapes, I wonder why I didn't press him further on this point. Possibly it seemed quite clear to me at the time!

5. Chez Germaine is a small, crowded, inexpensive restaurant on the rue Pierre Laroux, just off the rue de Sèvres, in the 7th arrondissement, very close to where I used to live. In the summer of 2003, it was still in operation. Despite what one might assume to be a common, indeed archetypal name, this is the only "Chez Germaine" listed in the Paris Yellow Pages.

6. See also "Barcelona, Spain" (31), in which the daily activities of eating (the "folded white napkin") and the simple grace ("for what we are about to receive") become the formulas for a deeply pure and moving prayer.

7. Rue des Rosiers is in the centre of the Jewish quarter in the Marais. It is a bustling, busy quarter, the streets crowded with men in Hassidic attire, and lined with groceries selling kosher food, bookstores specializing in Talmudic texts, and dozens of fast-food falafel restaurants. Indeed, #21 itself, which stands at a corner and rises three or four storeys, features now (2003) on its storefront a falafel take-out called Mi-Va-Mi.

8. See also 29, for a very explicit reference, and perhaps 14, for a more oblique one.

9. Actually, references to heels occur in other parts of *Aqueduct*, as well, even where the speaking voice is not so clearly fictionalized: "He remembers the heels...the sight of flesh of a woman's rigid heel, her tendons prisoned upright, walking away" (212); "heels on pavement, hard leather" (315).

10. A "travel of indeterminate / stops" might indeed be a good description of the whole of *Aqueduct*, and as such I have adopted it as the title of this chapter.

11. When I asked Shikatani if there was a deliberate Baudelaire reference here, he denied it. But the intertextual echo is very strong. The incident in Shikatani's poem takes place in the Café Drouot, boulevard des Italiens, edging out of the Marais and onto the Grands Boulevards, the territory of Baudelaire's poem, which takes place in the Café de la Paix, at the Opéra.

12. The reference is dated. Since the opening of the Musée d'Orsay, all the great Impressionist paintings referred to in this poem have been moved to the new museum. I am old enough to share Shikatani's evocation here: when I first saw, and came to love, these paintings, they were hanging on the cramped walls and crowded rooms of the Jeu du Paume.

13. Parts of the boulevard Haussmann were built before his death, but the whole project was not completed until many years later. In 1879, some politicians attempted to remove the name; Haussmann loftily replied "An inscription can be erased. As long as Paris lives, my name will be engraved in all its stones" (Carmona, 379). A hundred years later, the boulevard Haussmann is indeed still there, featuring a rather glum statue of the Baron.

14. The rue Treilhard (Shikatani omits the h) is a small street in the 8th arrondissement, close to the boulevard Haussmann. Even by Parisian standards, the concentration of restaurants and cafés on this short street is remarkable.

15. The actual point of the island used to be marked by two flourishing trees (willows, I think), but they were irreparably damaged by floods in the 1990s and have yet to be satisfactorily replaced. One of the new trees is struggling to survive; the other has been killed by vandalism. My favourite photo of Maureen was taken of her sitting at the point of the Vert Galant: in the background are the expanse of the Louvre, and the Pont des Arts. The state of flood is memorably captured in a painting by Marge Berry, which hangs on my wall.

16. The comparison "big as a cow" may seem somewhat incongruous here. Of course, the cow is one possible source for "something sautéed just to the point." But what I hear, as an intertextual echo (whether or not Shikatani intended it) is Gertrude Stein: "As a Wife Has a Cow: A Love Story."

17. The wordplay "neuf / to-the-9s" works only between French and English. Within French, one does not dress to the 9s: one can be "sur son trente et un" (on one's 31), or "tiré à quatre épingles" (dressed to four pins). My thanks to Marie Vautier, as always, for advice on translation.

PART SIX

16⟶ THE FIRST TIME I SAW PARIS (1970)

1. "La grève" originally meant a meadow or grassy space on the bank of a river, and it is in that sense that it gave its name to the place de Grève, where the Paris City Hall still stands. In the early nineteenth century, the place de Grève was where casual day labourers were hired. Richard D.E. Burton reports that: "Workers disgruntled about pay or conditions would walk off construction sites and head back to the square in the hope of being rehired on better terms, whence the expression *faire la grève*, which by the mid-nineteenth century had entered the national, and not just the Parisian, lexicon as the term for 'to strike'" (98).

2. Indeed, to a far greater extent than Maureen and I were aware of in our political naivety, 1970 was still a period of repressive crackdown on any vestiges of May 68. For a detailed account, see Kristin Ross, *May '68 and its Afterlives*. Ross writes: "anyone who visited Paris in the early 1970s will recall the concentration in the metros and on the sidewalks of armed police, the CRS vans stationed at regular, close intervals throughout the central city" (63). This image certainly corresponds with my memory, though I did not at the time realize its full implications.

3. Over the years, it has gone through several name-changes; most recently it is called Le Zimmer—a name that suggests to me a possible continuity of German, or more likely Alsatian ownership; but that also, of course, irresistibly reminds me of a certain Mr. Zimmerman! I had resisted going back to it, unwilling to meddle with memories, but I eventually broke down and had lunch there in December 2002. A very decent steak.

17⟶ CATASTROPHE AND SHAME

1. This chapter is based on journals I kept during a visit to Paris in April–May 2002. The journals have been extensively edited and revised for publication. This was my first visit to Paris since the death of my wife,

Maureen, with whom I had shared so much of the city; I have omitted much, though not all, of the more personal material relating to my memories of her.

2. President Mitterrand is reputed to have enjoyed, towards the end of his life, a final meal of songbirds whose killing and consumption are strictly forbidden by French law.

3. Actually, I was mistaken on this point. In the 1950s, the Cinémathèque had not yet moved to Trocadéro, but was situated on the avenue de Messine.

WORKS CITED

Adnan, Etel. *Paris, When It's Naked*. Sausalito, CA: The Post-Apollo Press, 1993.

Aragon, [Louis]. *Paris Peasant [Le Paysan de Paris]*. Trans. Simon Watson Taylor. London: Jonathan Cape, 1971; Picador, 1980.

Attwater, Douglas. *The Penguin Dictionary of Saints*. Harmondsworth: Penguin, 1965.

Barnes, Djuna. *Nightwood*. Ed. Cheryl J. Plumb. Illinois State University: Dalkey Archive Press, 1995. Original edition: 1936.

Barthes, Roland. *The Eiffel Tower and Other Mythologies*. Trans. Richard Howard. Berkeley: University of California Press, 1979.

_____ *Roland Barthes*. Paris: Seuil, 1975.

Baudelaire, Charles. *Selected Writings on Art and Artists*. Trans. P.E. Charvet. Penguin, 1972.

Bell, David A. "He wouldn't dare" [review of Burton]. *London Review of Books* 24:9, 9 May 2002, 19–20.

Benjamin, Walter. *The Arcades Project*. Trans. Howard Eiland and Kevin McLaughlin. Cambridge, MA: The Belnap Press of Harvard University Press, 1999.

_____ *Charles Baudelaire: A Lyric Poet in the Era of High Capitalism*. London: New Left Books, 1983.

Benstock, Shari. *Women of the Left Bank: Paris, 1900-1940*. Austin: University of Texas Press, 1986.

Berman, Marshall. *All That Is Solid Melts Into Air: The Experience of Modernity*. First edition 1982. New York: Penguin, 1988.

Bowering, George, ed. *Likely Stories*. Toronto: Coach House Press, 1992.

Boyer, M. Christine. *The City of Collective Memory: Its Historical Imagery and Architectural Entertainments*. Cambridge, MA: MIT Press, 1994.

Boyle, Kay. See McAlmon.

Breton, André. *Nadja*. Trans. Richard Howard. New York: Grove Press, 1960. First Edition: Paris: Gallimard, 1928.

Brinnin, John Malcolm. *The Third Rose: Gertrude Stein and Her World*. Boston: Little, Brown and Company, 1959.

Buck-Morss, Susan. *The Dialectics of Seeing: Walter Benjamin and the Arcades Project*. Cambridge, MA: MIT Press, 1991.

Burton, Richard D.E. *Blood in the City: Violence and Revolution in Paris 1789-1945*. Ithaca and London: Cornell University Press, 2001.

Caine, Peter and Oriel Caine. *Paris Then and Now*. San Diego, CA: Thunder Bay Press, 2003.

Callaghan, Morley. *That Summer in Paris: Memories of Tangled Friendships with Hemingway, Fitzgerald and Some Others*. Toronto: Macmillan, 1963. Paperback: 1973.

Carlson-Reddig, Thomas. *An Architect's Paris*. Boston: Bulfinch Press, 1993.

Carmona, Michael. *Haussmann: His Life and Times, and the Making of Modern Paris*. Trans. Patrick Camiller. Chicago: Ivan R. Doe, 2002. (Original French edition: 2000.)

Certeau, Michel de. *L'invention de quotidian*. Union générale d'éditions, 1980. Gallimard, 1990. *The Practice of Everyday Life*. Trans. Steven F. Rendall. Berkeley: University of California Press, 1984.

Chambers, Ross. *Loiterature*. Lincoln and London: University of Nebraska Press, 1999.

Chevalier, Louis. *The Assassination of Paris*, with a new epilogue by the author; foreword by John Merriman; trans. David P. Jordan. Chicago: University of Chicago Press, 1994. Original French edition: 1977.

Clark, T.J. "Reservations of the Marvellous" [review of *The Arcades Project*]. *London Review of Books* (22 June, 2000).

Clarkson, Adrienne. *Heart Matters: a memoir*. Toronto: Viking, 2006.

Cobb, Richard. *Paris and Elsewhere*. Ed. David Gilmour. London: John Murray, 1998.

Cohen, Leonard. *Death of a Lady's Man*. Toronto: McClelland and Stewart, 1978.

Colette. *Claudine in Paris*. Trans. Antonia White. London: Vintage, 2001. First
French edition: 1901.

Cope, Karin. *Passionate Collaborations: Learning to Live With Gertrude Stein*.
Victoria, BC: ELS Editions, 2005.

Crunden, Robert M. *American Salons: Encounters with European Modernism,
1885-1917*. New York: Oxford University Press, 1993.

Culbertson, Judi, and Tom Randall. *Permanent Parisians: An Illustrated Guide to
the Cemeteries of Paris*. Chelsea, VT: Chelsea Green Publishing Company,
1986.

Delbanco, Nicholas. *The Lost Suitcase: Reflections on the Literary Life*. New York:
Columbia University Press, 2000.

Douglas, Ann. *Terrible Honesty: Mongrel Manhattan in the 1920s*. New York:
Farrar, Strauss and Giroux, 1995.

D'Souza, Aruna, and Tom McDonough, eds. *The invisible flâneuse?: Gender,
public space and visual culture in nineteenth century Paris*. Manchester:
Manchester University Press, 2006.

Dyer, Geoff. *Paris Trance*. New York: Farrar, Strauss and Giroux, 1998.

Dylan, Bob. *Lyrics 1962-2001*. New York: Simon & Schuster, 2004.

Encyclopaedia Britannica. References are to the 200th Anniversary edition,
1970.

Engel, Howard. *Murder in Montparnasse: A Literary Mystery of Paris*.
Harmondsworth: Penguin, 1993.

Evenson, Norma. *Paris: A Century of Change, 1878-1978*. New Haven, CT and
London: Yale University Press, 1979.

Ferguson, Priscilla Parkhurst. *Paris as Revolution: Writing the 19th-Century City*.
Berkeley: University of California Press, 1994. Paperback edition: 1997.

Flahiff, F.T., *always someone to kill the doves: a life of Sheila Watson*. Edmonton,
AB: NeWest Press, 2005.

Gagnon, François-Marc. *Paul-Emile Borduas*. Ottawa: National Gallery of
Canada, 1976.

———— *Paul-Emile Borduas*. Montreal: Montreal Museum of Fine Arts, 1988.

Gallant, Mavis. *A Fairly Good Time*. Toronto: Macmillan, 1970.

————*Overhead in a Balloon: Twelve Stories of Paris*. New York: Random House,
1985.

———— *Paris Notebooks*. Toronto: Macmillan, 1986.

———— *In Transit*. Toronto: Penguin 1997. First edition: 1988.

———— *The Selected Stories of Mavis Gallant*. Toronto: McClelland and Stewart,
1996.

Glassco, John. *Memoirs of Montparnasse*. Toronto: Oxford University Press, 1970. 2nd edition, with a Critical Introduction and Notes on the Text by Michael Gnarowski. Toronto, Oxford University Press, 1995. (Page references are to the 2nd edition.)

———— *Selected Poems*. Toronto: Oxford University Press, 1971.

Gopnik, Adam, *Paris to the Moon*. New York: Random House, 2000.

———— ed. *Americans in Paris: a Literary Anthology*. The Library of America, 2004.

Gosling, Nigel. *The Adventurous World of Paris 1900-1914*. New York: William Morrow and Company, 1978.

Green, Julien. *Paris*. Paris: Champ Vallon, 1989. Reprint: Seuil, 1989. Bilingual edition: Trans. J.A. Underwood. New York and London: Marion Boyars, 1991.

Harvey, David. *Paris: Capital of Modernity*. New York and London: Routledge, 2003.

Hazan, Eric. *L'invention de Paris: Il n'ya pas de pas perdus*. Paris: Seuil, 2002. (My translations.)

Hébert, Anne. *Am I Disturbing You?* Paris: Seuil, 1998. Trans. Sheila Fischman. Toronto: Anansi, 1999.

Hemingway, Ernest. *The Sun Also Rises*. New York: Charles Scribner's Sons, 1926. Quotations from 2003 edition.

———— *A Moveable Feast*. New York: Charles Scribner's Sons, 1964. Quotations from 2003 edition.

Hemingway, Mary Welsh. *How It Was*. New York: Alfred A. Knopf, 1976.

Herring, Philip. *Djuna: The Life and Work of Djuna Barnes*. New York: Viking, 1995.

Higonnet, Patrice. *Paris: Capital of the World*. Trans. Arthur Goldhammer. Cambridge, MA: Harvard University Press, 2002.

Hine, Daryl. *Arrondissements*. Erin, ON: The Porcupine's Quill, 1989.

Hollier, David, ed. *A New History of French Literature*. Cambridge, MA: Harvard University Press, 1989.

Holy Bible. References are to the King James Authorized Version.

Hugo, Victor. *Les Misérables*. Harmondsworth: Penguin, 1982.

Huston, Nancy. *The Mark of the Angel*. Toronto: McArthur & Company, 1999. Originally: *L'Empreinte de l'ange*. Paris: Actes Sud, 1998. (English version by the author.)

———— *Longings and Belongings*. Toronto: McArthur & Company, 2005.

Illich, Ivan. "Utopia of an Odorless City." In Miles, *City Cultures Reader*, 249-52.

Jacobs, Allan B. *Great Streets*. Cambridge, MA: MIT Press, 1993.

James, Henry. *Autobiography*. Ed. Frederick W. Dupee. New York: Criterion
    Books, 1956. Original edition: 1913.

Jones, Colin. *Paris: The Biography of a City*. New York: Viking, 2004.

Kauffmann, Jean-Paul. *La Lutte avec l'Ange*. Paris: Éditions de la Table Ronde,
    2001. *Wrestling with the Angel*. Trans. Patricia Clancy. London: The Harvill
    Press, 2003.

Kennedy, J. Gerald. *Imagining Paris: Exile, Writing, and American Identity*. New
    Haven, CT and London: Yale University Press, 1993.

Kiki. *Kiki's Memoirs*. Ed. Billy Klüver and Julie Martin. Hopwell, NJ: The Ecco
    Press, 1996.

King, Geoff. *Mapping Reality: An Exploration of Cultural Cartographies*. London:
    Macmillan, 1996.

King, Ross. *The Judgment of Paris: The Revolutionary Decade that Gave the World
    Impressionism*. Toronto: Doubleday, 2006.

Kroetsch, Robert, with Shirley Neuman and Robert Wilson. *Labyrinths of Voice:
    Conversations with Robert Kroetsch*. Edmonton, AB: NeWest Press, 1982.

Kurnow, Stanley. *Paris in the Fifties*. New York: Random House, 1997.

Lafarge, Paul. *Haussmann or The Distinction*. New York: Farrar, Strauss and
    Giroux, 2001.

Lapprand, Marc. "Jacques Jouet, Metro Poet." *SubStance* 96 (Vol. 30, no. 3),
    2002, 17–26.

Lejeune, Philippe. *Le Pacte autobiographique*. Paris: Éditions du Seuil, 1975.

Levenstein, Harvey. *Seductive Journey: American Tourists in France from Jefferson
    to the Jazz Age*. Chicago: University of Chicago Press, 1998.

MacMillan, Margaret. *Paris 1919*. New York: Random House, 2002.

McAlmon, Robert. With Kay Boyle. *Being Geniuses Together*. New York:
    Doubleday & Company, Inc., 1968. Revised edition with Afterword: San
    Francisco: North Point Press, 1984.

――― *The Nightinghouls of Paris*. Ed. Sanford J. Smoller. Urbana and Chicago:
    University of Illinois Press, 2007.

Marnham, Patrick. *Crime and the Académie Française: Dispatches from Paris*.
    Harmondsworth: Penguin, 1994.

Miles, Barry. *The Beat Hotel: Ginsberg, Burroughs, and Corso in Paris, 1957–1963*.
    New York: Grove Press, 2000.

Miles, Malcolm, Tim Hall, and Iain Borden, eds. *The City Cultures Reader*.
    London and New York: Routledge, 2000.

Ondaatje, Michael. *The English Patient*. Toronto: MacClelland and Stewart,
    1992.

O'Reilly, James, Larry Habegger, and Sean O'Reilly, eds. *Paris*. San Francisco, CA: Travelers' Tales Guides, 1997.

Paris Circulation. Paris: Éditions A. Leconte, 9ème édition, 2006.

Perec, Georges. *Tentative d'epuisement d'un lieu parisien*. Union générale d'éditions, 1975. (My translation.)

Persky, Stan. *The Short Version: An ABC Book*. Vancouver: New Star Books, 2005.

Pinkney, David H. *Napoleon III and the Rebuilding of Paris*. Princeton, NJ: Princeton University Press, 1958.

Pizer, Donald. *American Expatriate Writing and the Paris Moment*. Baton Rouge: Louisiana University Press, 1996.

Plaskett, Joseph. *A Speaking Likeness*. Vancouver: Ronsdale Press, 1988.

Pound, Ezra. *Selected Poems*. New York: New Directions, 1957.

Prendergast, Christopher. *Paris and the Nineteenth Century*. Oxford: Blackwell, 1992.

Rearick, Charles. *Pleasures of the Belle Epoque: Entertainment & Festivity in Turn-of-the-Century France*. New Haven, CT and London: Yale University Press, 1985.

Réda, Jacques. *The Ruins of Paris*. Paris: Gallimard, 1977. Trans. Mark Treharne. London: Reaktion Books, 1996.

————— *Amen, Récitatif, La tourne*. Paris: Gallimard, 1999.

Rice, Shelley. *Parisian Views*. Cambridge, MA: MIT Press, 1997.

Richardson, Bill. *Waiting for Gertrude*. Vancouver: Douglas & McIntyre, 2001.

Rifkin, Adrian. *Street Noises: Parisian pleasure, 1900–1940*. Manchester: Manchester University Press, 1993.

Rilke, Rainer Maria. *Lettres d'autour d'un jardin*. Paris: La Délirante, 1977.

Roubaud, Jacques. *La forme d'une ville change plus vite, hélas, que le coeur des humains: cent cinquante poèmes 1991–1998*. Paris: Gallimard, 1999. *The form of a city changes faster, alas, than the human heart*. Trans. Keith and Rosmarie Waldrop. London: Dalkey Archive Press, 2006.

Ross, Kristin. *May '68 and Its Afterlives*. Chicago and London: The University of Chicago Press, 2002.

Russell, John. *Paris*. New York: Abrams, 1983. (Enlarged edition, with illustrations.) Original edition, with photos by Brassaï: London: B.T. Batsford Ltd., 1960.

Rybczynski, Witold. *City Life: Urban Reflections in a New World*. Toronto: HarperCollins, 1995.

Sasaki, Ken-Ichi. "For Whom is City Design: Tactility versus Visuality." In Miles, *City Cultures Reader*, 36–44.

Scobie, Stephen. *Stone Poems*. Vancouver: Talonbooks, 1970.

_____ "Love in the Burning City: the poetry of Wilfred Watson." *Essays on Canadian Writing*, 18/19 (Summer/Fall, 1980): 281-303.

_____ *McAlmon's Chinese Opera*. Dunvegan, ON: Quadrant Editions, 1980.

_____ *Dunino*. Montreal: Signal Editions, 1989.

_____ *Earthquakes and Explorations: Language and Painting from Cubism to Concrete Poetry*. Toronto: University of Toronto Press, 1997.

_____ *Alias Bob Dylan Revisited*. Calgary, AB: Red Deer Press, 2003.

_____ *The Spaces in Between: Selected Poems 1965—2001*. Edmonton, AB: NeWest Press, 2003.

_____ *Paris Québec*. With Marie Vautier, trans. Victoria, BC: Ekstasis Editions, 2003.

Scott, Gail. "My Paris Diary (Book of Gesture): Work-in-progress." *Contemporary Verse* Volume 18 No. 2 (Fall 1995).

_____ "The Porous Text." *Chain*. University of Hawaii, 1998.

_____ *My Paris: a novel*. Toronto: The Mercury Press, 1999.

Sheringham, Michael, ed. *Parisian Fields*. London: Reaktion Books, 1996.

Shikatani, Gerry. *Aqueduct: Poems and Texts from Europe 1979-1987*. Toronto: The Mercury Press, Underwhich Editions, and Wolsak and Wynn Publishers, 1996.

Sieburth, "Benjamin the Scrivener," *Assemblage* 6 (June, 1988): 8-9.

Smith, Steven. *Transient Light*. Stratford, ON: The Mercury Press, 1990.

Smoller, Sanford J. Introduction to McAlmon, *The Nightinghouls of Paris*. xi-liv.

Solnit, Rebecca. *Wanderlust: A History of Walking*. New York: Viking, 2000.

Stein, Gertrude. *Geography and Plays*. Originally published: Boston: Four Seas Company, 1922. Facsimile edition: New York: Something Else Press, 1968.

_____ *The Autobiography of Alice B. Toklas*. New York: The Literary Guild, 1933.

_____ *Lectures in America*. New York: Random House, 1935.

_____ *The World Is Round*. London: B.T. Batsford, Ltd., 1939.

_____ *Paris France*. New York: Liveright, 1970. Original edition: 1940.

_____ *The Yale Gertrude Stein*. Ed. Richard Kostelanetz. New Haven, CT and London: Yale University Press, 1980.

Szondi, Peter. "Walter Benjamin's City Portraits," in Gary Smith, ed., *On Walter Benjamin: Critical Essays and Recollections*. Cambridge, MA: MIT Press, 1988.

Tester, Keith, ed. *The Flâneur*. London and New York: Routledge, 1994.

Tostevin, Lola Lemire. *Frog Moon*. Dunvegan, ON: Cormorant Books, 1994.

_____ *Subject to Criticism*. Stratford, ON: The Mercury Press, 1995.

_____ *The Jasmine Man*. Toronto: Key Porter Books, 2002.

Tremain, Rose. *The Way I Found Her*. London: Vintage, 1998.

Turgeon, Pierre. "Fragments Parisiens." *Liberté* 210, Volume 35, Numéro 6. Décembre, 1993.

Valance, Georges. *Haussmann le grand*. Paris: Flammarion, 2000.

Verne, Jules. *Paris in the Twentieth Century*. Written 1863. Paris: Hachette, 1994. Trans. Richard Howard. New York: Random House, 1996.

Wagner-Martin, Linda. *"Favored Strangers": Gertrude Stein and her Family*. New Brunswick, NJ: Rutgers University Press, 1995.

Watson, Sheila, Paris Diaries. In Flahiff, *always someone to kill the doves*, 91–161.

_____ "What I'm Going To Do." Ed. Stephen Scobie. *Open Letter* 3:1 (1975).

Webb, Phyllis. *The Vision Tree: Selected Poems*. Vancouver: Talonbooks, 1982.

Weintraub, William. *Getting Started*. Toronto: McClelland and Stewart, 2002.

Weiss, Andrea. *Paris Was a Woman: Portraits from the Left Bank*. San Francisco: Harper, 1995.

White, Norval. *The Guide to the Architecture of Paris*. New York: Charles Scribner's Sons, 1991.

Wilson, Edmund. *The Flâneur: A Stroll through the Paradoxes of Paris*. New York: Bloomsbury, 2001.

Woods, Lebbeus. "Everyday War." In Miles, *City Cultures Reader*, 310–13.

IMAGE CREDITS

Art / Licensed by SCALA / Art Resource, NY. The Museum of Modern Art, New York, NY, U.S.A.

Page 253: Photo by Stephen Scobie, restored by Mary Scobie.

Dyer, Geoff, 86–87, 205
Dylan, Bob, 255–56, 285n24, 300n11

Earthquakes and Explorations
    (Scobie), 302n5
Eiffel Tower, 22–27, 61–62, 279n2,
    279n4, 287n31
elections, presidential (2002), 251–
    52, 256–57, 262–67, 273–74
Eliot, T.S., 108, 298n1
Emerson, Ralph Waldo, 288n4
Engel, Howard, 35
Engels, Friedrich, 12, 295n2
Étoile (place Charles de Gaulle), 73
Eugène-Melchior, Vicomte de
    Vogue, 23
Eunoia (Bök), 299n7
Evenson, Norma, 26, 30, 136–37,
    279n2
Everybody's Autobiography (Stein),
    38
expatriates in Paris
    absence of Tour Eiffel in writing
        by, 23–24
    economic independence of,
        136–37
    in Montparnasse, 7, 62, 90, 139,
        294n1
    overview of, xi–xii
    romanticization of 1920s, 33–36
    See also autobiography and
        memoir
"Exposé" (Benjamin), 102–03
"The Eyes of the Poor" (Baudelaire),
    233, 302n8

A Fairly Good Time (Gallant), 279n4
"*Favoured Strangers*" (Wagner-
    Martin), 298n10

Ferguson, Priscilla Parkhurst
    on flânerie, 70–73, 96–97, 101,
        119, 126–28, 289n7, 289n9
    on metonymy, 85–86
    on street names, 73, 84–85
Ferreri, Marco, 21
Ferron, Marcelle, 193
Finlay, Ian Hamilton, 157–58, 297n8,
    299n6
"First Sketches" (Benjamin), 68
Flahiff, Fred, 108, 290n1, 291n2
flânerie
    arcades and, 95
    as activities other than walking,
        94, 288n3
    as category of urban discourse,
        97
    as de Certeau's "long poem of
        walking," xii, 89, 93, 236
    as idioms of science and
        pleasure, 104–05
    as myth, 95
    as reading of the street, 85
    as resistance to speed, 99–100
    automobiles and, 288n5
    dreaming and, 121–25
    gastronomy and, 137–38
    Grands Boulevards and, 239–40
    history of, 96–98
    inscape and, 110–11, 292n12
    maps and, 89, 287n33
    modernity and, 94, 101, 290n10
    sanitation system and, 95
    shopping and, 101–03, 289n9
    street system and, 95–96, 288n5
    work ethic and, 135–37
flâneur
    as aimless walker, 71
    as changing type, 96–97

Gallant, Mavis, works
  "Across the Bridge," 27
  "Baum, Gabriel, 1935-( )," 27
  A Fairly Good Time, 279n4
  "In Plain Sight," 27
  In Transit, 24, 279n4
  Overhead in a Balloon, 279n4
  "A Painful Affair," 118
  Paris Notebooks, 27, 117-27, 280n7
  "Paris: The Taste of a New Age,"
    27-28
  "Questions and Answers," 91-92
  "A Report," 24
gardens, Palais-Royal, 162-64
Gare du Montparnasse, 75
Gare Saint-Lazare, 68
gastronomy
  as metaphor for sexuality, 227
  flânerie and, 137-38
  food markets in Les Halles,
    20-21
  in Glassco's *Memoirs*, 142-43, 227
  in Shikatani's *Aqueduct*, 227-29
  pleasure in, 137-38, 250, 269
  wine and wine bars, 162-63,
    295n2
Geography and Plays (Stein), 152
Germaine, Saint, 176
Getting Started (Weintraub), 279n4
Gilmour, David, 6
Glassco, John
  as flâneur, 61-62, 71, 94, 139,
    146-48
  dandyism and, 290n10
  fictional memoirs, 40-42, 46-47,
    281nn6-7, 283n5
  hedonism of, 146
  in McAlmon's *Nightinghouls of
    Paris*, 43
  in Montparnasse, 90
  Kay Boyle and, 281nn8-9
  life of, 40-41
  street itineraries in works by,
    57-59, 61-62, 70, 74-75, 81, 146
  theories of autobiography and,
    36, 40-42
  visas for, 130
  work ethic and, 135-48
Glassco, John, works
  "Brummell at Calais," 290n10
  See also Memoirs of Montparnasse
    (Glassco)
Gnarowski, Michael, 281nn8-9,
    283n1
gnomon astronomikon, 172-73, 178
Godard, Jean-Luc
  Alphaville, 14, 259, 277n1, 278n7
  *Deux ou trois choses que je sais
    d'elle*, 276n1
  King Lear, 255-56
Gopnik, Adam
  on choice, 296n5
  on Métro stops, 79
  on Paris as American myth of
    happiness, 136
  on street names, 62, 64, 80
Gopnik, Adam, works
  Americans in Paris, 136, 281n8
  "The Balzar Wars," 294n9
  "A Handful of Cherries," 294n9
  Paris to the Moon, 294n9
Gordon, Alastair, 276n4
"Graffiti, spray-painted through
    stencils, on the rue de l'École
    de Médecine" (Scobie),
    252-53
Grands Boulevards, 237-39

poetry and, 285n18
riders as flâneurs, 294n5
strikes, 248–49
Métro Trocadéro, 260
Métro Vaneau, 185–86
militarism
Haussmannization and, 11–13
maps and, 88
Mitterrand, François, 8, 26, 252, 306n2
modernity
flânerie and, 94, 101, 290n10
Paris as city of, 17, 23
The Moderns (Rudolph), 35
Mondrian, Piet, 263–64, 273
Montmartre, 7
Pigalle area, 161
See also Basilica of the Sacré-Coeur
Montparnasse
expatriates and, 7, 62, 90, 139, 294n1
railway station, 26–28
street names, 74–75
Montparnasse Tower, 26–28, 187, 279n5
monuments and statues
1920s expatriates and, 139
Haussmannization and, 13–16, 277n6
See also Arc de Triomphe;
Deportation Memorial; *Dora Maar* (Picasso); Lion de Belfort; Tour Eiffel
Moses, Robert, 8
"movable feast," 7
A Moveable Feast (Hemingway), 41, 62–63, 70, 142, 280n2
Muda, Dayang, 281n6

Muir, Frank, 155–56, 297n6
Murder in Montparnasse (Engel), 35
Musée d'Orsay, 263–64, 304n12
Musée du Louvre
1920s expatriates and, 139
Haussmannization and, 11
in *The Da Vinci Code*, 172, 280n6
Pyramid, 26, 28, 164–65, 280n6, 298n13
Musée Picasso, 208–09, 211, 215, 218, 301n2, 302n11
My Paris (Scott), 47–54, 66, 79–80, 127–33, 286n26, 294n4
mythological Paris
1920s expatriates, 33–36, 136
flânerie and, 95
Judgement of Paris (Greek myth) and, 46, 144–46, 275n2, 296n4
Métro names and, 78
theories of autobiography and, 36

Nadja (Breton), 57, 81–82, 286n27
names
deconstruction of, 82–83
proper names, 82, 286n27
sensory pleasures of, 65–67, 83
significance of, 71–73, 82–83
See also street names
Napoleon I, 77, 139, 260, 284n15, 286n28
Napoleon III, 7–8, 9, 12
National Front, 251
Nerval, Gérard de, 95, 99
New York City, 8, 77, 85, 87–88, 287n31
Niépce, Janine, 189, 193
Niépce, Nicéphore, 188–89

The Nightinghouls of Paris
(McAlmon), 43–44
Nightwood (Barnes)
churches in, 170, 174–76, 178–83,
269
Daniel Mahoney in, 57–58, 299n2
Robin Vote in, 170, 173–78, 294n6,
299n3
Norden, Dennis, 297n6
Nord-Sud (magazine), 159
"Nord-Sud" Metro line, 159
nostalgia. *See* "Paris perdu" (Paris
lost)
"Notes on Writing and Meals"
(Shikatani), 228–29
"Notice on the door of the Church
of Saint-Julien-le-Pauvre
(one of Djuna Barnes's
Nightwood churches)"
(Scobie), 269
"Notice on the railings of the
(rather small) garden on the
south side of the church of
Saint-Germain-des-Prés"
(Scobie), 268
Notre-Dame Cathedral, 15, 85, 169,
278n9
Notre Dame de Lorette, Church of,
70–71, 161
Notre-Dame-des-Champs, Métro,
158
novels, detective, 102–03

Oehler, Dolf, 277n6
Ondaatje, Michael, 91
Ordnance Survey maps, 88
The Other Paris (Weintraub), 279n4
Oulipo (group of experimental
writers), 67, 178, 299n7

Overhead in a Balloon (Gallant),
279n4
Ovid, *Metamorphoses*, 210

"A Painful Affair" (Gallant), 118
"The Painter of Modern Life"
(Baudelaire), 97–98, 101
Palais des Tuileries, 164
Palais du Luxembourg, ix
Palais-Royal gardens, 162–64
panoptic surveillance, 88–90, 92,
103
Parc Montsouris, 271–72
Paré, Ambrose, 112
Paris (Green), 100
Paris, city of
as linguistic system, 84–85
as unknowable, 102–03
gender of, 145
history of maps of, 88–89,
287n33
See also city planning in
Paris; Haussmannization;
monuments and statues;
"Paris perdu" (Paris lost);
street names; street systems
"Paris, Early July" (Shikatani),
227–28
Paris, Judgement of (Greek myth),
x, 46, 144–46, 275n2, 296n4
Paris 1919 (MacMillan), 287n32
Paris and Elsewhere (Cobb), 5–6
Paris and the Nineteenth Century
(Prendergast), 102–04, 289n9
Paris as Revolution (Ferguson),
71–72, 96, 289n9
Paris: Biography of a City (Jones), 6–7
See also Jones, Colin

place de la Nation, 176–77

place de la Odéon, 262

place Denfert-Rochereau, 75–76, 80, 283n1

place des Vosges, 208, 230

place du Carrousel, 164

place du Châtelet, 250

place du Marché-Saint-Honoré, 72

place du Tertre, 230

place du Théatre-Français, 73

place Emile Goudeau, 160

place Pigalle, 161

place Robespierre, 72

place Saint-Michel, 112, 277n6

place Vendôme, 111

"The Plan" (Shikatani), 236

Plaskett, Joseph, 7

pleasure, discourse of

   discourse of justification and, 138

   flânerie and, 97, 101–02, 104–05, 289n7

   food and wine, 137–38, 250, 295n2

   sexuality and, 137

   work ethic and, 138–40

The Pleasure of the Text (Barthes), 236

Pleasures of the Belle Epoque (Rearick), 139–41

Polanski, Roman, 209–11, 216

Pompidou, Georges, 8, 20

Pompidou Centre, Beaubourg, 8, 24–26, 28–29, 280n7

Pont de la Tournelle, 236

Pont des Arts, 62

Pont Neuf, 147, 240–43, 278n8, 304n15

"Pont Neuf" (Breton), 90

"The Pont Neuf" (Shikatani), 224, 240–43

"The Porous Text" (Scott), 52

Porte de Clignancourt, 79

Porte de la Chapelle, 158

"The Post-Impressionists" (Shikatani), 237

Pound, Ezra, 78, 86, 292n11

power

   city centre and, 13–14

   elevated viewpoints and, 87–88

   Haussmann and, 238

   mapmaking and, 73, 88

   proper names and, 82–83

   street names and, 71–73, 77–78, 285n25

Pozier, Bernard, 276n2

Prendergast, Christopher, 102–04, 137, 142, 289n9, 303n1

presidential elections (2002). *See* elections, presidential (2002)

prostitution

   in arcades, 21, 146, 296n4

   in areas of Paris, 161, 249

   in Shikatani's *Aqueduct*, 230–35

   use of term *lorettes* for, 161, 298n11

Proust, Marcel, 68, 123, 207

Putnam, George, 95

Putnam, Samuel, 145

Pyramid (Musée du Louvre), 26, 28, 164–65, 280n6, 298n13

quai des Grands Augustins, 109, 291n8

quays. *See* Seine and quays

"Questions and Answers" (Gallant), 91–92

rue Étienne-Marcel, 230

rue Georges Braque, 271

rue Gît-le-Coeur, 62, 109, 112, 283n4,
    291n9

rue Guillaume Apollinaire, x, 76,
    255, 285n16

rue Jacob, 181, 182

rue Léon-Maurice-Nordmann, 73,
    283n5

rue Maître Albert, 62

rue Marcel-Proust, 80

rue Marie Stuart, 73

rue Mouffetard, 79, 266

rue Notre-Dame-des-Champs, 255

rue Oudinot, 185–86, 265

rue Perronet, 169

rue Picpus, 174

rue Ravignan, 158, 160

rue Rembrandt, 77–78

rue Richelieu, 162

rue Robespierre, 72–73

rue Rousselet
    as a street, 185–88, 196, 301n1
    M. and S. Scobie's stays on, vii,
        xiv, 74–75, 185–89, 193, 196,
        260, 265
    Réda's poems on, 196–98
"Rue Rousselet" (Réda; trans.
    Scobie), 196–97

rue Royer-Collard, 123, 124

rue Saint-Denis, 230, 234

rue Saint-Jacques, 277n6

rue Saint-Romain, 170, 186

rue Saint-Sulpice, 268

rue Servandoni, 173

rue Solférino, 263, 286n28

rue St. André des Arts, 109

rue Treilhard, 240–41, 304n14

"Rue Vavin. 1988" (Smith), 81

rue Vignon, 108–09

rue Villiers de l'Isle-Adam, 80–81,
    205

rue Visconti, 256–57

rue Xavier Primas, 62

The Ruins of Paris (Réda), 67–68, 101,
    196

Russell, John, 10, 14, 24–25, 163, 176

Sacré-Coeur, Basilica of the, 22–23,
    161, 279n3

"Sacred Emily" (Stein), 152

Sacred Heart, cult of, 279n3

Sainte-Clothilde, Church of, 175–76,
    178

Saint-Germain-des-Prés, Church
    of. *See* Church of Saint-
    Germain-des-Prés

Saint-Germain l'Auxerrois, Church
    of, 116

Saint-Julien-le-Pauvre, Church of,
    174–76, 269

Saint-Sulpice, Church of. *See*
    Church of Saint-Sulpice

Salter, F.M., 115

sanitation system, 95

Santé prison, 58–59

Sasaki, Ken-Ichi, 15, 278n9

Scarfe, Eunice, vii

Schumann, Robert, 220–21

Scobie, Maureen
    in Paris, 74, 187–90, 193, 196,
        247–50
    life and passing of, 190, 241, 247,
        253
    photo of, vii, 253–54, 274, 304n15
    Shikatani's poem dedicated to,
        224, 240–43

work on murdered women
(unpublished), 129–30
Seductive Journey (Levenstein), 95,
137–39
"The Seine, the Oldest Paris"
(Benjamin), 19
Seine and quays
cultural resonances of, 61–62,
165
Gallant on, 123
Glassco on, 147
Haussmannization of, 19–20
S. and W. Watson on, 110–11, 116
sewage system, 95
sexuality
association with Paris, 137
flânerie and, 98
in Shikatani's *Aqueduct*, 227,
230–35
in Tostevin's.*Frog Moon*, 216–19,
302n9
See also prostitution
Shakespeare, William, 155
Shields, Rob, 95
Shikatani, Gerri
interview with, 224–26, 229, 231,
237–39, 303n3, 304n11
life of, 254, 303n2
on line length in poetry, 226–27
Shikatani, Gerri, works. *See*
Aqueduct (Shikatani)
shopping and shopping malls,
20–22, 29–30, 101–03, 279n1,
289n9
sidewalk cafés. *See* cafés, sidewalk
Smith, Steven, 81
Smoller, Sanford J., 43
social class
cultural tourism and, 138–39

flânerie and, 290n12
Haussmannization and, 8, 11–13,
16, 20, 238
Solnit, Rebecca, 61, 85, 94, 99–101,
119, 135–36, 289n9
Sorbonne, 120, 125
Sorbonne area, 249, 267
The Spaces In Between (Scobie),
282n2, 300n10
Spadina Expressway, Toronto,
238–39
Spang, Rebecca L., 137–38
A Speaking Likeness (Plaskett), 7
Spitzer, Leo, 83
Stahl, Fritz, 19
Stein, Gertrude
as expatriate writer, xii, 33–34
Colette and, 163
Gail Scott on, 52
grave of, 151, 166–68
Hemingway and, 34, 38–39
home of, x, 33, 74
knowledge of French, 298n12
on change, 2, 28
route from home to Picasso's
studio, 151, 158–68, 298n10
theories of autobiography and,
36
Stein, Gertrude, works
Autobiography of Alice B. Toklas,
34, 37–40, 45–46, 54, 153–54,
158
Bee Time Vine, 152–53
Everybody's Autobiography, 38
Paris France, 2
"Rose is a rose is a rose is a
rose," 151–57, 167, 297nn4–5
"Sacred Emily," 152
The World is Round, 153–55

marriage to Wilfred, 107, 112–13, 291nn2–3

on the flâneur, 93

on writer's life as circus, 115

use of street names, 109–10, 112

Watson, Sheila, works

The Double Hook, 108, 115

Paris Diaries, 107–16, 290n1

Watson, Wilfred

career of, 108, 291n4, 291n6

marriage to Sheila, 107, 112–13, 291nn2–3

on the Seine, 110–11

Watson, Wilfred, works

Friday's Child, 108, 298n1

The Waves (Woolf), 255–56

The Way I Found Her (Tremain), 65

Webb, Phyllis, 276n5

Weil, Simone, 114–15

Weintraub, William, 279n4

Weiss, Andrea, 145

White, Edmund, 97, 100, 289n6

White, Norval, 175

Willi's Wine Bar, 162–63

wine and wine bars, 162–63, 254, 295n2

Woods, Lebbeus, 8, 276n5

Woolf, Virginia, 255–56

work ethic

1920s expatriates and, 136–37

Benjamin and, 135, 140

flânerie and, 135–37, 140

Glassco and, 135

history of, 138–40

of Hemingway, 70–71, 136, 138, 142–43, 284n14

Scott and, 135

work permits, 115–16, 131, 295n7

The World is Round (Stein), 153–55

World Trade Center, 85, 87–88, 287n31

Wrestling with the Angel (Kauffmann), 300n13

xenophobia, 293n4

The Yale Gertrude Stein (Stein), 152–53

Ze Kitchen Galérie, 261

Zweig, Paul, 62